Ceramic Production in the American Southwest

CONTRIBUTORS

DAVID R. ABBOTT, Tucson, AZ

JAMES R. ALLISON, Department of Anthropology,
Arizona State University, Tempe

ERIC BLINMAN, Office of Archaeological Studies,
Museum of New Mexico, Santa Fe

JUDITH A. HABICHT-MAUCHE, Anthropology Board
of Studies, University of California, Santa Cruz

MELISSA B. HAGSTRUM, Department of Anthropology,
University of Washington, Seattle

MICHELLE HEGMON, Department of Anthropology,
Arizona State University, Tempe

WINSTON HURST, Blanding, UT

STEPHEN PLOG, Department of Anthropology,
University of Virginia, Charlottesville

BARBARA L. STARK, Department of Anthropology,
Arizona State University, Tempe

MARY-ELLEN WALSH-ANDUZE, SWCA, Inc.
(Environmental Consultants), Flagstaff, AZ

C. DEAN WILSON, Office of Archaeological Studies,
Museum of New Mexico, Santa Fe

MARÍA NIEVES ZEDEÑO, Department of Anthropology,
University of Arizona, Tucson

Ceramic Production in the American Southwest

edited by

Barbara J. Mills
and Patricia L. Crown

The University of Arizona Press
Tucson

The University of Arizona Press
Copyright © 1995
Arizona Board of Regents
All rights reserved

♾ This book is printed on acid-free, archival-quality paper.
Manufactured in the United States of America

00   6 5 4 3 2

Library of Congress Cataloging-in-Publication Data

Ceramic production in the American Southwest / edited by Barbara J.
  Mills and Patricia L. Crown.
      p.   cm.
    Includes bibliographical references and index.
    ISBN 0-8165-1508-5 (cloth)
      1. Pueblo pottery—Themes, motives.   2. Pueblo pottery—
  Classification.   3. Ceramic materials—Southwest, New—Analysis.
  4. Ethnoarchaeology—Southwest, New.   5. Southwest, New—
  Antiquities.   I. Mills, Barbara J., 1955- .   II. Crown, Patricia L.
  E99.P9C44   1995
  738.3'0979—dc20   95-8771
                                                            CIP

British Library Cataloguing-in-Publication Data
A catalogue record for this book is available from the British Library.

To our spouses

T. J. Ferguson and W. H. Wills

CONTENTS

1

Ceramic Production in the American Southwest

An Introduction

Barbara J. Mills and Patricia L. Crown

Production is the cornerstone of all economic models. Before the distribution and consumption of goods can be fully understood, the social and spatial contexts of production must be delineated. Despite this prerequisite, ceramic production has only recently received the intensive research that has characterized interest in exchange and consumption. In this book, we concentrate on the social, economic, and political organization of ceramic production. Examples of some recent models of the organization of ceramic production in the general archaeological literature include those of Arnold (1985), Benco (1987), Costin (1991), Peacock (1982), Pool (1992), Rice (1981, 1987, 1991), Sinopoli (1988), and van der Leeuw (1984). These works emphasize the variety of organizational forms within which ceramic production takes place and seek means by which these forms can be recognized in the archaeological record.

Ceramics are a particularly useful class of materials for investigating production in the archaeological record. They are ubiquitous components of the technological repertoire of most food-producing societies, and even some nonfood producers. Their many and varied constituents are especially useful for identifying different locations of production (e.g., Bishop and Neff 1989; Bishop et al. 1982; Neff 1992). Although always subject to natural and cultural formation processes (Schiffer 1987), ceramics are for the most part well preserved in the archaeological record. Ethnographers and ethnoarchaeologists have extensively studied ceramics, providing ample examples of contemporary contexts of production (see Longacre [1992] for a comprehensive bibliography on ceramic ethnoarchaeology).

This volume brings together the research of scholars currently working in the American Southwest on issues relating to the organization of ceramic production. The volume began as a symposium at the 56th Annual Meeting of the Society for American Archaeology. Our goals were to illustrate the variety of social and spatial contexts of ceramic production in the Southwest (fig. 1.1) and to provide a focused dialogue among different researchers. Although the participants are building and testing models using Southwestern data, their research has wide-ranging implications for the study of ceramics worldwide, especially those produced in middle-range societies.

In the remainder of this chapter, we discuss current approaches to the organization of ceramic production in the archaeological literature. Then we review many of the methods and results of past research on this topic by archaeologists working in the Southwest. Finally, we provide a brief summary of the papers in the volume, emphasizing the diversity of models, methods, and contexts for investigating the organization of ceramic production in the Southwest.

The Organization of Ceramic Production

The organization of ceramic production encompasses more than where, when, or how ceramics were made; it also includes who is producing for whom and why. Organizational approaches thus include the reconstruction of the social, economic, and political contexts of production and how these contexts change through time. Ideally, they also provide models that explain why organizational forms govern in some situations but not in others and why those forms change through time.

Héléne Balfet (1965) was one of the first archaeologists to acknowledge explicitly the interplay of technological and organizational components in ceramic production. Working among potters in North Africa, she compared different producing groups to illustrate two distinct modes of ceramic production, one household based and the other more specialized. Her examples illustrate how variation in productive specialization, gender, social organization, and modes of distribution coexisted.

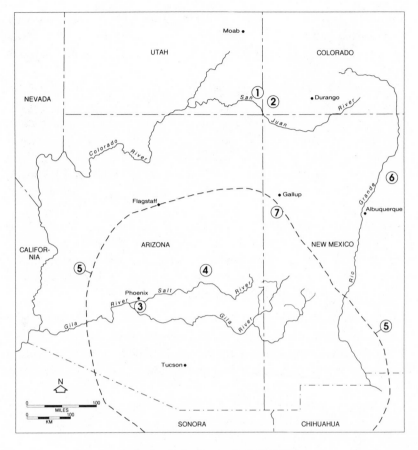

1. San Juan Region (Hegmon, Hurst, and Allison)
2. Northern San Juan Region (Wilson and Blinman)
3. Phoenix Basin (Abbott and Walsh-Anduze)
4. Grasshopper Region (Zedeño)
5. Salado Polychrome Distribution (Crown)
6. Northern Rio Grande (Habicht-Mauche)
7. Zuni (Mills)

Figure 1.1 Spatial distribution of ceramics used in case studies in this volume.

Although somewhat typological and transformational in its approach, her work has had an important influence on subsequent research, including that of Costin (1991), Peacock (1982), Rice (1981, 1991), and Sinopoli (1988).

Two recent syntheses emphasize the underlying multidimensional scales or parameters of existing typologies (Costin 1991; Pool 1992). Costin's model includes the dimensions of (1) context, (2) concentration, (3) scale, and (4) intensity of production, and she explicitly discusses how these different social dimensions can be measured using both direct and indirect measures. By contrast, Pool identifies (1) scale and efficiency, (2) size of the social unit of production, (3) segregation of activities, (4) location of production, and (5) variability of products as the important dimensions underlying the study of production. Although Costin's and Pool's models evoke similar terminology, close comparison reveals differences (table 1.1), including Costin's greater emphasis on organizational variability. Despite these differences, current approaches to the organization of production illustrate several themes:

1. The interrelatedness of production with the two other components of economic systems—distribution and consumption;
2. An emphasis on examining underlying variability to define modes or types of production, especially in terms of more continuous measures; and
3. Careful consideration of the match between archaeological methods and the specific dimensions of variation identified for investigation in a given archaeological setting.

Archaeologists studying craft production have also tied their research to broader issues related to social and political organization (e.g., Brumfiel and Earle 1987; Costin et al. 1989; Feinman et al. 1984). Cross-cultural research conducted by Clark and Parry (1990) has demonstrated that intensification of craft production and some general measures of cultural complexity covary, especially those variables of complexity related to social stratification and political integration. Their research suggests that archaeological identification of the social and political contexts of craft production will be most successful when distinctions between attached and independent, and part- and full-time specialists can be demonstrated.

As the above discussion reveals, previous models for the organization of ceramic production have been overwhelmingly based on analyses of complex societies. Much more attention needs to be paid to middle-

Table 1.1 Comparison of Costin's and Pool's Parameters or Dimensions of Production and Their Identified Archaeological Measures

Parameters		
Costin (1991)	Pool (1992)	Archaeological Measures
Context (degree of vertical control over production)		Location of production tools, debris, or facilities vis-à-vis high-status residences or administrative structures
Concentration (relative spatial organization of production)	Segregation of activities; location of production; variability of products	Relative spatial distribution of production tools, debris, or facilities; homogeneity or heterogeneity in assemblage composition (evenness)
Scale (size of producing unit and principles of recruitment)	Size of production entity	Size of production facilities; degree of standardization in raw-material preparation and finished products[a]
Intensity (amount produced per unit of time)	Scale, intensity, and efficiency	Number of vessels produced (controlling for population size and duration of occupation); range of economic activities represented; number of production steps used[b]; standardization in raw-material preparation and in finished products; degree of skill

[a]Standardization may be a measurement of both the size of the producing unit and the amount produced by that unit during a given period of time.

[b]This measure probably has a more curvilinear relationship with intensity; low intensity of production will result in few production steps as well as many cases in which items are mass produced.

range societies, such as those in the American Southwest. New methods for recognizing and interpreting variation in production organization currently being applied in the Southwest and elsewhere will allow more broad-based models to be developed.

The Study of Ceramic Production in the Southwest

Ceramic production has been a continuing topic of concern for archaeologists working in the Southwest. Even the earliest researchers were interested in who produced the abundant ceramics on the sites they studied, although most assumed that the historical Native Americans in the Southwest provided adequate analogs for ceramic production in prehistory.

Anna O. Shepard was the first to challenge this assumption with her detailed analyses of Southwestern ceramics. Through her pioneering use of petrography, Shepard demonstrated that in some areas of the Southwest production of ceramics exceeded what individual households needed and became a craft specialization. She based these conclusions on the identification of high frequencies of ceramics made from materials that could not be obtained near the sites at which the ceramics were found. The suggestion that every household did not manufacture its own ceramics was archaeological heresy to many Southwestern archaeologists of the mid-twentieth century (Cordell 1991; Judd 1954:235). Other interpretations were not widely accepted at the time she initially published them.

Shepard had her supporters, however, including Alfred Kidder, with whom she collaborated on the analysis of ceramics from Pecos Pueblo (Kidder and Shepard 1936; see also Shepard 1965a, b; Thompson 1991). This research led to her only monograph-length work on Southwestern ceramics, *Rio Grande Glaze Paint Ware: A Study Illustrating the Place of Ceramic Technological Analysis in Archaeological Research* (Shepard 1942). Other archaeologists in the Southwest with whom she worked included Wesley Bradfield in the Mimbres area (Shepard 1930), Earl Morris in the La Plata district (Shepard 1936, 1939), Paul Reiter at Unshagi (Shepard 1938), Deric O'Bryan at Mesa Verde (Shepard 1950), Fred Wendorf in the Petrified Forest (Shepard 1953), Neil Judd at Pueblo Bonito (Shepard 1954), and Watson Smith at Awatovi (Shepard 1971). Her work provides a benchmark for later work on the ceramics of the Southwest, especially on the Colorado Plateau.

Archaeologists continue to draw on Shepard's work as a model of research methods and presentation. In undertaking the study of the organization of ceramic production, Southwestern archaeologists typically use three sources of data: direct evidence for production in the form of tools, raw materials, unfired vessels, and production facilities; identification of limited production loci and widespread exchange through chemical and mineralogical analyses; and indirect evidence from the finished products.

Direct Evidence of Ceramic Production

The strongest evidence of ceramic production comes from the tools, materials, and features used in the production process. To date, no ceramic production workshops have been identified in the prehistoric Southwest, and many facilities associated with household production have left few identifiable traces (B. Stark 1985; Sullivan 1988). However, increasing excavation outside domestic spaces has led to the identification of a few ceramics firing facilities. At Snaketown, Emil Haury discovered clay mixing basins, pit "kilns," potting clay, and portable tools used in the production process in a single outside work area surrounded by six Sacaton phase structures (Haury 1976:194–197). Production features have also been identified at the Tucson Basin Hohokam West Branch Site (Huntington 1986). First recorded in the Mesa Verde area in the early 1970s (Helm 1973), trench kilns are now being recognized more often (Brown and Earls 1989; Brown et al. 1989; Fuller 1984; Hibbets 1984; Hibbets and Harden 1982). Archaeologists would undoubtedly discover more production features if excavation included more horizontal stripping of exterior areas.

Although relatively few firing facilities have been identified, many excavations recover tools used in manufacturing ceramics, including scrapers, polishing stones, ground stone with clay residues, and pukis (e.g., Geib and Callahan 1988; Haury 1931; Hill 1985; Jones 1986; Judd 1954; Sullivan 1988; Triadan 1989). Unfortunately, some of these tools, particularly the scrapers and polishing stones, may have been used for other activities as well; thus, it is not always possible to argue for ceramic production on the basis of their presence alone. Although caution is advised in the identification of potting tools and materials (Christenson 1991; Sullivan 1988; Waterworth and Blinman 1986), the probability of finding artifacts associated with the production process is so high that researchers should expend more effort in examining the distribution patterns of such tools. Blinman and Wilson (1988) have used regional data on the distribution of these artifacts to look at change through time in the scale of production from A.D. 600 to 800 in the Dolores area of southwestern Colorado. Careful excavation often reveals raw materials as well, including clays, tempers, or pigments, and even unfired vessels (Martin et al. 1961). Other scholars identify clusters of tools and materials of potters or places where potters lived and worked (Crotty 1983; Herr 1993), and some burials have been identified as those of potters on the basis of an associated toolkit (Ravesloot 1992; Shafer 1985). Herr's (1993) comparison of ceramic scrapers recovered from sites along a long transect through northern New Mexico and Arizona found a predictable drop off in these tools at sites where the vessels were finished via the paddle-and-anvil rather than scraping technique.

Differential distributions of tools, materials, and facilities have been used primarily to examine intrasite variability in ceramic production, the dimension of production termed *concentration* (Costin 1991) or *segregation* (Pool 1992). In this volume, Wilson and Blinman use distributions of potting tools to examine the presence of potting and nonpotting households, and thus, the number of potters working within sites.

Identification of Production Loci Through Compositional Analysis

Use of compositional data has become commonplace in studies of production loci and exchange. These data are often used to construct arguments concerning the organization of production as well. Mineralogical and chemical analyses form the basis for determining the source of pottery, identifying the relative concentration of producers within an area, and comparing the relative intensity of production among sites and regions. When pottery is shown to have been manufactured from materials available in a limited area or is found to be compositionally homogeneous despite widespread distribution, scholars have a strong foundation for interpreting limited production loci and subsequent exchange of pottery. Alternatively, it is often possible to identify in site assemblages pottery that was not produced locally. Small-scale exchange of pottery does not necessarily imply production by specialists, but large-scale exchange often does. Therefore, the identification of limited production loci combined with evidence for widespread distribution of a particular pottery type usually indicates specialization. Relative frequencies of local and nonlocal types within and between sites may reveal variable production, exchange, and use of vessels (see Wilson and Blinman, this volume).

A suite of compositional techniques is also used to identify where ceramics were produced in the Southwest. The petrographic microscope remains a mainstay for ceramic analysis (e.g., Danson and Wallace 1956; Douglass 1987; Garrett 1982, 1986; Miksa 1992; Rose and Fournier 1981; Warren 1980). For many studies, petrographic analysis is sufficient for identifying location of production, especially if the sources for aplastics used for temper are restricted in their distribution.

Chemical compositional techniques have become increasingly popular in studies of ceramic production in the Southwest. These methods include the electron microprobe (Abbott 1983; Abbott and Schaller 1991; Abbott and Walsh-Anduze, this volume; Vint 1992); X-ray fluorescence (Crown 1984; Crown et al. 1988; Olinger 1987a, 1987b, 1988; Olinger and Woosley 1989); atomic absorption (Foust et al. 1989; Walker 1992); inductively coupled plasma spectroscopy (Burton and Simon 1993; Duff 1993; Stone 1992; Zedeño 1994; Zedeño et al. 1993); and instrumental neutron activation analysis (Bishop et al. 1988; Crown and Bishop 1991; Deutchman 1980; Elam et al. 1992; Neitzel and Bishop 1990; Ravesloot 1989; Tani 1986; Whittlesey et al. 1992). Compositional data have been important in identifying problems with assigning "local" vs. "nonlocal" status to particular wares based on surface treatment and gross technological characteristics (Crown 1984; Crown and Bishop 1991; Crown et al. 1988; Doyel and Elson 1985; Toll et al. 1980).

Compositional studies have been particularly helpful in showing that the relative concentration of potters within regions of the Southwest may be highly variable. Researchers now agree that some potters were producing more intensively than others in the Hohokam area (Crown 1990: 239; Doyel 1991:233; Neitzel 1991:185–196). In the Anasazi area, Toll has confirmed Shepard's early observations on the intensity of Chuskan ceramic production by demonstrating that this region supplied up to 50 percent of the culinary ceramics used at Chacoan sites (Toll 1984, 1985; Toll and McKenna 1987). The concentration of production at some Rio Grande villages may have been even greater: most vessels of a particular functional class were supplied by a single village or group of villages (Warren 1969).

Compositional data are thus typically used in examining intersite variability in ceramic production. In this volume, the organization of production of Southwestern pottery was assessed using a variety of analytic techniques for determining composition, including petrography (papers by Abbott and Walsh-Anduze; Habicht-Mauche); instrumental neutron activation analysis (papers by Hegmon, Hurst, and Allison; Zedeño; Crown); X-ray fluorescence (paper by Habicht-Mauche); atomic absorption (paper by Mills); inductively coupled plasma spectroscopy (papers by Abbott and Walsh-Anduze; Zedeño); and the electron microprobe (paper by Abbott and Walsh-Anduze).

Indirect Evidence of Ceramic Production Through Examination of Vessels

Southwestern archaeologists have used vessels and sherds for evaluating the organization of production, although interpretations based on the finished products alone are weaker than those based on other forms of data. Many researchers argue that the number of potters producing vessels for a village affects the finished products in identifiable ways; in particular, the frequency of production (greater specialization indicates an increase in each potter's output) is related to the degree of standardization and skill evinced in ceramic vessels. Although ethnoarchaeological research supports this association (Arnold and Nieves 1992; Longacre et al. 1988; Stark, this volume), the relationships are quite complex (Arnold 1991; M. Stark 1993). Some investigators have suggested that measures of mechanical skill are the most appropriate for evaluating the organization of production (e.g., Costin and Hagstrum 1995).

Using analysis of gestures or morphological standardization in products, several investigators in the Southwest have assessed change in the degree of skill apparent in archaeological assemblages over time. Haury (1976) argued that the use of fewer, larger motifs on Sedentary Hohokam red-on-buff pottery indicated mass production, with design quality and detail declining with increased vessel output. Hagstrum (1985) evaluated gestures and morphological standardization for black-on-white ceramics from the northern Rio Grande and found evidence for change toward greater standardization in the Classic period. Motsinger (1992) reached similar conclusions for ceramics from the Galisteo Basin and also found a decrease in the degree of standardization at the end of the sequence. Intriguingly, Toll (1981) found only minor differences in morphological standardization between the heavily imported Chuskan wares at Chaco and local Cibola wares. Longacre et al. (1988) compared the degree of morphological standardization in cooking vessels from the Grasshopper Ruin with ethnoarchaeological data on assemblages from the Philippines. They argued that measures such as the coefficient of variation mean little unless archaeologists first identify appropriate morphological classes in their assemblages. Lindauer (1988) evaluated morphological standardization for a large assemblage of Hohokam red-on-buff vessels and argued that specialists may have produced a few forms.

Morphological characteristics have also been used to evaluate exchange in prehistoric vessels. Whittlesey (1974) argued that bowls produced for exchange should nest for easier and more economical transport. Evaluation of several types of bowls from the Grasshopper Ruin suggested that specific types were produced for exchange and others were not.

A few Southwestern archaeologists have also employed the production-step measure (Feinman et al. 1981) to evaluate the relative labor investment in ceramics. A decline in the measure may indicate increasing cost-efficiency in producing vessels, as would be expected when vessels were manufactured for domestic consumption. Alternatively, vessels with finely executed and highly decorated designs reflect the high labor investment expected on vessels manufactured for consumption by an attached elite. Upham et al. (1981) used the production-step measure, together with varying distributions of particular types, to argue for status differentiation within several settlement systems on the Colorado Plateau. Neitzel (1991) estimated the production costs for several Hohokam pottery types and argued that the differential labor investments reflected differences in the organization of production of those types.

Many of the papers in this volume rely on vessel attributes for evaluating the organization of production. Various researchers examined the skill of potters as revealed by morphological standardization (papers by Mills; Crown; Hegmon, Hurst, and Allison); the frequency of misfired vessels (paper by Hegmon, Hurst and Allison); and the quality of design execution (papers by Crown; Hegmon, Hurst, and Allison). In their paper, Abbott and Walsh-Anduze evaluated the development of manufacturing traditions by examining covariation in a suite of finishing techniques on Hohokam red ware vessels. Stark's paper examines the assumptions made by archaeologists who use morphological standardization to evaluate specialization.

Most research on the organization of production in the Southwest has concentrated on evaluating the existence and degree of craft specialization. Very few studies have attempted to assess the social and political contexts of production. Nonetheless, the high degree of variation in prehistoric Southwestern societies suggests that both social and political contexts were not static (Mills 1995). As the papers in this volume indicate, debates about specific socio-political forms have been rephrased and questions are now being asked that treat these phenomena in more continuous terms. In the absence of clear-cut evidence for attached specialists, different intensities of social and political complexity are dependent upon interpretations of degree of specialization—the amount produced by potters for extra-household consumption (Clark and Parry 1990).

Principles of recruitment into the social units of production are difficult to reconstruct from the archaeological record. Archaeological identification of production cohorts within the Southwest has often been based on ethnographic analogy. Ethnographic descriptions of ceramic production in the Southwest indicate that women were primarily responsible for the manufacture of ceramic vessels (Bunzel 1929; Fontana et al. 1966; Tschopik 1941). Prehistoric burials that contain potters' tool kits (e.g., Ravesloot 1992; Shafer 1985) also confirm that pottery production was a task primarily associated with adult females. Cross-cultural studies indicate that pottery that is hand-built by nonspecialists or part-time specialists in the context of the dispersed household industry is almost always made by women (Arnold 1985; Murdock and Provost 1973). Based on these data and studies, most Southwestern archaeologists assume that women produced the prehistoric pottery found in the Southwest. Historically, however, men at some pueblos participated in decorating vessels made by women (Bunzel 1929). The subject matter of representational painting on Mimbres White Ware vessels has led some researchers to suggest that men participated in at least the painting stage of producing this prehistoric pottery (Brody 1977:116; Jett and Moyle 1986:716–717; Skibo and Schiffer 1995). Although the papers in this volume do not directly address gender issues, recent research on the topics of gender and Southwestern ceramic production has included discussions on the origins of ceramic production (Crown and Wills 1994, 1995) and on ceramic production in the Anasazi (Hays-Gilpin 1993), Zuni (Mills 1994), and Hohokam (Crown and Fish 1994) areas. Further gender research on the organization of production is clearly warranted (Arnold 1985; Wright 1991).

Summary of Volume Chapters

The papers in this volume incorporate diverse methods for approaching the organization of ceramic production in the American Southwest. They also reflect a wide geographic expanse (from southern Colorado to northern Chihuahua) and lengthy time period (from the A.D. 500s to the Protohistoric period). In combination, these papers indicate that specialized production began early in the Southwest, during Basketmaker III (A.D. 575–725) times (see Wilson and Blinman, this volume). Differential distributions of tools, facilities, raw materials, and finished products indicate that some households at this time were producing pottery and others were not, and that potters at some sites were producing some wares more intensively than potters at other sites. Through the following millennium, ceramics were produced with variable concentration and intensity in the Southwest, with evidence for specialized production of some types, wares, or forms in essentially all areas and time periods examined. In addition to these important conclusions, all of the researchers agree on two other points: (1) in none of these case studies was ceramic production organized beyond the level of the dispersed household industry; and (2) in none of these case studies were the specialists attached to an elite. A brief review of the papers emphasizes additional implications.

Hegmon, Hurst, and Allison review evidence for production of red ware and white ware vessels in the San Juan region from approximately A.D. 800–950. Combining data on distribution, composition, and standardization of morphological and design attributes, they argue that red ware production was specialized at the community level, whereas evidence for specialization in the production of white ware is less convincing. Contradictory results from compositional data and morphological and design standardization led these authors to conclude that the wares were made at similar levels of intensity and scale, despite the evidence for more geographically limited production of red ware vessels.

Wilson and Blinman examine white ware manufacture in the Northern San Juan region. Because of the differential distributions of tools, raw materials, and facilities, they argue that the intensity of production varied by site and household through time. Using direct evidence for production, macroscopic compositional differences, and a variety of vessel attributes, they examine changes in the degree of specialization in white ware production over time. Production of white ware vessels intensified during the Pueblo III period, in conjunction with the appearance of formal firing facilities.

Abbott and Walsh-Anduze examine Classic period Hohokam red ware production. Their compositional analysis allows them to determine production loci within the Salt and Gila River basins. Analysis of covariation among surface finish, color, and composition indicates that patterns previously believed to be related to temporal changes in manufacturing traditions is instead due to spatial differences in production techniques. Their results reveal high levels of pottery exchange in the Classic period, and, perhaps most significantly, high levels of exchange among irrigation communities. The authors suggest that the vessels were exchanged on a formalized basis between socially distant parties.

Zedeño evaluates the manufacture and exchange of pottery in the Grasshopper region between approximately A.D. 1250 and 1400. Her research indicates how pottery and the knowledge to make pottery might have circulated in the prehistoric Southwest. Relying on compositional data, she interprets variable sources for the pottery in this region; even single types were apparently manufactured both locally and in other areas. She notes three mechanisms for the movement of ceramic vessels and knowledge: (1) mobile settlement patterns led to contact with populations in surrounding areas and movement of pottery; (2) immigration brought new pots and potters applying their technology to local materials; and (3) ethnic coresidence led to technology transfer from immigrants to local potters. She emphasizes the importance of technological change as a signal of changes in the potting group.

Crown examines the organization of production of the Salado polychromes from approximately A.D. 1275 to 1450. These types are widespread, but compositional analysis indicates that they were manufactured in most areas in which they are found. Analysis of use-wear and context of recovery reveals primarily domestic use, with common placement in burials after use. Examination of morphological standardization and design efficiency suggests production of most vessels at the household level. Product specialization, however, is probable for some large bowl and jar forms. Crown argues that only highly skilled potters had the expertise to manufacture these difficult forms, but that low demand kept this production from intensifying. Her results suggest that women may have begun producing above the needs of the household because of their skill at producing difficult forms rather than their disenfranchisement.

Using the assemblage from Arroyo Hondo Pueblo in the northern Rio Grande, Habicht-Mauche employs compositional data to examine craft specialization and exchange in the Classic period (A.D. 1300–1450). She argues that the early black-on-white types were made over a large area and exchanged among neighboring communities. In contrast, the later glaze ware was produced in a few centers located close to the resources necessary for the glaze paint. Biscuit ware production apparently was also controlled by a few communities. This increasing community specialization was associated with a shift from household production for domestic consumption to a household industry for exchange. The late Classic period decorated ceramics signaled the appearance of a regional tribal alliance with highly integrated economic interaction.

Mills assesses the production of two protohistoric decorated wares in the Zuni area to evaluate possible changes in political organization associated with European contact. She examines standardization in raw-material use through compositional data and in morphology through vessel dimensions. She concludes that the later vessels were produced by fewer potters, with increasing exchange of pottery from fewer production locales after European contact. These results do not support models of greater political complexity in the Zuni area before contact. Indeed, the author suggests that production was consistently at the level of the household, with informal exchange networks between potting and non-potting households.

Stark presents a critique of the concept of standardization. Using ethnographic data from a variety of sources, she challenges the notion that specialized production is necessarily associated with greater morphological standardization. This theoretical overview does not deal specifically with Southwestern data but has important implications for many of the papers presented in this volume. The authors of the regional papers reference this research, which has been widely cited (in unpublished form) for several years. Inclusion of this paper makes Stark's conclusions available to a wider audience, particularly those who are interested in the use of morphological standardization as an argument for specialized production in the Southwest.

Finally, the two symposium discussants, Stephen Plog and Melissa Hagstrum, provide their perspectives on these papers. Each of these authors places the papers in the broader context of research on ceramic production and exchange.

Conclusions

The papers in this volume address ceramic production in a variety of environmental and economic contexts in the American Southwest. In addition, they cover nearly 1,000 years of Southwestern prehistory and history. The resulting spatial and temporal cross section illustrates the diversity of approaches currently in use in the Southwest and the variability in the organization of production within this area.

The papers demonstrate that compositional and noncompositional data provide important clues about the organization of production. Changes in analytic techniques have been accompanied by changes in interpretive paradigms. Prehistoric and early historical ceramic production in the Southwest was far from the uniform system in which each household made all of its own ceramics. Anna O. Shepard would find much more company among archaeologists working in the Southwest today than she did in her own day.

Acknowledgments

We thank Carla Sinopoli and an anonymous reviewer for their many helpful suggestions on this chapter and the other chapters in this volume. We would especially like to thank Chris Szuter, our editor at the press, for all of her encouragement in getting this volume into print, and Evelyn M. VandenDolder for her excellent copyediting. Ronald Stauber drafted figure 1.1.

References Cited

Abbott, David R.
1983   A Technological Assessment of Ceramic Variation in the Salt-Gila Aqueduct Area: Toward a Comprehensive Documentation of Hohokam Ceramics. In *Hohokam Archaeology Along the Salt-Gila Aqueduct, Central Arizona Project, Vol. VIII: Material Culture*, edited by Lynn S. Teague and Patricia L. Crown, pp. 3–117. Arizona State Museum Archaeological Series 150. University of Arizona, Tucson.

Abbott, David R., and David M. Schaller
1991   Electron Microprobe and Petrographic Analyses of Prehistoric Hohokam Pottery to Determine Ceramic Exchange Within the Salt River

Valley, Arizona. In *Materials Issues in Art and Archaeology II,* edited by Pamela B. Vandiver, James Druzik, and George Seagan Wheeler, pp. 441–453. Symposium Proceedings No. 185. Materials Research Society, Pittsburgh.

Arnold, Dean E.
1985　*Ceramic Theory and Cultural Process.* Cambridge University Press, Cambridge.

Arnold, Dean E., and Alvaro L. Nieves
1992　Factors Affecting Ceramic Standardization. In *Ceramic Production and Distribution: An Integrated Approach,* edited by George J. Bey III and Christopher A. Pool, pp. 93–113. Westview Press, Boulder, Colorado.

Arnold, Philip J., III
1991　Dimensional Standardization and Production Scale in Mesoamerican Ceramics. *Latin American Antiquity* 2(4):363–370.

Balfet, Héléne
1965　Ethnographical Observations in North Africa and Archaeological Interpretation: The Pottery of the Maghreb. In *Ceramics and Man,* edited by Frederick R. Matson, pp. 161–177. Aldine Publishing Co., Chicago.

Benco, Nancy L.
1987　*The Early Medieval Pottery Industry at al-Basra, Morocco.* BAR International Series 341. British Archaeological Reports, Oxford.

Bishop, Ronald L., Veletta Canouts, Suzanne P. De Atley, Alfred Qoyawayma, and C. W. Aikins
1988　The Formation of Ceramic Analytical Groups: Hopi Pottery Production and Exchange, A.D. 1300–1600. *Journal of Field Archaeology* 15:317–337.

Bishop, Ronald L., and Hector Neff
1989　Compositional Data Analysis in Archaeology. In *Archaeological Chemistry IV,* edited by Robert O. Allen, pp. 57–86. Advances in Chemistry Series No. 220. American Chemical Society, Washington, D.C.

Bishop, Ronald L., Robert L. Rands, and George R. Holley
1982　Ceramic Compositional Analysis in Archaeological Perspective. In *Advances in Archaeological Method and Theory,* vol. 5, edited by Michael B. Schiffer, pp. 275–330. Academic Press, New York.

Blinman, Eric, and C. Dean Wilson
1988　Overview of A.D. 600–800 Ceramic Production and Exchange in the Dolores Project Area. In *Dolores Archaeological Program: Supportive Studies: Additive and Reductive Technologies,* compiled by Eric Blinman, Carl J. Phagan, and Richard H. Wilshusen, pp. 395–423. U.S. Bureau of Reclamation, Engineering and Research Center, Denver.

Brody, J. J.
1977   *Mimbres Painted Pottery*. School of American Research, Santa Fe, and the University of New Mexico Press, Albuquerque.

Brown, Gary M., and Amy C. Earls
1989   Preliminary Report on Archaeological Data Recovery at LA 61844 (NA-60) and LA 61848 (NA-64), La Plata Mine, San Juan County, New Mexico. Ms. on file, Mariah Associates, Inc., Albuquerque.

Brown, Gary M., Amy C. Earls, and W. Nicholas Trierweiler
1989   Preliminary Report on Archaeological Data Recovery at LA 59954 (OSM-C), LA 61823 (NA-39), LA 61888 (NA-104), and LA 61896 (NA-112), La Plata Mine, San Juan County, New Mexico. Ms. on file, Mariah Associates, Inc., Albuquerque.

Brumfiel, Elizabeth M., and Timothy K. Earle
1987   Specialization, Exchange, and Complex Societies: An Introduction. In *Specialization, Exchange, and Complex Societies*, edited by Elizabeth M. Brumfiel and Timothy K. Earle, pp. 1–9. Cambridge University Press, Cambridge.

Bunzel, Ruth L.
1929   *The Pueblo Potter: A Study of Creative Imagination in Primitive Art*. Columbia University Press, New York.

Burton, James H., and Arleyn W. Simon
1993   Acid Extraction as a Simple and Inexpensive Method for Compositional Characterization of Archaeological Ceramics. *American Antiquity* 58(1):45–59.

Christenson, Andrew L.
1991   Identifying Pukis or Potter's Turntables at Anasazi Sites. *Pottery Southwest* 18(1):1–6.

Clark, John E., and William J. Parry
1990   Craft Specialization and Cultural Complexity. *Research in Economic Anthropology* 12:289–346.

Cordell, Linda S.
1991   Anna O. Shepard and Southwestern Archaeology: Ignoring a Cautious Heretic. In *The Ceramic Legacy of Anna O. Shepard*, edited by Ronald L. Bishop and Frederick W. Lange, pp. 132–153. University Press of Colorado, Niwot.

Costin, Cathy L.
1991   Craft Specialization: Issues in Defining, Documenting, and Explaining the Organization of Production. In *Archaeological Method and Theory*, vol. 3, edited by Michael B. Schiffer, pp. 1–56. University of Arizona Press, Tucson.

Costin, Cathy L., Timothy Earle, Bruce Owen, and Glenn Russell

1989   The Impact of Inca Conquest on Local Technology in the Upper Mon-
taro Valley, Peru. In *What's New? A Closer Look at the Process of Innova-
tion*, edited by Sander E. van der Leeuw and Robin Torrence, pp.
107–139. Unwin Hyman, London.

Costin, Cathy L., and Melissa B. Hagstrum

1995   Standardization, Labor Investment, Skill, and the Organization of Ceramic Production in Late Pre-Hispanic Highland Peru. *American Antiquity*, in press.

Crotty, Helen K.

1983   *Honoring the Dead: Anasazi Ceramics from the Rainbow Bridge–Monument
Valley Expedition*. UCLA Monograph Series No. 22. Museum of Cultural History, University of California, Los Angeles.

Crown, Patricia

1984   An X-ray Fluorescence Analysis of Hohokam Ceramics. In *Hohokam
Archaeology Along the Salt-Gila Aqueduct, Central Arizona Project, Vol.
VIII: Material Culture*, edited by Lynn S. Teague and Patricia L. Crown,
pp. 277–310. Arizona State Museum Archaeological Series 150. University of Arizona, Tucson.

1990   The Hohokam of the American Southwest. *Journal of World Prehistory*
4(2):223–255.

Crown, Patricia L., and Ronald L. Bishop

1991   Manufacture of Gila Polychrome in the Greater American Southwest:
An Instrumental Neutron Activation Analysis. In *Homol'ovi II: Archaeology of an Ancestral Hopi Village, Arizona*, edited by E. Charles Adams
and Kelley Ann Hays, pp. 49–56. Anthropological Papers of the University of Arizona No. 55. University of Arizona Press, Tucson.

Crown, Patricia L., and Suzanne K. Fish

1994   Gender and Power in the Hohokam Pre-Classic to Classic Transition.
Paper presented at the 59th Annual Meeting of the Society for American Archaeology. Anaheim, California.

Crown, Patricia L., Larry A. Schwalbe, and J. Ronald London

1988   X-ray Fluorescence Analysis of Materials Variability in Las Colinas Ce-
ramics. In *Excavations at Las Colinas, Vol. 4: Material Culture*, edited by
David A. Gregory, pp. 29–37. Arizona State Museum Archaeological
Series 162. University of Arizona, Tucson.

Crown, Patricia L., and W. H. Wills

1994   The Origins of Southwestern Ceramic Containers: Women's Time Allocation and Economic Intensification. Paper presented at the 4th Southwest Symposium, Tempe, Arizona.

1995   Economic Intensification and the Origins of Ceramic Containers in the American Southwest. In *The Emergence of Pottery*, edited by W. Barnett and J. Hoopes. Smithsonian Institution Press, Washington, D.C.

Danson, Edward B., and Robert M. Wallace

1956   A Petrographic Study of Gila Polychrome. *American Antiquity* 22:180–182.

Deutchman, Haree L.

1980   Chemical Evidence of Ceramic Exchange on Black Mesa. In *Models and Methods in Regional Exchange*, edited by Robert E. Fry, pp. 119–133. SAA Papers No. 1. Society for American Archaeology, Washington, D.C.

Douglass, Amy A.

1987   *Prehistoric Exchange and Sociopolitical Development: The Little Colorado White Ware Production-Distribution System.* Unpublished Ph.D. dissertation, Department of Anthropology, Arizona State University, Tempe.

Doyel, David E.

1991   Hohokam Exchange and Interaction. In *Chaco and Hohokam, Prehistoric Regional Systems in the American Southwest*, edited by Patricia L. Crown and W. James Judge, pp. 225–252. School of American Research Press, Santa Fe.

Doyel, David E., and Mark D. Elson

1985   *Hohokam Settlement and Economic Systems in the Central New River Drainage, Arizona.* Publications in Archaeology No. 4. Soil Systems, Inc., Phoenix.

Duff, Andrew I.

1993   *An Exploration of Post-Chacoan Community Organization Through Ceramic Sourcing.* Unpublished M.A. thesis, Department of Anthropology, Arizona State University, Tempe.

Elam, J. Michael, Christopher Carr, Michael D. Glascock, and Hector Neff

1992   Ultrasonic Disaggregation and INAA of Textural Fractions of Tucson Basin and Ohio Valley Ceramics. In *Chemical Characterization of Ceramic Pastes in Archaeology*, edited by Hector Neff, pp. 93–112. Prehistory Press, Madison, Wisconsin.

Feinman, Gary, Steven A. Kowaleski, and Richard E. Blanton

1984   Modelling Archaeological Ceramic Production and Organizational Change in the Pre-Hispanic Valley of Oaxaca. In *The Many Dimensions of Pottery: Ceramics in Archaeology and Anthropology*, edited by Sander E. van der Leeuw and Alison C. Pritchard, pp. 295–334. Albert Egges van Giffen Instituut voor Prae-en Protohistorie, Universiteit van Amsterdam, Amsterdam.

Feinman, Gary M., Steadman Upham, and Kent G. Lightfoot
1981   The Production Step Measure: An Ordinal Index of Labor Input in Ceramic Manufacture. *American Antiquity* 46:871–884.

Fontana, Bernard L., William J. Robinson, Charles W. Cormack, and
Ernest E. Leavitt, Jr.
1966   *Papago Indian Pottery.* University of Washington Press, Seattle.

Foust, Richard D., Jr., J. Richard Ambler, and L. D. Turner
1989   Trace Element Analysis of Pueblo II Kayenta Anasazi Sherds. In *Archaeological Chemistry 4,* edited by Ralph O. Allen, pp. 125–143. Advances in Chemistry Series No. 220. American Chemical Society, Washington, D.C.

Fuller, Steven L.
1984   *Late Anasazi Pottery Kilns in the Yellow Jacket District, Southwestern Colorado.* CASA Papers No. 4. Complete Archaeological Service Associates, Cortez, Colorado.

Garrett, Elizabeth M.
1982   *A Petrographic Analysis of Ceramics from Apache-Sitgreaves National Forests, Arizona: On Site or Specialized Manufacture?* Unpublished Ph.D. dissertation, Science Education, Western Michigan University, Kalamazoo.
1986   A Petrographic Analysis of Black Mesa Ceramics. In *Spatial Organization and Exchange: Archaeological Survey on Northern Black Mesa,* edited by Stephen Plog, pp. 114–142. Southern Illinois University Press, Carbondale.

Geib, Phil, and Martha Callahan
1988   Clay Residue on Polishing Stones. *The Kiva* 53(4):357–362.

Hagstrum, Melissa B.
1985   Measuring Prehistoric Ceramic Craft Specialization: A Test Case in the American Southwest. *Journal of Field Archaeology* 12:65–75.

Haury, Emil W.
1931   Showlow and Pinedale Ruins. In *Recently Dated Ruins in Arizona,* by E. W. Haury and L. L. Hargrave, pp. 4–79. Smithsonian Miscellaneous Collections Vol. 82, No. 11. Smithsonian Institution, Washington, D.C.
1976   *The Hohokam: Desert Farmers and Craftsmen.* University of Arizona Press, Tucson.

Hays-Gilpin, Kelley
1993   Symbolic Archaeology, Science, and Other False Dichotomies: Learning About the Broken Flute Basketmakers. Paper presented at the New Mexico Archaeological Council Symposium, "Archaeological Theory: An Examination of Current Perspectives and Applications," Albuquerque.

Helm, Claudia
1973   The Kiln Site. In *Highway U-95 Archaeology: Comb Wash to Grand Flat*, edited by Gardiner Dalley, pp. 209–219. Ms. on file, Department of Anthropology, University of Utah, Salt Lake City.

Herr, Sarah
1993   Broken Pots as Tools. In *Across the Colorado Plateau: Anthropological Studies Along the San Juan Basin and Transwestern Mainline Expansion Pipeline Routes, Vol. 16, Ceramic Interpretations*, by Barbara J. Mills, Christine E. Goetze, and Marja Nieves Zedeño, pp. 347–376. Office of Contract Archeology and Maxwell Museum of Anthropology, University of New Mexico, Albuquerque.

Hibbets, Barry N.
1984   *Excavation and Evaluation of Archeological Site 5MT8451, and a Report of Archeological Monitoring of Celsius [sic] Energy's Cutthroat No. 1 Well Site and Access Road, Montezuma County, Colorado.* LAC Report 8428. La Plata Archeological Consultants, Inc., Dolores, Colorado. Submitted to Celsius [sic] Energy Co., Rock Springs, Wyoming.

Hibbets, Barry N., and Patrick L. Harden
1982   *Archeological Monitoring of Celcius Energy Corporation's Woods Unit 1-S Well Pad and Access Road, and a Report of the Excavation and Evaluation of Site 5MT7143, Montezuma County, Colorado.* LAC Report 8205a. La Plata Archeological Consultants, Inc., Dolores, Colorado. Submitted to Celcius Energy Corp., Rock Springs, Wyoming.

Hill, David V.
1985   Pottery Making at the Ewing Site (5MT927). *Southwestern Lore* 51:19–31.

Huntington, Frederick W.
1986   *Archaeological Investigations at the West Branch Site: Early and Middle Rincon Occupation in the Southern Tucson Basin.* Institute for American Research Anthropological Papers No. 5. Tucson.

Jett, Stephen C., and Peter B. Moyle
1986   The Exotic Origins of Fishes Depicted on Prehistoric Mimbres Pottery from New Mexico. *American Antiquity* 51(4):688–720.

Jones, A. Trinkle
1986   *A Cross-Section of Grand Canyon Archaeology: Excavations at Five Sites Along the Colorado River.* Publications in Anthropology No. 28. Western Archeological and Conservation Center, Tucson.

Judd, Neil
1954   *The Material Culture of Pueblo Bonito.* Smithsonian Miscellaneous Collections No. 24. Smithsonian Institution, Washington, D.C.

Kidder, Alfred V., and Anna O. Shepard

1936 *The Pottery of Pecos: The Glaze-Paint, Culinary, and Other Wares*, vol. 2. Papers of the South West Expedition No. 7. Phillips Academy, Andover, and Yale University Press, New Haven.

Lindauer, Owen

1988 *A Study of Vessel Form and Painted Designs to Explore Regional Interaction of the Sedentary Period Hohokam.* Unpublished Ph.D. dissertation, Department of Anthropology, Arizona State University, Tempe.

Longacre, William A.

1992 *Ceramic Ethnoarchaeology.* University of Arizona Press, Tucson.

Longacre, William A., Kenneth L. Kvamme, and M. Kobayashi

1988 Southwestern Pottery Standardization: An Ethnoarchaeological View from the Philippines. *The Kiva* 53:101–112.

Martin, Paul S., John B. Rinaldo, and William A. Longacre

1961 *Mineral Creek Site and Hooper Ranch Pueblo, Eastern Arizona.* Fieldiana: Anthropology, vol. 52. Chicago Natural History Museum, Chicago.

Miksa, Elizabeth

1992 Appendix A: Petrographic Evaluation of Sand and Sherd Samples: Methodology for the Quantitative and Qualitative Analyses. In *The Rye Creek Project: Archaeology in the Upper Tonto Basin, Vol. 3: Synthesis and Conclusions*, by Mark D. Elson and Douglas B. Craig, pp. 157–184. Center for Desert Archaeology Anthropological Papers No. 11. Tucson.

Mills, Barbara J.

1994 Gender and the Reorganization of Historic Zuni Craft Production. Paper presented at the 4th Biennial Southwest Symposium, Tempe, Arizona.

1995 The Social Context of Production. In *Interpreting Southwestern Diversity: Underlying Principles and Overarching Patterns*, edited by Paul R. Fish and J. Jefferson Reid. Anthropological Research Papers. Arizona State University, Tempe, in press.

Motsinger, Thomas

1992 *The Rise and Fall of a Village Industry: Specialized Ceramic Production in Protohistoric New Mexico.* Unpublished M.A. thesis, Department of Anthropology, Northern Arizona University, Flagstaff.

Murdock, G. P., and C. Provost

1973 Factors in the Division of Labor by Sex: A Cross-Cultural Analysis. *Ethnology* 12:203–225.

Neff, Hector (editor)

1992 *Chemical Characterization of Ceramic Pastes in Archaeology.* Prehistory Press, Madison, Wisconsin.

Neitzel, Jill

1991   Hohokam Material Culture and Behavior: The Dimensions of Organi-
        zational Change. In *Exploring the Hohokam, Prehistoric Desert Peoples of
        the American Southwest*, edited by George J. Gumerman, pp. 177–230.
        University of New Mexico Press, Albuquerque.

Neitzel, Jill E., and Ronald L. Bishop

1990   Neutron Activation of Dogoszhi Style Ceramics: Production and Ex-
        change in the Chacoan Regional System. *The Kiva* 56(1):67–85.

Olinger, Bart

1987a   Pottery Studies Using X-ray Fluorescence. Part 1: An Introduction,
        Nambe Pueblo as an Example. *Pottery Southwest* 14(1):1–5.

1987b   Pottery Studies Using X-ray Fluorescence. Part 2: Evidence of Prehis-
        toric Reoccupation of the Pajarito Plateau. *Pottery Southwest* 14(2):2–5.

1988   Pottery Studies Using X-ray Fluorescence. Part 3: The Historic Pottery
        of the N. Tewa. *Pottery Southwest* 15(4):1–6.

Olinger, Bart, and Anne I. Woosley

1989   Pottery Studies Using X-ray Fluorescence. Part 4: The Pottery of Taos
        Pueblo. *Pottery Southwest* 16(1):1–8.

Peacock, D. P. S.

1982   *Pottery in the Roman World: An Ethnoarchaeological Approach.* Longman,
        London.

Pool, Christopher A.

1992   Integrating Ceramic Production and Distribution. In *Ceramic Produc-
        tion and Distribution, An Integrated Approach*, edited by George J. Bey
        III and Christopher A. Pool, pp. 275–313. Westview Press, Boulder,
        Colorado.

Ravesloot, John C.

1989   Chemical Compositional Analysis of Rillito Red-on-Brown and Santa
        Cruz Red-on-Buff Pottery. In *Hohokam Archaeology Along Phase B of the
        Tucson Aqueduct Central Arizona Project. Volume 1: Syntheses and Interpre-
        tations, Part II*, edited by Jon S. Czaplicki and John C. Ravesloot, pp.
        341–374. Arizona State Museum Archaeological Series 178. University
        of Arizona, Tucson.

1992   The Anglo-American Acculturation of the Gila River Pima: The Mortu-
        ary Evidence. Paper presented at the 25th Annual Conference on His-
        torical and Underwater Archaeology, Kingston, Jamaica.

Rice, Prudence M.

1981   Evolution of Specialized Pottery Production: A Trial Model. *Current
        Anthropology* 22:219–240.

1987   *Pottery Analysis.* University of Chicago Press, Chicago.

1991 Specialization, Standardization, and Diversity: A Retrospective. In *The Ceramic Legacy of Anna O. Shepard*, edited by Ronald L. Bishop and Frederick W. Lange, pp. 257–279. University Press of Colorado, Niwot, Colorado.

Rose, Jerome C., and Dale M. Fournier
1981 Appendix F: Petrographic Analysis of Gray Ware and Brown Ware Ceramics. In *Prehistory of the St. Johns Area, East-Central Arizona: The TEP St. Johns Project*, by Deborah A. Westfall, pp. 405–420. Arizona State Museum Archaeological Series 153. University of Arizona, Tucson.

Schiffer, Michael B.
1987 *Formation Processes of the Archaeological Record*. University of New Mexico Press, Albuquerque.

Shafer, H. J.
1985 A Mimbres Potter's Grave: An Example of Mimbres Craft-Specialization? *Bulletin of the Texas Archaeological Society* 56:185–200.

Shepard, Anna O.
1930 Preliminary Tests Applied in the Classification of Mimbres Pottery: A Summary of Laboratory Studies in Archaeology: July 1927 to October 1929. Ms. on file, Shepard Archive, University of Colorado Museum, Boulder.
1936 The Technology of Pecos Pottery. In *The Pottery of Pecos*, vol. 2, by Alfred V. Kidder and Anna O. Shepard, pp. 389–587. Papers of the South West Expedition No. 7. Phillips Academy, Andover, and Yale University Press, New Haven.
1938 Technological Notes on the Pottery from Unshagi. In *The Jemez Pueblo of Unshagi, New Mexico*, part 2, by Paul Reiter, pp. 205–211. School of American Research and University of New Mexico Monographs No. 6. University of New Mexico Press, Albuquerque.
1939 Technology of La Plata Pottery. In *Archaeological Studies in the La Plata District*, by Earl H. Morris, pp. 249–287. Carnegie Institution of Washington Publication No. 519. Washington, D.C.
1942 *Rio Grande Glaze Paint Ware: A Study Illustrating the Place of Ceramic Technological Analysis in Archaeological Research*. Carnegie Institution of Washington Publication No. 528. Washington, D.C.
1950 Technological Notes on Mesa Verde Pottery. In *Excavations in Mesa Verde National Park, 1947–1948*, by Deric O'Bryan, pp. 89–91, 93–99. Medallion Papers No. 39. Gila Pueblo, Globe, Arizona.
1953 Notes on Color and Paste Composition. In *Archaeological Studies in the Petrified Forest National Monument*, by Fred Wendorf, pp. 177–193. Bulletin No. 27. Museum of Northern Arizona, Flagstaff.

1954   Rebuttal. In *The Material Culture of Pueblo Bonito,* by Neil Judd, pp. 236–238. Smithsonian Miscellaneous Collections No. 24. Smithsonian Institution, Washington, D.C.

1965a   *Ceramics for the Archaeologist.* Publication No. 609. Carnegie Institution of Washington, Washington, D.C.

1965b   Rio Grande Glaze-Paint Pottery: A Test of Petrographic Analysis. In *Ceramics and Man,* edited by Frederick R. Matson, pp. 62–87. Viking Fund Publications in Anthropology No. 41. Wenner-Gren Foundation for Anthropological Research, New York.

1971   Technological Note on Awatovi Pottery. In *Painted Ceramics of the Western Mound at Awatovi,* by Watson Smith, pp. 179–184. Papers of the Peabody Museum of American Archaeology and Ethnology Vol. 38 (Reports of the Awatovi Expedition No. 8). Harvard University, Cambridge.

Sinopoli, Carla M.

1988   The Organization of Craft Production at Vijayanagara, South India. *American Anthropologist* 90:580–597.

Skibo, J. M., and M. B. Schiffer

1995   The Clay Cooking Pot: An Exploration of Women's Technology. In *Expanding Archaeology,* edited by J. M. Skibo, W. Walker, and A. Nielson. University of Utah Press, Salt Lake City.

Stark, Barbara

1985   Archaeological Identification of Pottery Production Locations: Ethnoarchaeological and Archaeological Data from Mesoamerica. In *Decoding Prehistoric Ceramics,* edited by Ben A. Nelson, pp. 158–194. Southern Illinois University Press, Carbondale.

Stark, Miriam

1993   *Ceramic Production and Distribution: An Ethnoarchaeological Case Study of the Kalinga.* Unpublished Ph.D. dissertation, Department of Anthropology, University of Arizona, Tucson.

Stone, Tammy

1992   *The Process of Aggregation in the American Southwest: A Case Study from Zuni, New Mexico.* Unpublished Ph.D. dissertation, Department of Anthropology, Arizona State University, Tempe.

Sullivan, Alan P., III

1988   Prehistoric Southwestern Ceramic Manufacture: The Limitations of Current Evidence. *American Antiquity* 53(1):23–35.

Tani, Masakazu

1986   Chemical Composition Analysis: Southwestern Clays and Sherds. Ms. on file, Department of Anthropology, University of Arizona, Tucson.

Thompson, Raymond H.
1991   Shepard, Kidder, and Carnegie. In *The Ceramic Legacy of Anna O. Shepard*, edited by Ronald L. Bishop and Frederick W. Lange, pp. 11–41. University Press of Colorado, Niwot.

Toll, H. Wolcott
1981   Ceramic Comparisons Concerning Redistribution in Chaco Canyon, New Mexico. In *Production and Distribution: A Ceramic Viewpoint*, edited by Hilary Howard and Elaine L. Morris, pp. 83–122. BAR International Series 120. British Archaeological Reports, Oxford.
1984   Trends in Ceramic Import and Distribution in Chaco Canyon. In *Recent Research on Chaco Prehistory*, edited by W. James Judge and John D. Schelberg, pp. 115–135. Reports of the Chaco Center No. 8. National Park Service, Albuquerque.
1985   *Pottery, Production, Public Architecture, and the Chaco Anasazi System.* Ph.D. dissertation, University of Colorado, Boulder. University Microfilms, Ann Arbor.

Toll, H. Wolcott, and Peter J. McKenna
1987   The Ceramography of Pueblo Alto. In *Artifactual and Biological Analyses, Investigations at the Pueblo Alto Complex, Chaco Canyon, New Mexico, 1975–1979*, vol. 3, part 1, edited by F. Joan Mathien and Thomas C. Windes, pp. 19–230. Publications in Archaeology No. 18F. National Park Service, Santa Fe.

Toll, H. Wolcott, Thomas C. Windes, and Peter J. McKenna
1980   Late Ceramic Patterns in Chaco Canyon: The Pragmatics of Modeling Ceramic Exchange. In *Models and Methods in Regional Exchange*, edited by Robert E. Fry, pp. 95–118. SAA Papers No. 1. Society for American Archaeology, Washington, D.C.

Triadan, Daniel
1989   *Defining Local Ceramic Production at Grasshopper Pueblo, Arizona.* Unpublished M.A. thesis, Freien Universität, Berlin. (Copy on file, Arizona State Museum, Tucson).

Tschopik, Harry, Jr.
1941   *Navaho Pottery Making, An Inquiry into the Affinities of Navaho Painted Pottery.* Papers of the Peabody Museum of American Archaeology and Ethnology Vol. 17, No. 1. Harvard University, Cambridge.

Upham, S., K. Lightfoot, and G. Feinman
1981   Explaining Socially Determined Ceramic Distributions in the Prehistoric Plateau Southwest. *American Antiquity* 46:822–833.

van der Leeuw, Sander
1984   Dust to Dust: A Transformational View of the Ceramic Cycle. In *The Many Dimensions of Pottery: Ceramics in Archaeology and Anthropology,*

edited by Sander E. van der Leeuw and Alison C. Pritchard, pp. 707–778. Albert Egges van Giffen Instituut voor Prae-en Protohistorie, Universiteit van Amsterdam, Amsterdam.

Vint, James
1992   *Electron Microprobe Analysis of Agua Fria Glaze-on-Red Ceramics from Bandelier National Monument, New Mexico.* Unpublished M.A. thesis, Department of Anthropology, Northern Arizona University, Flagstaff.

Walker, Frank Spencer
1992   *Chemical Differentiation of Clays by Atomic Spectroscopy.* Unpublished M.S. thesis, Department of Chemistry, Northern Arizona University, Flagstaff.

Warren, A. Helene
1969   Tonque, One Pueblo's Glaze Pottery Dominated Middle Rio Grande Commerce. *El Palacio* 76:36–42.
1980   A Petrographic Study of the Pottery from Gran Quivera. In *Contributions to Gran Quivera Archaeology, Gran Quivera National Monument, New Mexico,* edited by Alden C. Hayes, pp. 57–75. Publications in Archaeology No. 17. National Park Service, Washington, D.C.

Waterworth, Robert, and Eric Blinman
1986   Modified Sherds, Unidirectional Abrasion, and Pottery Scrapers. *Pottery Southwest* 13(2):4–7.

Whittlesey, Stephanie
1974   Identification of Imported Ceramics Through Functional Analysis of Attributes. *The Kiva* 40:101–112.

Whittlesey, Stephanie, Paul R. Fish, Suzanne K. Fish, Hector Neff, Michael D. Glascock, and J. Michael Elam
1992   An Evaluation of the Production and Exchange of Tanque Verde Red-on-Brown Ceramics in Southern Arizona. In *Chemical Characterization of Ceramic Pastes in Archaeology,* edited by Hector Neff, pp. 233–254. Monographs in World Archaeology No. 7. Prehistory Press, Madison, Wisconsin.

Wright, Rita
1991   Women's Labor and Pottery Production in Prehistory. In *Engendering Archaeology,* edited by Joan M. Gero and Margaret W. Conkey, pp. 194–223. Basil Blackwell, Oxford.

Zedeño, María Nieves
1994   *Sourcing Prehistoric Ceramics at Chodistaas Pueblo, Arizona: The Circulation of People and Pots in the Grasshopper Region.* Anthropological Papers of the University of Arizona No. 58. University of Arizona Press, Tucson.

Zedeño, María Nieves, James Busman, James Burton, and Barbara J. Mills
1993   Ceramic Compositional Analyses. In *Across the Colorado Plateau: An-
        thropological Studies Along the San Juan Basin and Transwestern Mainline
        Expansion Pipeline Routes, Vol. 16, Ceramic Interpretations*, by Barbara J.
        Mills, Christine E. Goetze, and María Nieves Zedeño, pp. 187–234. Of-
        fice of Contract Archeology and Maxwell Museum of Anthropology,
        University of New Mexico, Albuquerque.

2

Production for Local Consumption and Exchange

Comparisons of Early Red and White Ware Ceramics in the San Juan Region

Michelle Hegmon, Winston Hurst,
and James R. Allison

Archaeologists have long recognized that different kinds of ceramics were distributed very differently in the prehistoric Southwest; some appear to have been widely exchanged, whereas others had a much more restricted and localized distribution. Ceramic exchange and its implications for regional economic systems have been the focus of recent research (e.g., Doyel 1991; Plog 1986; Toll 1991). However, the production of those ceramics—including whether and to what degree production was specialized—has received much less attention (though see Bishop et al. 1988; Crown 1994; Graves 1994). Our goal here, as part of this volume, is to focus specifically on understanding ceramic production in relation to distribution and exchange.

This chapter addresses the problem by comparing ceramics that were distributed at different scales in the prehistoric Southwest. Specifically, the focus is on red and white ware ceramics in the Northern San Juan region (fig. 2.1) during the ninth and early tenth centuries A.D., the late Pueblo I and very early Pueblo II periods. The white ware types appear to have been made and used locally, whereas the red ware types were distributed well beyond their zone of production. We proceed by first examining data on ceramic distribution. Then we consider compositional data to gain information about production sources. Finally, we evaluate the standardization of the ceramics to understand the organization of production in more detail.

Production, Distribution, and Standardization

Recent research has demonstrated, not surprisingly, that ceramic production and its relationship to standardization are complex issues. Both production and standardization are multidimensional concepts, and their relationship is by no means constant. Much research on ceramic production and specialization focuses on administratively complex societies with fairly high degrees of specialization (e.g., Brumfiel and Earle 1987; Clark and Parry 1990; Costin 1991; Feinman et al. 1984; Peacock 1981, 1982; Rice 1981; Sinopoli 1988; van der Leeuw 1977, 1984). These studies devote relatively little attention to less complex societies, such as those present in the early Puebloan Southwest. We hope here to contribute to research on prehistoric production by expanding archaeologists' understanding of less complex systems.

Production Systems

In considering production systems, we draw most heavily on Costin's recent formulation (1991:8–18; see also Mills and Crown, this volume), in which she conceives of the organization of production in terms of four parameters: context, concentration, scale, and intensity. Her formulation considers only specialized production, but it can be expanded to include unspecialized household production as well. We use Spielmann's (1988) definition of specialization because it is particularly well suited to relatively low levels of complexity. *Specialization* is defined as "production above the needs of the household for purposes of exchange. . . . The term implies a relatively small number of producers in relation to the number of consumers" (Spielmann 1988:1). The focus is primarily on what Rice (1991:265) calls producer specialization, though, as will become apparent, her concepts of site and resource specialization are also relevant.

Because the levels of administrative complexity and specialization were fairly limited in early Pueblo societies, this discussion of production systems is limited to three of Costin's parameters: concentration, scale, and intensity. Although some (e.g., Kane 1989) have argued that

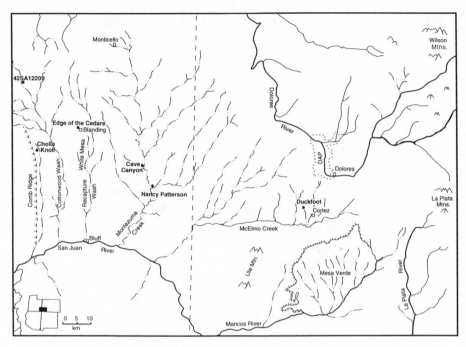

Figure 2.1 Portion of the San Juan region in southeastern Utah and southwestern Colorado, showing the locations of the sites used in the analysis. Sites are indicated with dots and names are in bold. Modern towns are indicated by open squares. The location of the Dolores Archaeological Program (DAP) study area is indicated by a dotted line.

social hierarchies were present in the northern Southwest during the ninth century, there is no evidence of the kind of elite control of production or well-developed administrative complexity that may have been present in later periods (e.g., Upham 1982). Thus, the production context is assumed to have been one of *independent* producers rather than producers attached to elites or government institutions. In addition, given the absence of any evidence of elaborate workshops with expensive technology such as true kilns or wheels, the scale of production is assumed to have been fairly limited, involving nothing larger than interhousehold work groups (see Wilson and Blinman, this volume). Finally, although intensity is difficult to assess archaeologically (Costin 1991:30; Rice 1991: 263), pottery producers are assumed to have been, at most, part-time specialists who were not totally dependent on others for their sustenance.

This last assumption is based on the presence of generalized inventories of goods in Pueblo I households, which indicate that these households engaged in a variety of activities (Varien and Lightfoot 1989).

Given these assumptions, we focus on two basic issues regarding the organization of ceramic production and specialization. First, is there any evidence for specialized production of the red or white ware ceramics? Second, if production was specialized, how were specialists distributed (i.e., were they dispersed across the area or were they concentrated in certain communities)? We consider three basic modes of production: (1) unspecialized household production, in which each household makes pottery for its own use; (2) dispersed individual specialization, in which a few individuals or households make pottery for an entire community; and (3) community specialization, in which individual specialists, aggregated in a limited number of communities, produce pottery for regional distribution.

Dispersed individual specialization and community specialization differ mainly in the spatial distribution of both the producers and their goods. Other aspects of the organization of production may be very similar. For example, in both cases households or interhousehold groups produce surpluses, usually on a part-time basis. In the first case, certain individuals produce a surplus of goods that are used primarily by other members of their community. In the second case, some or all households in certain communities produce surpluses that are distributed to other communities. Although examples of community specialization are common in both the ethnographic and archaeological literature (e.g., Allen 1984; Dietler and Herbich 1989; Ford 1972; Harding 1967; Irwin 1978; Shepard 1942), the concept of community specialization as a system of production has only recently been discussed explicitly (Costin 1991; Rice 1987: 191; Spielmann 1988; see also Muller [1984, 1987] and Rice [1991:262] on site and resource specialization). Community and site specialization are important in archaeological research because they should be discernible in the archaeological record, even if individual specialization is not.

Specialization and Standardization

Archaeologists often assume that craft products will become more standardized as their production becomes more specialized, and several studies give some support to this assumption (e.g., Hagstrum 1985; Longacre et al. 1988; Rice 1981:222–223; Sinopoli 1988:582; Whittaker 1987: 474; see also Stark, this volume). Specialists are expected to make more standardized products both because they are more skillful and because they may be motivated to increase their efficiency by simplifying and standardizing their products (Allen 1984:422–423; Hagstrum 1985:68). In addition, an assemblage will appear to be more standardized if it is made by fewer producers because of what Stark (this volume) calls the "ratio effect"; i.e., standardization will increase as the ratio of producers to products decreases.

Other recent studies, however, show that the relationship between specialization and standardization is highly complex and does not apply in all cases. In her comparison of the products of specialist and nonspecialist potters from Papua New Guinea, Guatemala, and the Amazon Basin, Stark (this volume) reports that the products of individual specialists are, on the average, more standardized than those of nonspecialists. However, she also reports a great deal of variation in the degree of standardization exhibited by specialists, and some specialists produced less standardized ceramics than some nonspecialists.

The complexity of this relationship between specialization and standardization can be understood, at least to some extent, by studying four components of ceramic standardization (or variability): intentional stylistic, gross formal, compositional, and mechanical and technological characteristics (see Costin 1991; Costin and Hagstrum 1995; Rice 1987: 202–204).

Intentional stylistic components of ceramics (e.g., decoration) are strongly affected by social variables and, thus, have a tenuous relationship to the system of production. In some cases, ceramics with apparently standardized designs were produced at different locations and at a fairly small scale (e.g., Salado polychromes [Crown 1994]). On the other hand, some specialists created highly variable designs to express their individuality (Costin 1991:34, citing Earle 1982).

Gross formal characteristics, such as size and shape, are strongly associated with the intended use of the ceramics. It is therefore unlikely that these characteristics and specialization are strongly related. These characteristics are still valuable, however, to the study of specialization and standardization. For example, size and shape are important attributes of ceramics that are made for long-distance distribution, especially in areas where community specialization is prevalent. Smaller vessels are easier to transport, and standard-sized bowls that can be stacked and nested are especially desirable (Rice 1987:202; Whittlesey 1974). Some specialists may produce a wider variety of forms than do nonspecialists. Even if each form is highly standardized, it may be difficult to separate them in an archaeological context. Longacre et al. (1988) note that lumping emic functional classes in their Kalinga and Paradijon data greatly inflates their measures of variation, making the assemblages appear less standardized. It is therefore important to measure standardization separately on different sizes and shapes of ceramic vessels whenever distinct classes can be recognized.

Material composition (i.e., the chemical and mineralogical characteristics of the clay and temper) can provide important information on sources of production (e.g., Bishop et al. 1988; Crown 1994; Fish et al. 1992; Foust et al. 1989; Shepard 1942). Compositional data may be used to infer the number of production sources. The number of sources, however, is not equivalent to the number of potters or workshops because several potters may exploit one source and one potter may use several sources. Compositional data at least provide general information on the concentration and distribution of production sources.

Mechanical or technological variables are probably most directly related to productive specialization, and they are most often measured in research on standardization (Costin and Hagstrum 1995; Motsinger 1990; Rice 1989:113). These subtle variables reflect how a pot was made (e.g., rim form), decorated (e.g., line width), or fired (e.g., paste color). As the scale of production increases and a potter produces a greater volume, production techniques become more routinized and skill levels increase, resulting in more standardization (see Hill 1977).

This chapter considers stylistic and gross formal characteristics only briefly (see Allison 1991 and Hegmon 1995a for a more detailed discussion of style). The focus is on material composition and mechanical and technological variables. After discussing ceramic distribution, we use compositional data to gain basic information on the number of sources and general organization of production. We then use the standardization of mechanical and technological variables to gain a more detailed understanding of the organization of production.

The Database: Red and White Wares

We examine the relationship between production and distribution by comparing red and white ware ceramics from the San Juan region of the northern Southwest during the ninth and early tenth centuries A.D. We specifically focus on Bluff Black-on-red (Breternitz et al. 1974:57–59), Piedra Black-on-white (Breternitz et al. 1974:29–31), and White Mesa Black-on-white (Blinman and Wilson 1989:15; Hurst et al. 1985; fig. 2.2). These types can be distinguished on the basis of technological criteria (slip, polish, and paint color) as well as painted designs. Sherds that could be classified by these criteria were included in the analysis to maximize the sample size.

Previous research provides important background information on the production and distribution of these three types. Both the red and white wares are tempered primarily with crushed igneous rock (commonly andesite or diorite). This rock is available in most parts of the San Juan region north of the San Juan River. It is therefore likely that all three types were made somewhere in the San Juan region. At least three subtraditions of Pueblo I white ware are known in the Northern San Juan region (i.e., White Mesa Black-on-white in southeastern Utah, Piedra Black-on-white in southwestern Colorado, and Glaze-painted Piedra Black-on-white farther east along the Animas River in Colorado [see Wilson and Blinman, this volume]). These subtraditions suggest that the white ware types were made in several areas and that the distribution of each type was limited. Citing this evidence of subtraditions and drawing on data on ceramic manufacturing debris and tools, Wilson and Blinman (this volume; see also Blinman 1988:76–95) argue that white ware production was specialized at a small scale (i.e., a few potters produced material for an entire community). Thus, the white ware would have been exchanged locally and perhaps within the region. San Juan Red Ware has been found throughout the Northern San Juan region; no subtraditions have been identified, nor are there differences within this ware from different areas. Red ware is most abundant in southeastern Utah; many researchers assume that most or all of the San Juan Red Ware was made in that area and exchanged widely (Hurst 1983; Lucius and Breternitz 1981). Red-firing clays also appear to be most abundant in southeastern Utah, although they are available in other parts of the Northern San Juan region.

Our research is based on a detailed analysis of ceramics from five sites (fig. 2.1): the Duckfoot Site (5MT3868, Lightfoot 1992; Lightfoot and Etzkorn 1993) in southwestern Colorado; Nancy Patterson Village (42sa2110, Thompson et al. 1988) in Montezuma Canyon in southeasternmost Utah; and Edge of the Cedars Pueblo (42sa700, Green 1970; Hurst

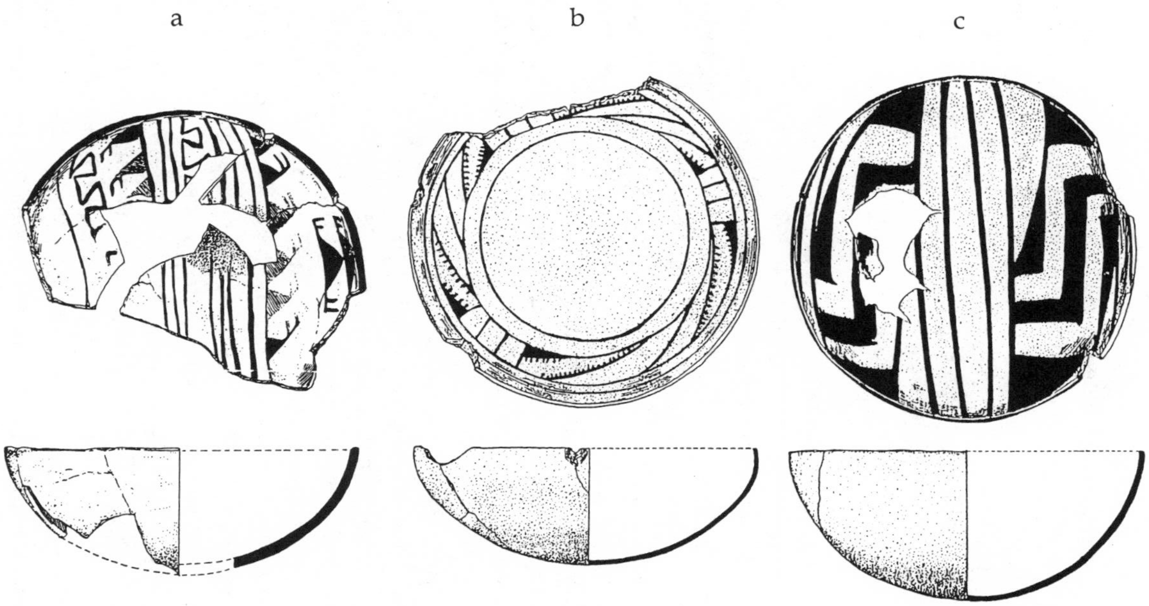

Figure 2.2 Illustrations of the ceramic types used in the analysis: (a) Piedra Black-on-white; (b) White Mesa Black-on-red; (c) Bluff Black-on-white. Diameter of Piedra bowl is 19 cm; others are drawn to same scale. Illustrations by B. J. Earle; (b) and (c) reproduced, with permission, from Forsyth (1977:figs. 58 and 10).

1990), 42sa12209 (Fetterman et al. 1988), and Cholla Knoll (42sa555, Nelson 1978), all located west of Montezuma Canyon in southeastern Utah. In many of the analyses, the latter three sites are combined and referred to as the "Utah West" group. Some of the sites (e.g., Duckfoot) were occupied during a short, tightly dated period; others were occupied for longer periods and are less well dated (e.g., Edge of the Cedars). Where possible, analyses focus on deposits dated to the ninth and early tenth centuries. However, because the analysis is typologically based and all three types are associated with the Pueblo I period, temporal control of the ceramic samples could be maintained, even where the deposits are mixed.

The Distribution of Red and White Wares

The Pueblo I red and white wares were distributed differently across the Northern San Juan region and beyond. The general distributions are shown in Table 2.1, and more detailed distributions are shown in Table 2.2. Bluff Black-on-red and other San Juan Red Ware types are most abundant (as a percentage of the total ceramic assemblage) in southeastern Utah, particularly in Montezuma Canyon. Red ware is also relatively common in the eastern part of the San Juan region, in southwestern Colorado. Furthermore, San Juan Red Ware is consistently present (though in low frequencies) in areas beyond the San Juan region, such as Black Mesa in northeastern Arizona more than 100 km south of the San Juan River. In contrast, the two black-on-white types were distributed over more restricted areas (less than 50 km in diameter). With the exception of trace quantities, Piedra Black-on-white is found only in southwestern Colorado and northernmost New Mexico, and White Mesa Black-on-white is found only in southeastern Utah. The latter is most common west of Montezuma Canyon; thus, its distribution in southeastern Utah is somewhat complementary to that of the red wares.

The distributions alone indicate that red and white wares were produced and distributed at different scales in the ninth century San Juan region. San Juan Red Ware sherds are found across a broad area. Their presence in northeastern Arizona is clear evidence that they were distributed well beyond their zone of production (i.e., somewhere in the Northern San Juan region). If most or all of the red ware was made in southeastern Utah, then its distribution across the San Juan region suggests

Table 2.1 Summary Distribution of Red and White Wares, Showing
Counts and Percentages of Total Ceramic Assemblage

Area	Red Wares	White Wares	Total Ceramics	Red/White Ratio
Montezuma Canyon	18,316[a]	1,667[b]	94,543	10.99
	19.4%	1.8%		
Utah West	3,434[a]	1,159[b]	25,796	2.96
	13.3%	4.5%		
Mesa Verde	1,093[a]	979[b]	25,705	1.12
(SW CO)	4.3%	3.8%		
Dolores & Duckfoot	10,946[a]	9,968[b]	203,076	1.10
(SW CO)	5.4%	4.9%		
Black Mesa	498[a]	18,907[c]	59,739	0.03
(NE AZ)	0.8%	31.6%		

SOURCES: Montezuma Canyon includes Cave Canyon Village (Christensen 1980; Harmon 1979), Monument Village (Patterson 1975) and Nancy Patterson Village (J. R. Allison's analysis for this chapter). Utah West includes sites west of Montezuma Canyon: Cholla Knoll (Emery 1981; Nelson 1978), Edge of the Cedars Pueblo (proveniences with less than 3 percent corrugated gray ware; Walker 1980), Woodrat Knoll (Nickens 1977), 42sa12209 (Fetterman et al. 1988), and 42sa8014 (Davis 1985). Mesa Verde includes ninth-century proveniences from Site 1676 (Hayes and Lancaster 1975). Dolores includes refuse collections dated A.D. 800–920 (Blinman 1988:240). Duckfoot includes total ceramic assemblage from Crow Canyon Archaeological Center's database. Black Mesa includes D:11:2023, D:11:2025, D:11:2027 (Nichols and Smiley 1984), and D:11:2030 (Christenson and Parry 1985)

[a]Most or all are San Juan Red Wares.
[b]Most or all are San Juan White Wares, considered local to the San Juan region.
[c]Most or all are Tusayan White Wares, considered local to northeastern Arizona.

Table 2.2 Distribution of San Juan Red and White Wares, Showing Counts and
Percentages of Total Ceramic Assemblage

Site	Bluff B/R	San Juan Red Ware	White Mesa B/W	Piedra B/W	San Juan White Ware	Tusayan White Ware	Total
Edge of Cedars	1,089 2.8%	2,413 6.1%	1,138 2.9%	trace	5,555 14.0%	trace	39,616
Cholla Knoll	250 7.4%	456 13.5%	73 2.2%	0?	204 6.0%	trace	3,374
42Sa 12209	412 10.7%	505 13.1%	132 3.4%	0	132 3.4%	0	3,862
Dolores	572 0.9%	3,963 6.2%	trace	584 0.9%	3,328 5.2%	trace	90,879
Duckfoot	2,023 1.8%	5,795 5.2%	0?	1,175 1.0%	5,624 5.0%	0?	112,197
Black Mesa	?	409 0.7%	0?	0?	0?	18,907 31.6%	59,439

SOURCES: Edge of the Cedars data include entire site tallies. Specimens originally classified
by Walker as Cortez Black-on-white are here interpreted as White Mesa Black-on-white,
based on Winston Hurst's reanalysis for this chapter. Cholla Knoll data are from Nelson
(1978). Specimens originally classified as Kana'a Black-on-white are here interpreted as
White Mesa Black-on-white, based on Hurst's reanalysis. Dolores data are from selected
assemblages used in ceramic dating, A.D. 775–910 (Blinman 1986:73). Others as referenced
in Table 2.1.

that its production was specialized at the community level, with one or
more communities in southeastern Utah producing it for exchange.

In contrast, both white ware types had relatively limited distributions,
and there is no evidence that they were distributed beyond the areas
where they were produced. These data suggest that the white ware ceramics were produced and distributed at a local level. Although these
data provide little information regarding the scale of white ware produc-

tion, they do not contradict the suggestion that it was specialized on a small scale.

The reddish orange color of San Juan Red Ware is made by firing the ceramics in an oxidizing atmosphere, at least in the final stages of the firing. However, some apparently misfired red ware sherds are gray, suggesting that the proper atmosphere was not achieved. When refired in an oxidizing atmosphere, these misfired sherds become reddish orange. Although we cannot be certain that sherds classified as "misfired" were perceived as mistakes by early Pueblo potters, analysis of these sherds does provide a means of comparing production techniques at different sites.

The distribution of misfired red wares is shown in Table 2.3. Misfired pieces are very common (17 percent of the red ware sherd assemblage) at Nancy Patterson Village, they are less common on sites farther west, and they are least common at the Duckfoot Site. It is likely that mistakes (i.e., misfired pieces) will most often be left where they are produced and less often be exported (Russell 1988, cited in Costin 1991:20). If misfired sherds represent mistakes in some sense, the distribution of misfired red wares supports the argument that red wares were produced in southeastern Utah and exported to southwestern Colorado. This distribution also suggests that the Montezuma Canyon area (where Nancy Patterson Village is located) was the locus (or at least the core area) of red ware production. The very high percentage of misfired sherds (nearly one-fifth of the assemblage) at Nancy Patterson Village suggests that specialization, if present, may have involved considerable variability in production techniques.

Table 2.3 Distribution of Misfired Red Wares

Site or Area	% Red Wares Misfired
Red Knobs (along Cottonwood Wash, near Utah West group)	9
Utah West	10
Nancy Patterson (Montezuma Canyon)	17
Duckfoot (southwestern Colorado)	5

Compositional Analyses

To understand the ceramic production sources, we conducted a series of analyses of the ceramics' temper and chemical composition. Some of these results are preliminary, though further work is planned (Hegmon and Allison 1990); therefore, the analyses are described only briefly here. Petrographic analysis (done by Michelle Hegmon and Elizabeth Garrett) was used to examine the igneous rock temper in 61 samples of Piedra Black-on-white and generalized Pueblo I white ware from southwestern Colorado (Garrett 1990; Hegmon 1995b). Fifteen of these samples were from the Duckfoot Site; the remaining 46 were from three sets of sites excavated by the Dolores Archaeological Program (DAP; see fig. 2.1). Most of the nonplastic inclusions in the ceramics were porphyries with phenocrysts of twinned and untwinned feldspars, biotite, and in some inclusions, hornblende and pyroxene. However, the specific characteristics of the rocks, especially of the feldspar minerals, are quite variable with some consistent intersite differences. Specifically, three sets of characteristics differentiate the Duckfoot and Dolores samples. First, rock characterized as cryptocrystalline groundmass with quartz fragments is much more common in the Duckfoot sample (20 percent) than in the Dolores sample (2 percent). Second, feldspars characterized as moderately or heavily clouded (the clouding is an indication of decomposition) are much more common in the Dolores sample (67 percent) than in the Duckfoot sample (7 percent). Third, abundant twinning of feldspars is much more common in the Duckfoot sample (69 percent) than in the Dolores sample (16 percent).

Igneous rocks apparently suitable for ceramic temper are available from igneous outcrops and from streams and terraces across much of the Northern San Juan region. Various potential source materials were analyzed but were not found to be a close match for the ceramic temper. Despite this failure to identify specific sources, the analyses still provided important information regarding ceramic production. First, the differences noted between the Duckfoot and Dolores samples indicate that different sources were used to produce the two samples and that Piedra Black-on-white was made at several locations across southwestern Colorado. These differences also support the argument that white ware was produced locally (i.e., at a scale of tens of kilometers) at many sites across the area. Second, the rock temper is much less variable than the suite of locally available igneous rocks. It appears that potters making Pueblo I white ware in southwestern Colorado carefully selected certain kinds of rocks and that the same selection criteria were applied at several production locales.

Instrumental neutron activation analysis (INAA) was used to determine the chemical composition of the ceramics and assess the compositional homogeneity or variability of each type. INAA is a sensitive multielemental technique that determines the chemical composition of a sample. Numerous archaeological applications have demonstrated its use for research on ceramic production and exchange (e.g., Bishop et al. 1988; Neff 1989, 1992; Perlman and Asaro 1969; Wilson 1978). Interpretation of the INAA data involves searching for groups of chemically similar samples, working under the general assumption that a group was probably made from the same materials and in the same place (Bishop et al. 1982). We performed the INAA analysis using facilities at the National Institute of Standards and Technology, in association with Ronald Bishop and James Blackman of the Smithsonian Institution's Conservation Analytical Laboratory.

The analysis assessed the bulk chemical composition of the ceramics, i.e., the composition of the clay and temper combined. Igneous rock temper is potentially problematic for this kind of procedure because igneous rocks are heterogeneous, chemically complex, and rich in many of the elements (such as iron, scandium, and the rare earths) that are commonly used to differentiate clay sources. Igneous rock temper, therefore, is expected to add "noise" to the analysis. A group of ceramics made from a single clay source and single igneous rock source would be expected to be somewhat heterogeneous chemically. The extent of the heterogeneity and whether groups can be differentiated depend on the sources and the differences among them.

To determine the utility of INAA for this situation, we conducted a pilot study with samples of each type. We analyzed 19 samples of Bluff Black-on-red (18 from Edge of the Cedars and 1 from Black Mesa, Arizona), 17 samples of White Mesa Black-on-white (from Edge of the Cedars), and 11 samples of Piedra Black-on-white (10 from Duckfoot and 1 from Dolores). The distributions of the samples based on the concentrations of iron and scandium are shown in figure 2.3. These two elements are particularly useful for this kind of analysis because they can be detected with a high level of precision. In addition, they tend to substitute

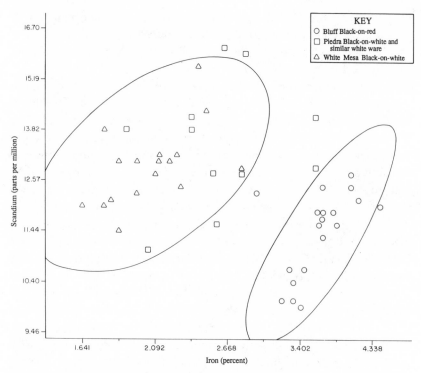

Figure 2.3 Distribution of Bluff Black-on-red, Piedra Black-on-white, and White Mesa Black-on-white, showing the concentrations of iron and scandium. Ellipses show 95-percent confidence interval. The ellipse for the Bluff group was calculated excluding the one outlier. Figure courtesy of Crow Canyon Archaeological Center, Cortez, Colorado.

for each other chemically, so sources can often be distinguished on the basis of the iron-scandium ratio, graphically seen as a cigar-shaped plot (Sayre 1975).

Eighteen of the 19 red ware specimens group together quite tightly; they are neatly bounded by a 95-percent confidence interval. The single specimen from Arizona groups together with 17 of the Edge of the Cedars specimens. The one outlier is from Edge of the Cedars. The White Mesa Black-on-white specimens also group together and are bounded by a 95-percent confidence interval, though they are more broadly distributed than the red ware specimens. In contrast, the Piedra Black-on-white specimens are broadly scattered and do not form a distinguishable chemical group. These compositional analyses, combined with the data on distribution, can be used to offer some tentative conclusions regarding the production of the three ceramic types.

Bluff Black-on-red is widely distributed across the Northern San Juan region and beyond. The sample of Bluff Black-on-red from Edge of the Cedars forms a tight chemical-composition group, and the one specimen from Black Mesa, Arizona, is chemically indistinguishable from the Utah sample. These data provide fairly strong evidence that Bluff Black-on-red was produced in southeastern Utah and distributed—probably exchanged—across the San Juan region and beyond. Because Bluff Black-on-red was apparently produced in a relatively small area but was widely distributed, we believe it was produced by specialized communities. However, more research is needed to determine the number of production centers, their locations, and the scale and intensity of red ware production.

White Mesa Black-on-white also forms a relatively tight chemical-composition group. Unlike Bluff Black-on-red, however, its distribution is limited to southeastern Utah. The compositional homogeneity suggests that the production of White Mesa Black-on-white was somehow restricted, though its limited distribution indicates that production was probably not specialized at the community level. We suggest that White Mesa Black-on-white was produced by dispersed individual specialists.

Piedra Black-on-white is quite heterogeneous compositionally, and petrographic analysis indicates that temper sources are fairly localized. Furthermore, Piedra, like White Mesa, has a relatively restricted distribution. There is no evidence for community specialization in the production of Piedra Black-on-white. The chemical heterogeneity argues against large-scale or intense production. It is possible that it was produced by dispersed individual specialists. However, this chemical heterogeneity indicates that more sources were used to produce Piedra than White Mesa ceramics and that Piedra was produced on a smaller scale and/or with less intensity.

Mechanical and Technological Standardization

Data on ceramic distribution and composition provide important information regarding the sources of ceramic production. However, these data

provide relatively little information about the details of productive organization, including the scale and intensity of production. To investigate
these factors, we reviewed data on the standardization of the ceramics,
focusing on detailed attributes of form and design. We expected that as
scale (the size of the work unit) and intensity (the volume per producer)
increased, standardization would have resulted because of increases in
skill, efficiency, and the consumer-to-producer ratio. In our analysis of
standardization, we compared ceramic types from the same site or area
to ensure relative temporal equivalence (a procedure advocated by Stark,
this volume). We also compared ceramic types between regions and with
each other to gain a broader understanding of the relative standardization of each type. Furthermore, to control for vessel form (Longacre et al.
1988), we considered only bowls because bowls account for 85 to 100 percent of the assemblages, and samples of other forms are too limited.

Form and Design

Variation in ceramic form and design was assessed by evaluating several
attributes on rim sherds (fig. 2.4). Most of these attributes (e.g., line width
and rim shape) likely resulted from the mechanics of the production
process and should be closely related to the scale and intensity of production. A few attributes (e.g., the presence or absence of a rim line) are
probably stylistic in nature and were assessed in relation to the mechanical variables.

   We considered three continuous variables: bowl radius, line width,
and wall thickness. We examined frequency distributions of the variables
for each type at each site or area to determine whether any had a multimodal distribution. Multiple modes would have provided important information regarding different classes of ceramics that must be separated
in assessing standardization (see Longacre et al. 1988). Multiple size
modes have been noted in analyses of later Southwestern ceramics (Mills
1989; Turner and Lofgren 1966). However, none of the Pueblo I types exhibited a multimodal distribution (e.g., fig. 2.5), so we proceeded with
quantitative summaries of the data, focusing on the coefficient of variation. The results, arranged in terms of three sets of comparisons, are
shown in Tables 2.4 to 2.6. Within each table, the coefficients of variation
are ranked, with the highest rank (1) indicating the greatest variability.

   Variation in Bluff Black-on-red divided by area is shown in Table 2.4.
The Duckfoot sample is least variable in radius and thickness but most

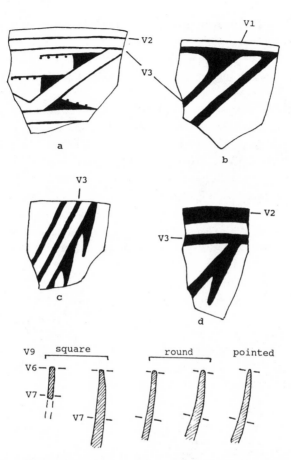

Figure 2.4 Variables measured on rim sherds and used in the analysis of standardization. (a) White Mesa Black-on-white; (b) Bluff Black-on-red; (c) Piedra Black-on-white; (d) Bluff Black-on-red; (V1) Line on rim (present or absent); (V2) Line below and parallel to rim (present or absent); (V3) Modal line width (mm); (V4) *not used*; (V5) Interior radius (cm) (*not illustrated*); (V6) Thickness of walls directly below rim (mm); (V7) Thickness of walls measured two centimeters below rim (mm); (V8) Relation of walls at rim: If V7-V6 < 1, the walls are considered to be *parallel*; If V7-V6 > 1, the walls are considered to be *tapered*; (V9) Rim shape (square, round, or pointed).

variable in line width. Although the trend is not strong, these results suggest that red ware vessels exported to southwestern Colorado were more standardized than those used in southeastern Utah. These results complement the finding that misfired pieces are least abundant in southwestern Colorado.

Comparisons of the three types, either overall (table 2.6) or divided by site (tables 2.4 and 2.5), show that Bluff Black-on-red is consistently the most variable in all three attributes (fig. 2.6). White Mesa and Piedra Black-on-white vessels display roughly equal degrees of variability. When the white ware types are compared as a whole (table 2.6), Piedra appears to be less variable, though the difference may be due to the contexts of the different samples; i.e., the Piedra assemblage is from a single site, whereas the White Mesa is from four sites. When single-site assemblages are compared (table 2.5), White Mesa is slightly less variable than Piedra.

We also considered three categorical variables: rim form (square, round, or pointed), line on rim (present or absent), and rim walls (tapered or parallel; fig. 2.4). States of these variables by type are listed in Table

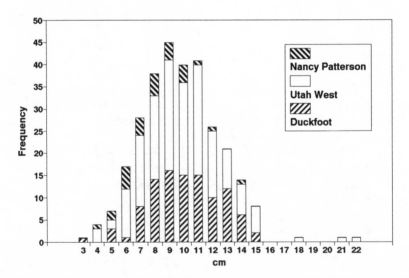

Figure 2.5 Histogram of bowl radius measurements on Bluff Black-on-red, showing a unimodal distribution.

Table 2.4 Summary Statistics of Continuous Variables on Bluff Black-on-
Red Bowls, Divided by Site and Area

Site or Area	Variable	N	Mean	C.V.	Rank	Min.	Max.
Duckfoot	Radius	103	10.10	23.76	3	3	15
	Line Width	79	3.90	62.56	1	2	20
	Thickness	135	4.82	15.56	3	3	7
Utah	Radius	162	9.90	28.99	1.5	4	22
West	Line Width	82	3.79	41.16	2	2	10
	Thickness	264	4.20	20.71	2	4	8
Nancy	Radius	28	8.02	27.68	1.5	4	14
Patterson	Line Width	44	4.03	31.51	3	2	8
	Thickness	49	4.39	24.60	1	2	6

2.7. With the exception of the rim line, the attribute states are quite variable across all three types; i.e., none is present in more than 73 percent of
the cases. Only the rim lines are highly consistent: they are present on 98
percent of the White Mesa sample. However, the significance of the rim
lines is difficult to evaluate because a rim line is a stylistic attribute that
may be affected by social factors. Using contingency tables, we examined
the association of these attributes, but the tables also revealed no consistent differences between the types.

Standardization and Specialization

The results of these analyses of both continuous and categorical variables
are surprising. They reveal relatively few differences in the standardization of ceramic form. Bluff Black-on-red, the type for which we have the
strongest evidence of specialized production based on the compositional
data, is the least standardized in form and design. In other words, we
have fairly strong evidence that Bluff Black-on-red was produced by specialized communities and traded widely, whereas the white ware was

Table 2.5 Summary Statistics of Continuous Variables for All Three Ceramic
Types on Sites Where They Are Most Abundant

Site/Type	Variable	N	Mean	C.V.	Rank	Min.	Max.
Edge of Cedars/	Radius	58	10.07	23.63	3	5	20
White Mesa	Line Width	142	1.07	26.17	3	1	3
B/W	Thickness	126	3.77	18.83	2	3	6
Duckfoot/	Radius	89	9.34	24.63	2	3	15
Piedra B/W	Line Width	85	2.36	35.17	1	1	7
	Thickness	134	4.89	14.31	3	3	7
Nancy	Radius	28	8.02	27.68	1	4	14
Patterson/	Line Width	44	4.03	31.51	2	2	8
Bluff B/R	Thickness	49	4.39	24.60	1	2	6

Table 2.6 Summary Statistics of Continuous Variables by Type,
Assemblages from All Sites Combined

Type	Variable	N	Mean	C.V.	Rank	Min.	Max.
Bluff	Radius	293	9.79	27.78	1	3	22
B/R	Line Width	205	3.88	49.74	1	2	20
	Thickness	488	4.41	19.95	1.5	2	8
Piedra	Radius	89	9.34	24.63	3	3	15
B/W	Line Width	85	2.36	35.17	2	1	7
	Thickness	134	4.89	14.31	3	3	7
White	Radius	95	9.67	26.16	2	5	20
Mesa	Line Width	201	1.09	29.36	3	1	3
B/W	Thickness	176	3.76	19.15	1.5	3	6

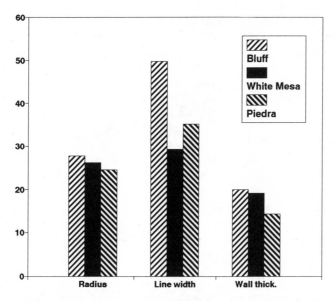

Figure 2.6 Histogram of coefficients of variation for Bluff Black-on-red, White Mesa Black-on-white, and Piedra Black-on-white.

produced and distributed on a more restricted and localized basis. Yet it appears that potters in the specialized communities produced less standardized forms than potters who produced for more local consumption. The high frequency of misfired red ware sherds in the production area (i.e., at Nancy Patterson Village) further suggests that red ware production was not highly standardized.

This apparent disassociation between specialization and standardization may be explained by considering the various dimensions of specialization. The concentration of specialists, the primary factor in community specialization, should have little effect on standardization. However, the scale and intensity of production, which may be similar for dispersed individual specialists and specialized communities, are expected to be most strongly related to standardization.

Although red ware production was clearly more spatially concentrated than white ware production, there may have been relatively few qualitative differences in the production processes. Both wares were

Table 2.7 States of Categorical Variables by Type

	Rim Form		Line on Rim		Rim Walls	
Type	Round	Square	Present	Absent	Tapered	Parallel
Bluff B/R	143	349	405	99	187	281
	29%	71%	80%	20%	40%	60%
Piedra B/W	119	54	103	76	96	55
	69%	31%	58%	42%	64%	36%
White Mesa	45	130	184	3	56	127
B/W	26%	74%	98%	2%	31%	69%

hand-built by coiling and scraping; both are likely to have been made on the same small scale, at the level of a household or small work group. Because the red ware in our sample appears to be slightly less standardized than the white ware, we conclude that red ware was produced at the same or a slightly lower level of intensity than white ware. In other words, red ware vessels appear to have been made by many producers, some of whom produced a small surplus for distribution beyond their household. Most or all households within the producing communities may have been involved in red ware production.

Conclusions

This paper considers the production of three Pueblo I pottery types in the Northern San Juan region in relation to their distribution. Bluff Black-on-red is widely distributed across the region and beyond, whereas Piedra Black-on-white and White Mesa Black-on-white have much more restricted distributions (in southwestern Colorado and southeastern Utah, respectively). The red ware and White Mesa Black-on-white are quite standardized compositionally, whereas Piedra Black-on-white is much more heterogeneous. In combination, these data suggest that red ware production was specialized at the community level, perhaps with the core production area in easternmost Utah (including Montezuma Canyon), where red ware is most abundant. The high percentage of misfired red ware in Montezuma Canyon supports this conclusion. There is less evidence for the specialized production of either white ware type, although many researchers have argued that white ware vessels were made by dispersed individual specialists. However, the limited distribution of both white ware types argues against any large-scale or intensive production of these ceramics.

Analysis of the standardization of rim form and design on these three ceramic types resulted in an unexpected conclusion. Bluff Black-on-red, the type for which there is the strongest evidence of specialized production, was the least standardized, though overall differences in standardization are not great. The apparent inverse correlation between specialization and standardization can be understood only if one considers both as multidimensional phenomena. Specialization includes the dimensions of concentration, intensity, and scale, whereas standardization includes stylistic variation and composition as well as mechanical and technological variation.

The red ware is highly standardized compositionally, indicating that it was made at only a few sources and its production was concentrated in specialized communities. However, this one dimension (i.e., concentration) is not necessarily associated with the other dimensions of specialization. The overall similar degree of mechanical, technological, and stylistic variation in both red and white wares suggests that their production was not qualitatively different and they were made at roughly the same scale and intensity. The variability and abundance of the red ware suggest that it was produced by a relatively large number of producers at a low level of intensity.

These conclusions, particularly those regarding the scale and intensity of production, are tentative rather than definitive, though we hope we have contributed to an understanding of Pueblo I ceramic production. We also hope that we have demonstrated the importance of considering many dimensions when assessing production systems. Although we have focused on the production process, understanding production is only one step toward understanding the prehistoric economic system. San Juan Red Ware may be the earliest documented example of community specialization in the Southwest. Further research is needed to consider how and why this system developed.

Acknowledgments

Several individuals and institutions contributed to this research. The Anasazi Heritage Center (U.S. Bureau of Land Management), Museum of Peoples and Cultures (Brigham Young University), Center for Archaeological Investigations (Southern Illinois University), Crow Canyon Archaeological Center, and Edge of the Cedars State Park provided us with access to their collections. Joel Janetski and Charmaine Thompson assisted us with collections from Nancy Patterson Village, and Crow Canyon Archaeological Center provided Michelle Hegmon with space and time to conduct some of the research. The compositional analyses were supported by a Smithsonian postdoctoral fellowship (for Hegmon), the Karen S. Greiner Foundation (Colorado State University), and the Wenner-Gren Foundation for Anthropological Research. Jack Ellingson and William Melson assisted Hegmon with the petrographic analysis, and Ricky Lightfoot contributed to the research on temper sources. The INAA was done at the Smithsonian Institution's Conservation Analytical Laboratory, with assistance and advice from Ronald Bishop and James Blackman. Katherine Spielmann and Barbara Stark provided valuable advice regarding the study of specialization and generously shared unpublished manuscripts with us. The volume editors and two anonymous reviewers provided useful comments and suggestions.

References Cited

Allen, Jim
1984   Pots and Poor Princes: A Multidimensional Approach to the Role of Pottery Trading in Coastal Papua. In *The Many Dimensions of Pottery*, edited by Sander E. van der Leeuw and A. C. Pritchard, pp. 409–463. Universiteit van Amsterdam, Amsterdam.

Allison, James R.
1991   Style, Exchange, and Social Networks in the Northern Southwest. Paper presented at the 56th Annual Meeting of the Society for American Archaeology, New Orleans.

Bishop, Ronald L., Veletta Canouts, Suzanne P. De Atley, Alfred Qoyawayma, and C. W. Aikins
1988   The Formation of Ceramic Analytical Groups: Hopi Pottery Production and Exchange. *Journal of Field Archaeology* 15:317–337.

Bishop, Ronald L., Robert L. Rands, and G. Holley
1982   Ceramic Compositional Analysis in Archaeological Perspective. *Advances in Archaeological Method and Theory* 5:275–330.

Blinman, Eric

1986   Additive Technologies Group Final Report. In *Dolores Archaeological Program: Final Report*, compiled by D. A. Breternitz, C. K. Robinson, and G. T. Gross, pp. 53–102. U.S. Bureau of Reclamation, Engineering and Research Center, Denver.

1988   *The Interpretation of Ceramic Variability: A Case Study from the Dolores Anasazi.* Unpublished Ph.D. dissertation, Department of Anthropology, Washington State University, Pullman.

Blinman, Eric, and C. Dean Wilson

1988   Ceramic Data and Interpretation: The McPhee Community Cluster. In *Dolores Archaeological Program: Anasazi Communities at Dolores: McPhee Village*, compiled by A. E. Kane and C. K. Robinson, pp. 1,295–1,341. U.S. Bureau of Reclamation, Engineering and Research Center, Denver.

1989   Mesa Verde Region Ceramic Types. Prepared for the New Mexico Archaeological Council, Albuquerque.

Breternitz, David A., Arthur H. Rohn, Jr., and Elizabeth A. Morris

1974   *Prehistoric Ceramics of the Mesa Verde Region.* Ceramic Series No. 5. Museum of Northern Arizona, Flagstaff.

Brumfiel, Elizabeth M., and Timothy K. Earle (editors)

1987   *Specialization, Exchange, and Complex Societies.* Cambridge University Press, Cambridge.

Christensen, Diana

1980   *Excavations at Cave Canyon Village, 1977, Montezuma Canyon, Utah.* Unpublished Master's thesis, Department of Anthropology, Brigham Young University, Provo, Utah.

Christenson, Andrew L., and William J. Parry

1985   *Excavations on Black Mesa, 1983: A Descriptive Report.* Research Paper No. 46, Center for Archaeological Investigations, Southern Illinois University, Carbondale.

Clark, John, and William J. Parry

1990   Craft Specialization and Cultural Complexity. *Research in Economic Anthropology* 12:289–346.

Costin, Cathy Lynne

1991   Craft Specialization: Issues in Defining, Documenting, and Explaining the Organization of Production. *Archaeological Method and Theory* 3:1–56.

Costin, Cathy L., and Melissa B. Hagstrum

1995   Standardization, Labor Investment, Skill and the Organization of Ceramic Production in Late Prehispanic Highland Peru. *American Antiquity,* in press.

Crown, Patricia A.

1994   *Ceramics and Ideology: Salado Polychrome Pottery.* University of New Mexico Press, Albuquerque.

Davis, William A.

1985   *Anasazi Subsistence and Settlement on White Mesa, San Juan County, Utah.* University Press of America, Lanham, Maryland.

Dietler, Michael, and Ingrid Herbich

1989   Tich Matek: The Technology of Luo Pottery Production and the Definition of Ceramic Style. *World Archaeology* 21:148–164.

Doyel, David E.

1991   Hohokam Exchange and Interaction. In *Chaco and Hohokam: Prehistoric Regional Systems in the American Southwest,* edited by P. L. Crown and W. J. Judge, pp. 225–252. School of American Research Press, Santa Fe.

Earle, Timothy K.

1982   The Ecology and Politics of Primitive Valuables. In *Culture and Ecology: Eclectic Perspectives,* edited by J. Kennedy and R. Edgerton, pp. 65–83. Special Publication No. 15. American Anthropological Association, Washington, D.C.

Emery, Sloan E.

1981   *Cholla Knoll Ceramics, Butler Wash, San Juan County, Utah.* Unpublished Master's thesis, Department of Anthropology, University of Denver, Denver.

Feinman, Gary, Richard Blanton, and Stephen Kowalewski

1984   Modelling Ceramic Production and Organizational Change in the Pre-Hispanic Valley of Oaxaca, Mexico. In *The Many Dimensions of Pottery,* edited by Sander E. van der Leeuw and A. C. Pritchard, pp. 295–338. Universiteit van Amsterdam, Amsterdam.

Fetterman, Jerry, Linda Honeycutt, and Kristin Kuckelman

1988   *Salvage Excavations of 42sa12209: A Pueblo I Habitation Site in Cottonwood Canyon, Manti-LaSal National Forest, Southeastern Utah.* Submitted to USDA Forest Service, Manti-LaSal National Forest, Monticello, Utah.

Fish, Paul R., Suzanne K. Fish, Stephanie Whittlesey, Hector Neff,
Michael D. Glascock, and J. Michael Elam

1992   An Evaluation of the Production and Exchange of Tanque Verde Red-on-Brown Ceramics in Southern Arizona. In *Chemical Characterization of Ceramic Pastes in Archaeology,* edited by H. Neff, pp. 233–254. Monographs in World Archaeology No. 7, Prehistory Press, Madison, Wisconsin.

Ford, Richard I.
1972   Barter, Gift, or Violence: An Analysis of Tewa Intertribal Exchange. In *Social Exchange and Interaction*, edited by E. N. Wilmsen, pp. 21–45. Anthropological Papers of the Museum of Anthropology, University of Michigan, Ann Arbor.

Forsyth, Donald W.
1977   *Anasazi Ceramics of Montezuma Canyon, Southeastern Utah.* Publications in Archaeology, New Series No. 2. Brigham Young University, Provo, Utah.

Foust, Richard D., Jr., J. Richard Ambler, and Larry D. Turner
1989   Trace Element Analysis of Pueblo II Kayenta Anasazi Sherds. In *Archaeological Chemistry IV*, edited by Ralph O. Allen, pp. 125–143. American Chemical Society, Washington, D.C.

Garrett, Elizabeth
1990   Petrographic Analysis of Selected Ceramics from the Northern Southwest. Ms. on file, Department of Sociology and Anthropology, New Mexico State University, Las Cruces.

Graves, Michael W.
1994   Community Boundaries in Late Prehistoric Puebloan Society: Kalinga Ethnoarchaeology as a Model for the Southwestern Production and Exchange of Pottery. In *The Ancient Southwestern Community: Models and Methods for the Study of Prehistoric Social Organization*, edited by. W. H. Wills and R. D. Leonard, pp. 149–169. University of New Mexico Press, Albuquerque.

Green, Dee
1970   First Season Excavations of Edge of the Cedars Pueblo, Blanding, Utah. Ms. on file, Edge of the Cedars State Park, Blanding, Utah.

Hagstrum, Melissa B.
1985   Measuring Prehistoric Ceramic Craft Specialization: A Test Case in the American Southwest. *Journal of Field Archaeology* 12(1):65–75.

Harding, Thomas G.
1967   *Voyagers of the Vitiaz Strait.* University of Washington Press, Seattle.

Harmon, Craig B.
1979   *Cave Canyon Village: The Early Pueblo Components.* Publications in Archaeology, New Series No. 5. Brigham Young University, Provo, Utah.

Hayes, Alden C., and James A. Lancaster
1975   *Badger House Community, Mesa Verde National Park, Colorado.* Publications in Archeology No. 7E. National Park Service, Washington, D.C.

Hegmon, Michelle
1995a *The Social Dynamics of Pottery Style in the Early Puebloan Southwest*. Occasional Papers No. 4. Crow Canyon Archaeological Center, Cortez, Colorado.
1995b Pueblo I Ceramic Production in Southwest Colorado: Analyses of Igneous Rock Temper. *The Kiva* 60:371–390.

Hegmon, Michelle, and James R. Allison
1990   *The Local Economy and Regional Exchange: Early Red Ware Production in the Northern Southwest*. Proposal for Archaeological Neutron Activation Services from the Missouri University Research Reactor (approved), Columbia.

Hill, James N.
1977   Individual Variability in Ceramics and the Study of Prehistoric Social Organization. In *The Individual in Prehistory*, edited by J. N. Hill and J. Gunn, pp. 55–108. Academic Press, New York.

Hurst, Winston
1983   The Prehistoric Peoples of San Juan County, Utah. In *San Juan County, Utah*, edited by A. K. Powell, pp. 17–44. Utah State Historical Society, Salt Lake City.
1990   Site Description and Setting. In *Edge of the Cedars State Park, Ruin Management Plan*. Ms. on file, Edge of the Cedars State Park, Blanding, Utah.

Hurst, Winston, Mark Bond, and Sloan E. Emery Schwindt
1985   Type Description: Piedra Black-on-White, White Mesa Variety. *Pottery Southwest* 12(3):1–7.

Irwin, G. J.
1978   Pots and Entrepots: A Study of Settlement, Trade, and the Development of Economic Specialization in Papuan Prehistory. *World Archaeology* 9:299–319.

Kane, Allen E.
1989   Did the Sheep Look Up? Sociopolitical Complexity in Ninth Century Dolores Society. In *The Sociopolitical Structure of Prehistoric Southwestern Societies*, edited by S. Upham, K. G. Lightfoot, and R. A. Jewett, pp. 307–361. Westview Press, Boulder, Colorado.

Lightfoot, Ricky R.
1992   Architecture and Tree-Ring Dating at the Duckfoot Site in Southwestern Colorado. *The Kiva* 57:213–236.

Lightfoot, Ricky R., and Mary C. Etzkorn (editors)
1993   *The Duckfoot Site. Volume 1: Descriptive Archaeology*. Occasional Papers No. 3. Crow Canyon Archaeological Center, Cortez, Colorado.

Longacre, William A., Kenneth L. Kvamme, and Masashi Kobayashi
1988   Southwestern Pottery Standardization: An Ethnoarchaeological View from the Philippines. *The Kiva* 53(2):101–112.

Lucius, William A., and David A. Breternitz
1981   The Current Status of Red Wares in the Mesa Verde Region. In *Collected Papers in Honor of Erik Kellerman Reed*, edited by A. H. Schroeder, pp. 99–111. Papers of the Archaeological Society of New Mexico No. 6, Albuquerque.

Mills, Barbara J.
1989   *Ceramics and Settlement in the Cedar Mesa Area, Southeastern Utah: A Methodological Approach.* Unpublished Ph.D. dissertation, Department of Anthropology, University of New Mexico, Albuquerque.

Motsinger, Thomas
1990   Craft Specialization in the Galisteo Basin, New Mexico. Paper presented at the 55th Annual Meeting of the Society for American Archaeology, Las Vegas.

Muller, Jon
1984   Mississippian Specialization and Salt. *American Antiquity* 49:489–501.
1987   Salt, Chert, and Shell: Mississippian Exchange and Economy. In *Specialization, Exchange, and Complex Societies*, edited by E. M. Brumfiel and T. K. Earle, pp. 10–21. Cambridge University Press, Cambridge.

Neff, Hector
1989   The Effect of Interregional Distribution on Plumbate Pottery Production. In *Ancient Trade and Tribute*, edited by B. Voorhies, pp. 249–267. University of Utah Press, Salt Lake City.

Neff, Hector (editor)
1992   *Chemical Characterization of Ceramic Pastes in Archaeology.* Monographs in World Archaeology No. 7, Prehistory Press, Madison, Wisconsin.

Nelson, Sarah M.
1978   Investigation at Cholla Knoll, 1978. Ms. on file, Department of Anthropology, University of Denver, Denver.

Nichols, Deborah L., and F. E. Smiley (editors)
1984   *Excavations on Black Mesa, 1982: A Descriptive Report.* Center for Archaeological Investigations Research Paper No. 39. Southern Illinois University, Carbondale.

Nickens, Paul R.
1977   *Wood Rat Knoll: A Multicomponent Site in Butler Wash, Southeastern Utah.* University of Denver, Denver.

Patterson, Gregory R.

1975   *A Preliminary Study of an Anasazi Settlement (42sa971) Prior to* A.D. *900 in Montezuma Canyon, San Juan County, Southeastern Utah.* Unpublished Master's thesis, Brigham Young University, Provo, Utah.

Peacock, D. P. S.

1981   Archaeology, Ethnology, and Ceramic Production. In *Production and Distribution: A Ceramic Viewpoint,* edited by H. Howard and E. Morris, pp. 187–194. BAR International Series 120. British Archaeological Reports, Oxford.

1982   *Pottery in the Roman World: An Ethnoarchaeological Approach.* Longman, London.

Perlman, I., and F. Asaro

1969   Pottery Analysis by Neutron Activation. *Archaeometry* 11:21–52.

Plog, Stephen

1986   Change in Regional Trade Networks. In *Spatial Organization and Exchange: Archaeological Survey on Northern Black Mesa,* edited by Stephen Plog, pp. 282–309. Southern Illinois University Press, Carbondale.

Rice, Prudence M.

1981   Evolution of Specialized Pottery Production: A Trial Model. *Current Anthropology* 22(3):219–240.

1987   *Pottery Analysis: A Sourcebook.* University of Chicago Press, Chicago.

1989   Ceramic Diversity, Production, and Use. In *Quantifying Diversity in Archaeology,* edited by Robert D. Leonard and George T. Jones, pp. 109–117. Cambridge University Press, Cambridge.

1991   Specialization, Standardization, and Diversity: A Retrospective. In *The Ceramic Legacy of Anna O. Shepard,* edited by Ronald L. Bishop and Frederick W. Lange, pp. 257–279. University Press of Colorado, Niwot, Colorado.

Russell, Glenn

1988   *The Impact of Inka Policy on the Domestic Economy of Wanka, Peru: Stone Tool Production and Use.* Ph.D. dissertation, University of California, Los Angeles. University Microfilms, Ann Arbor.

Sayre, Edward V.

1975   *Brookhaven Procedures for Statistical Analysis of Multivariate Archaeometric Data.* Working paper BNL-21693. Brookhaven National Laboratory, Upton, New York.

Shepard, Anna O.

1942   *Rio Grande Glaze Paint Ware: A Study Illustrating the Place of Ceramic Technological Analysis in Archaeological Research.* Contributions to American Anthropology and History, No. 39, Publication 528. Carnegie Institute of Washington, Washington, D.C.

Sinopoli, Carla M.
1988   The Organization of Craft Production at Vijayanagara, South India. *American Anthropologist* 90:580–597.

Spielmann, Katherine A.
1988   *Craft Specialization and Exchange in Tribal Societies.* Proposal to the National Science Foundation, Washington, D.C.

Thompson, Charmaine, James R. Allison, Shane A. Baker, Joel C. Janetski, Byron Loosle, James D. Wilde
1988   *The Nancy Patterson Village Archaeological Research Project: Field Year 1986–Preliminary Report No. 4.* Museum of Peoples and Cultures, Technical Series No. 87-24. Brigham Young University, Provo, Utah.

Toll, H. Wolcott
1991   Material Distributions and Exchange in the Chaco System. In *Chaco and Hohokam: Prehistoric Regional Systems in the American Southwest,* edited by Patricia L. Crown and W. James Judge, pp. 77–107. School of American Research Press, Santa Fe.

Turner, Christy G., II, and Laurel Lofgren
1966   Household Size of Prehistoric Western Pueblo Indians. *Southwestern Journal of Anthropology* 22:117–132.

Upham, Steadman
1982   *Polities and Power: An Economic and Political History of the Western Pueblo.* Academic Press, New York.

van der Leeuw, Sander E.
1977   Towards a Study of the Economics of Pottery Making. In *Ex Horreo,* edited by B. L. van Beek, R. W. Brandt, and W. Groenman-van Watteringe, pp. 68–76. Albert Egges van Giffen Instituut voor Prae-en Protohistorie, Universiteit van Amsterdam, Amsterdam.

1984   Pottery Manufacture: Some Complications for the Study of Trade. In *Pots and Potters: Current Approaches in Ceramic Archaeology,* edited by P. M. Rice, pp. 55–69. UCLA Institute of Archaeology Monograph No. 24. University of California, Los Angeles.

Varien, Mark D., and Ricky R. Lightfoot
1989   Ritual and Nonritual Activities in Mesa Verde Region Pit Structures. In *The Architecture of Social Integration in Prehistoric Pueblos,* edited by W. D. Lipe and M. Hegmon, pp. 73–87. Occasional Papers No. 1. Crow Canyon Archaeological Center, Cortez, Colorado.

Walker, J. Terry
1980   Untitled Ceramic Tallies for Edge of the Cedars Ruin, 1969–1974 Excavations. Ms. on file, Edge of the Cedars State Park, Blanding, Utah.

Whittaker, John C.
1987   Individual Variation as an Approach to Economic Organization: Pro-
        jectile Points at Grasshopper Pueblo, Arizona. *Journal of Field Archaeol-
        ogy* 14:465–479.

Whittlesey, Stephanie M.
1974   Identification of Imported Ceramics Through Functional Analysis of
        Attributes. *The Kiva* 40:101–112.

Wilson, A. L.
1978   Elemental Analysis of Pottery in the Study of Its Provenance: A Review.
        Journal of Archaeological Science 5:219–236.

3

Changing Specialization of White Ware Manufacture in the Northern San Juan Region

C. Dean Wilson and Eric Blinman

The Northern San Juan (or Mesa Verde) region refers to the northernmost extension of the Anasazi. This region includes most of the areas drained by the northern tributaries of the San Juan River (fig. 3.1). The confluence of the Colorado and San Juan rivers forms the southwestern boundary, and the Colorado River forms the western boundary of this region. The eastern boundary is sometimes drawn at the Animas River but is probably best placed slightly to the east. The northern boundary is usually defined by the watershed limits of the northern tributaries of the San Juan River, but it extends slightly farther north to include the southernmost portions of the Dolores River and its tributaries.

Anasazi sites dating from the Basketmaker III through the Pueblo III periods (A.D. 575 to 1300) are scattered throughout this region. Evidence from these sites indicates dynamic changes in settlement distribution, subsistence emphases, and social and economic networks. These changes influenced, and are reflected in, patterns of pottery production, decoration, use, and exchange. Although white ware pottery production is the focus of this paper, pottery production is a multilayered phenomenon also entailing social and economic contexts of vessel use and the transport and exchange of ceramics; white ware production cannot be considered in the absence of the other wares (Blinman 1988; Blinman and Wilson 1992, 1993; Rice 1984).

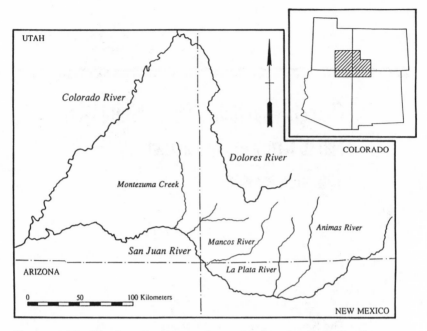

Figure 3.1 The Northern San Juan region and its location in the Southwest.

Characterization of Ceramic Production

Most models of pottery production and specialization have been derived from ethnographic data and have focused on the relationship between producers and consumers, the volume of production by individuals, or the proportion of an individual's subsistence obtained from pottery production (Arnold 1985; Balfet 1981; Costin 1991; Peacock 1982; Rice 1987: 180–191). Within these models, examples of ceramic production are ranked along continua, from full-time specialists and formalized distribution systems in large and complex societies to household production and consumption in smaller and less complex societies. Although production levels among the Northern San Juan Anasazi did vary, production appears to have almost always been organized at the low end of this scale, generally at or below the level of a household industry. This narrow range limits the usefulness of production typologies in the study of production change. It is more useful to explore estimated producer-consumer ratios and evidence of the geographic distribution of production.

Northern San Juan pottery production patterns are influenced by factors similar to those identified in studies of traditional potters: the geographic distribution of suitable raw materials; the size, organization, and subsistence emphases of populations; the technological complexities associated with the different wares; and utilitarian and social roles of vessels (Arnold 1985; Rice 1984, 1987). These factors can be related to synchronic differences in the production of different wares, as well as diachronic change in production patterns.

Wares and Production

Anasazi pottery production must be understood in terms of wares (Brisbane 1981; Fry 1980, 1981; Rice 1987; Vince 1981). Although Northern San Juan Anasazi vessel forms and decorative styles vary widely, the overwhelming majority of sherds and vessels fall within three distinctive ware classes: gray, white, and red (Abel 1955; Breternitz et al. 1974; Rohn 1977; Wilson and Blinman 1991). These wares are defined as vessels and sherds that share broad technological and decorative treatments (Blinman et al. 1984; Wilson and Blinman 1991). The ware definitions also have strong, but not perfect, functional correlates: gray ware vessels appear to have been used for cooking and bulk storage, and white and red ware vessels appear to have been used for serving and specialized storage functions. Gray wares are unpainted, unslipped, and generally unpolished and were fired in a neutral atmosphere. Decoration, when present, is in the form of surface texture such as coiled and corrugated treatments. White wares are painted vessels that are typically polished and slipped and were fired in a neutral atmosphere. Red wares are painted or polished vessels made of high-iron clays that were fired in a strong oxidizing atmosphere, which produced red or orange surface colors.

Two factors, vessel function and clay properties, appear to have had the strongest roles in determining the production organization of the different wares. Gray ware vessels were commonly used for cooking. As such, they were subject to more frequent breakage than other forms and needed to be replaced rapidly as part of household maintenance, especially as agricultural intensification increased reliance on boiling as a cooking technique (Blinman 1988). Also, the size and shape of cooking jars made them awkward to transport over long distances, and they were less likely than other vessel classes to be widely exchanged (Rice 1987).

Gray ware decoration was limited to surface texture, a decoration style that would remain visible during use despite the effects of sooting. The emphasis on surface texture rather than painted decoration also decreased the importance of surface color, allowing the use of clays with a wider range of properties than was possible with the other wares. Clays suitable for pottery production are ubiquitous within the region (Leonhardy and Clay 1985; Molenaar 1977; Wilson et al. 1988), and resource availability was not a constraint on gray ware production.

White ware vessels were generally used for serving and storage, but these functions were also met by both gray and red ware vessels. Bowl breakage should have been less frequent than cooking-jar breakage, and storage containers tended to have even longer use lives, requiring less frequent manufacture of replacement white ware than gray ware vessels (DeBoer 1985; Nelson 1985). Although gray ware vessels could readily fulfill the functions of white ware vessels, the poor heat-shock performance of many of the white ware clay-temper combinations limited their use as cooking containers except in emergencies (Bronitsky and Hamer 1986).

The most striking feature distinguishing white from gray wares is their decoration: dark brown or black designs executed in mineral or organic pigments contrast against a light gray or white background. Although this contrast can be achieved with most clays, moderate- or high-iron clays can only be used if the potter exercises precise control over the firing atmosphere. The firing process must allow just enough oxidation to remove organic material from the clay, but not so much oxygen to transform iron compounds from their ferrous (gray) to ferric (red) state. This "neutral" atmosphere is difficult to maintain, and consistent results are more easily achieved if low-iron clays are selected for white ware production. In the Northern San Juan region, low-iron clays are much less common than moderate- to high-iron clays. Low-iron clays, however, are relatively widely distributed; only localized portions of the region lack such clays. An additional factor in white ware production is the difference in organic-paint retention among clays, which requires that individual clays be matched with suitable paint types. These sources of variation may have influenced the geographic distribution of white ware production, but low-iron clays can be used as slips, and the small quantities needed could have been obtained given the large extent of the slip catchments of modern potters (Arnold 1985). Thus, clay resource distribution could have influenced white ware production, but that influence need not have been strong or consistent through time.

Red ware vessels fulfilled the same range of functions (serving and storage) as white ware vessels, but fewer large vessels were executed as red wares. As a result of this functional similarity, red ware vessels were subject to the same breakage rates as white wares. Also red ware functions were not exclusive, and vessels of other wares could have been substituted for red wares when necessary.

The most obvious distinguishing characteristic of the red wares is the combination of clay selection and strong oxidation firing. Whereas both gray and white wares were fired under neutral conditions, red ware potters selected high-iron clays and consciously oxidized those clays during at least the final stages of firing. The common presence of gray cores within red ware sherds indicates that naturally gray clays were used for most red ware production. If these clays had been subjected to the same firing regime as gray and white wares, the reddish orange colors would not have been achieved, which indicates that a distinctly different firing technique was used. Even though iron-rich slips were used for some later red wares, the slips were never applied over low-iron clays. Although they may be most abundant in southeastern Utah, sources of high-iron clays are widespread within the Northern San Juan region. Resource restriction by itself, therefore, should not have been a significant constraint on production (contra Lucius and Breternitz 1981; Lucius and Wilson 1980). Other aspects of San Juan Red Ware production are discussed by Hegmon et al. (this volume).

Cultural Context of Ceramic Production

Although it is dangerous to generalize the cultural history of the Northern San Juan region, numerous developments may have influenced pottery production (Brew 1946; Fuller 1987; Hayes 1964; Hayes and Lancaster 1975; Irwin-Williams and Shelley 1980; Kane 1986; Kuckelman and Morris 1988; Orcutt et al. 1990; Reed 1958; Rohn 1989; Schlanger 1988; Toll and Hannaford 1989; Wilshusen and Blinman 1992). Many of these developments, such as aggregation, were cyclical rather than unidirectional. Population size and organizational complexity, however, appear to have increased over time.

Anasazi occupations before the late sixth century are represented by a few small, scattered sites that contain either no pottery or low frequencies of undecorated brown ware pottery (Wilson and Blinman 1994). By A.D. 600, sites with pottery conforming to the Anasazi Basketmaker III tradition occur throughout much of the Anasazi region. During the seventh century, the Basketmaker III population increased dramatically, consisting of widely dispersed habitations housing nuclear or extended families. The population was still widely scattered at the beginning of the Pueblo I period (circa A.D. 725) but began to move to areas of higher rainfall at about A.D. 760. Although some large villages appeared during this time, much of the population remained in isolated hamlets. Most habitations consisted of suites of pit structures and surface rooms containing several households. Subsistence may have been more strongly based on agriculture, apparently as a response to population pressure on nonagricultural resources (Earle 1980; Orcutt 1987). Many of these villages appear to have been abandoned before A.D. 810, only to re-form about A.D. 830. Some of these later villages were abandoned by about A.D. 860 (Wilshusen and Blinman 1992), whereas others persisted and grew.

A major population decline occurred by the end of the ninth century, and much of the population returned to widely dispersed settlements (Blinman 1994). Possible exceptions to this dispersal are on Mesa Verde and in Mancos Canyon. Dispersed settlements continued to be common during the later tenth and eleventh centuries, although the number and size of habitations appear to have increased significantly. By the late eleventh century, much of the population moved into very large organized villages or communities, some of which are classified as Chacoan outliers, although such developments probably cannot be attributed to direct Chaco Canyon influence. Many of the villages formed during the Pueblo II period continued to serve as important centers during the Pueblo III period, and additional large nucleated settlements were also formed. Isolated households and hamlets persisted, but larger pueblos formed focal points for outlying populations. Canyon-head settlements and water-control features were common, indicating a greater concern for water, and some sites were placed in defensible settings. These developments ended sometime between A.D. 1250 and 1300 as the Anasazi abandoned the greater Four Corners area, coincident with the onset of a period of prolonged climatic deterioration (Dean 1994).

Increases in population and the movement into larger villages may have contributed to an increase in ceramic specialization in several ways.

Increased reliance on agriculture would have raised the demand for vessels, especially gray ware cooking jars, increasing production volume.
Climate-driven settlement movement would have changed the relationships between potters and resources, and population pressure may have
also restricted access to agricultural land in some areas. This pressure
could have encouraged some groups located in areas of poor agricultural
productivity to specialize in pottery production as a subsistence supplement (Arnold 1975; 1985). Concentration of population could also have
affected the organization of pottery production through the depletion of
wood as a result of heavy use for construction and fuel (Kohler and
Matthews 1988; Toll 1981; Toll and McKenna 1987). Village development
may also have fostered either interhousehold divisions of labor or social
inequalities that could have encouraged either specialization or restric-
tions on access to specific wares.

Documentation of Ceramic Production

Although many factors may have influenced pottery production in the
Northern San Juan region, little effort has been directed toward actually
documenting the organization of this production. The inferences that
have been drawn have usually been based on characteristics or distributions of pottery rather than on direct evidence of production organization (Cordell and Plog 1979:420; F. Plog 1983, 1984; S. Plog 1980; Rice
1980; Shepard 1965; Toll 1981). Some of these researchers have confused
the measurement of specialization with measurements that sometimes
reflect specialization (such as level of execution and standardization),
oversimplifying what appears to be an extremely complex situation.

The best indication that ceramic production took place in a particular
setting is evidence of vessel construction or firing. Activity areas are
valuable evidence of production (Sullivan 1988), but production waste
(tempered clay) and tool fragments (pottery scrapers with distinctive
edge wear [Waterworth and Blinman 1986]) are also unequivocal evidence (Blinman 1988; Blinman and Wilson 1988a; Hill 1985; Rye 1981;
Wilson 1988b, 1991). The distinction between reliance on dedicated work
or firing areas vs. the presence of tools or waste as adequate evidence of
production is important because dedicated facilities are more likely to be
associated with greater specialization where large production volume
warrants greater investment (Arnold 1985; Stark 1985). Both types of

evidence are rare. Large collections are necessary for the detection of production, as well as for the determination that residents of a particular site or structure did not produce pottery (Blinman 1988; Blinman and Wilson 1992). An inherent difficulty is that evidence may indicate that production took place, but the evidence may not be sufficient to determine what wares were produced.

In addition to direct evidence of production, resource selection (clay, temper, and paint) can provide circumstantial evidence of production on a subregional level. Local unavailability of some materials (such as igneous rock in the beanfield and canyon country of the Northern San Juan region) forms the basis of local subtraditions or pottery manufacturing tracts (Blinman 1988; Lucius 1981; Wilson 1988b). Tract characteristics can be used to argue that sherds originated from a particular portion of the region. Systematic associations of tract hallmarks and particular wares are circumstantial evidence of regionally differentiated production.

Temporal Changes in Ceramic Production

A comprehensive examination of Northern San Juan ceramic production is not possible now because of the lack of extensive and comparable data both through time and across space. Collections must be large enough and made with enough care that evidence of ceramic production could be recovered if production had taken place at the site. The collections must also be adequately analyzed so that items indicating ceramic production are consistently identified (pottery clay, ceramic scrapers, and tract affiliation of sherds), and data analysis must be presented in a comparable manner. As a result of these constraints, detailed examination of ceramic production evidence (and lack of evidence) has been carried out for only a few small portions of the region and for only limited spans of time (Blinman 1988; Blinman and Wilson 1992; Wilson 1988b). Anecdotal data (nonsystematic reports of production evidence) are available from a wider range of contexts (e.g., Hill 1985), circumstantial data in the form of temper descriptions are available for additional collections (e.g., Bond 1985; Hurst 1985; Lucius 1982), and some large systematic data sets are currently being formed (e.g., Toll and Hannaford 1989; Wilson 1993). The production inferences that follow rely on a mix of these uneven data to characterize ceramic production during the various occupations of the Northern San Juan region.

Basketmaker III Production (A.D. 575–725)

Most, but not all, large Basketmaker III collections include at least some evidence of pottery manufacture (Blinman 1988; Blinman and Wilson 1988b, 1992). Households not yielding production evidence are rare, and there were probably several pottery producing households to every non-producing household. The accurate identification of nonproducing households is circumstantially supported by the association of higher frequencies of nonlocal gray ware sherds with those households. Most of the individual instances of pottery production evidence are consistent with gray ware manufacture, but that does not preclude production of white wares. No significant volume of red ware vessels was produced during this period. The lack of distinct pottery-firing features at or near these Basketmaker III sites indicates that firing features were simple (such as open firings or multipurpose pits). Firing features could have been well removed from habitations because of fuel requirements, but measurable fuel depletion is first associated with the later and denser Pueblo I villages rather than Basketmaker III settlements (Kohler and Matthews 1988).

One instance of production evidence provides support for specialized white ware production. This evidence is from a cluster of three sites located south of Cortez, Colorado (Mary Errickson, personal communication 1991). These sites contained an unusually large amount of processed-clay and hematite grinding stones, polishing stones, and white ware vessels with fugitive red exteriors. From 18 to 27 percent of the sherds from these sites were white wares, which is extremely high for Basketmaker III assemblages where frequencies of less than 10 percent are normal (Blinman 1988:Table 5.2).

Specialization of Basketmaker III white wares is further indicated by several lines of indirect evidence. A narrower range of tempers and clays is found in white ware sherds than gray ware sherds (Wilson 1988b, 1991). At sites along the La Plata Valley and upper San Juan Valley, the majority of gray ware sherds contain sand temper and locally available, low-quality, silty alluvial clay with high-iron content. These contrast with the majority of white ware sherds that are tempered with crushed igneous rock and are made of high-quality clays with low-iron content (Wilson 1988b, 1991). In areas of the Montezuma Valley where igneous rock is not locally available, the majority of gray wares and all tempered, unfired clays recovered to date are tempered with local sandstone and have highly variable iron content. The majority of the white ware sherds from the same sites are tempered with crushed igneous rock, and the clays have consistently low-iron content (Wilson 1988b, 1991). The iron content of the clay itself cannot be used as an argument for specialization because all white ware potters would have tried to use low-iron clays. The temper data, however, are strong indications that most white wares were not locally manufactured in these areas.

Another circumstantial argument is provided by differences between frequencies of nonlocal white and gray ware sherds in the producing and nonproducing households in the Dolores area (Blinman 1988:Table 5.10). Whereas more nonlocal gray wares were present in the nonproducing households, nonlocal white wares were similarly distributed across both sets of households, with some indication of more nonlocal white wares at the producing households. If any of these pottery-producing households were making white wares, we would expect more local rather than non-local white wares in their collections. It appears that even the pottery-producing households obtained their white wares by exchange.

All of the evidence indicates that many Basketmaker III households produced gray wares, whereas white ware production was more limited, probably corresponding to a dispersed household-industry model.

Pueblo I Production (A.D. 725–900)

Pottery production underwent several major changes during the Pueblo I period, including an improvement in production technology after A.D. 800 (at least in gray wares) and the large-scale introduction of San Juan Red Ware. An increased incidence of pottery scrapers and evidence of interior scraping of gray ware vessels dating after A.D. 800 suggest an improvement in forming technology, and increased vitrification indicates shifts to higher temperature firing, resulting in increased vessel strength (Blinman 1988:70–74). These technical improvements are accompanied by a decrease in gray ware production specialization, as inferred from a lack of evidence for nonproducing households (Blinman 1988:76–97). These changes in technology and specialization coincided with an increase in demand for cooking vessels because of agricultural intensification and with the aggregation of much of the population into large villages. Despite extensive excavation of Pueblo I sites, only a single firing feature has been reported that may date to the Pueblo I period, and even in this case, the dating is uncertain (Hibbets 1984).

Production of San Juan Red Ware began in the mid-eighth century, and the ware is present in most Pueblo I collections dating after A.D. 775. Clines in red ware abundance in contemporary sites across the region point to regionally specialized production that was dominated by potters in southeastern Utah (Blinman 1983, 1988; Hurst 1983; Lucius and Breternitz 1981; Lucius and Wilson 1980). Red ware production volume was so great that red ware sherds account for more than 8 percent of A.D. 800 sherd collections in the Dolores Valley, 50 km from the source (Blinman 1988). From this period of peak production, red ware frequencies decline; they account for only about 4 percent of Dolores Valley collections by the late ninth century.

One effect of the regionally specialized red ware production and distribution was the suppression of white ware production over parts of the region (fig. 3.2). Gray ware sherd frequencies can be used as a constant for ratio calculations to avoid the constraint of percentages in the comparison of red and white ware production trends. The ratio of white to gray ware sherds is 0.091 in Dolores Basketmaker III collections (Blinman 1988:Table 5.1). This ratio declines to 0.050 in collections from the early Pueblo I period, when red wares were introduced, and plummets to 0.035 in collections from the time when red ware production was at its height. Collections from this same period show an increase in total decorated sherds from about 8 to 11 percent in the Dolores area. Depression of white ware production was most pronounced in the western portion of the region and least pronounced in the eastern portion, where white wares constitute about 6 percent of A.D. 800 collections and red wares less than 1 percent (Ellwood 1980; Wilson 1988a). Some evidence shows that red wares were preferred serving vessels at public gatherings (Blinman 1989). It is likely that their short-term popularity and availability negatively affected white ware production.

Within this complex context, Pueblo I white ware production appears to have been specialized in scattered areas. This specialization is apparent in regional differences in pigment and design of Piedra Black-on-white. In the eastern region, along the Animas River, glaze and organic paints were used to execute designs very similar to those associated with Rosa Phase sites to the south and east (Lucius 1982; Wilson 1988a; Wilson and Blinman 1993). This glaze-paint tradition began in the Basketmaker III period, became stylistically differentiated during the early Pueblo I period, and died out as the Animas Valley was abandoned in the mid-ninth century. In the central and southern region, mineral-painted white wares continued the ceramic tradition established in the seventh century, and white wares became more and more abundant through the ninth century. In the western part of the region, a distinctive white ware, with organic paint and designs similar to those found in Kana'a Black-on-white of the Kayenta region, was produced after the mid-ninth century. This type has been classified as White Mesa Black-on-white (Bond 1985; Hurst et al. 1985; Wilson and Blinman 1991) and was produced through the early Pueblo II period. Boundaries for these different white ware production areas are fairly abrupt; in contrast to the trends noted for red wares, distribution outside their proposed production areas appears to have been limited. Unfortunately, although regional differentiation is evident, we know nothing about white ware specialization at the site or household level.

Pueblo II Production (A.D. 900–1125)

Relatively little is known with confidence about Pueblo II pottery production because of a scarcity of systematic observations, but this was a period of significant change in the production of decorated wares. Direct evidence of ceramic manufacture is reported for several Northern Anasazi Pueblo II sites (Hill 1985; Wilson 1988b, 1991), whereas only one extensively excavated site has not yielded evidence of pottery production (Wilson 1988b). Several Pueblo II kilns have been excavated on Chapin Mesa, Mesa Verde National Park, but they are relatively small compared with later kilns (Oppelt 1991). If these observations are representative, the level of specialization is low, with many pottery-producing households for each nonproducing household. We assume that most households produced gray wares, although we have little direct information on what wares were produced.

Direct data on white ware production are too scarce to infer production organization or volume. Production change is evident, however, from the dramatic rise in the proportion of white ware sherds in total assemblages (fig. 3.2). Because white ware vessels of this period were predominantly serving and storage containers, the change in their breakage and replacement rates relative to cooking jars implies a functional shift in the roles of pottery within the household (or a change in the dynamics of use and breakage).

Regardless of its cause, this shift resulted in several changes within the white wares as a whole. Potters began to fine-tune their selection of

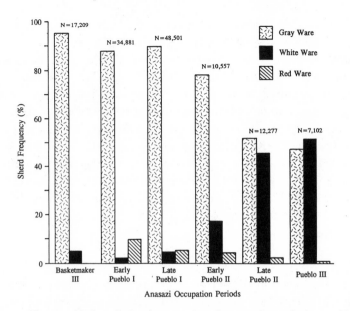

Figure 3.2 Changes in the relative frequencies of wares through time in Northern San Juan region collections. Data are derived from Dolores Archaeological Program collections (Blinman 1988; Wilson and Blinman 1988) and South Canal and Hovenweep Lateral collections (Wilson 1988b, 1991).

resources and firing regimes for white ware production, resulting in a higher proportion of well-fired vessels with very white surfaces. The contrast between clays used for gray ware and white ware manufacture continued to increase (Wilson 1985, 1991). Slipped vessels, rare in the Basketmaker III period and consistently present but not plentiful in the Pueblo I period, became much more common. Tempers were more finely crushed, and sherd temper was more widely used alongside the established varieties of igneous and sedimentary rocks. With a few exceptions, the regional stylistic variants that could be discerned in the Pueblo I period converge; styles became more uniform across the Northern San Juan region. This uniformity, however, was accompanied by an increase in the diversity of styles in contemporary use (see Toll et al. 1992; this perception differs from that of Braun and Plog [1982] and S. Plog [1980]). Within this mix of stylistic attributes, constellations of clay, temper, slip, and paint become more consistent. These features, along with increased evidence for movement of vessels over longer distances, suggest that production and distribution became increasingly formalized.

Some of the increase in white ware production may be attributed to unstable red ware production. Red ware production continued as a regional specialty in southeastern Utah through A.D. 1100, but it never regained the "market share" it had during the mid-Pueblo I period. Beginning about A.D. 1050, the center of red ware manufacture shifted southwest into the Kayenta region, and Tsegi Orange Ware replaced San Juan Red Ware. Although red wares are abundant in the northern Kayenta region, their production declined sharply in the Northern San Juan region after A.D. 1075. They are present in only trace amounts in late Pueblo II collections.

Pueblo III Production (A.D. 1125–1300)

Too few data are available for a discussion of pottery production in Pueblo III households, but this period hosts the strongest evidence for a significant change in the level of specialized production. By A.D. 1150, numerous distinctive firing features appeared in the Northern San Juan region. These consist of shallow 0.8- to 1.2-m-wide trenches up to 8 m long, most of which date from the early to late Pueblo III period (Brown and Wilson 1990; Fuller 1984; Helm 1973; Hibbets and Hardin 1982; Purcell 1993). Almost all of the pottery recovered from these features is white ware, with a few gray ware sherds and no red ware sherds. Most of these features are in isolated locations, and clusters of several features are common (Brown and Wilson 1990; Fuller 1984). These trench kilns could have been used cooperatively by unspecialized household potters, and vessels from one kiln did reveal two distinctive paste combinations. A single setting, however, would have been capable of supplying enough vessels for many households. These features appear to have been used exclusively for firing white wares, suggesting increasingly specialized white ware production. Interpretations concerning the exact nature and context of this specialization are tenuous because the location of kilns near fuel and away from all habitations does not allow us to relate specialized production to the social contexts at these settlements. Evidence of pottery production is present at most extensively excavated Pueblo III sites. It is likely that gray wares continued to be produced at most households, as they had been during the preceding periods.

Ceramic trends noted for Pueblo III contexts reflect increased and more specialized production of white ware vessels. The proportion of white wares in some Pueblo III assemblages is very high, and in some areas, the number of white ware sherds is actually higher than gray ware sherds. This abundance indicates an increased demand for and use of white ware vessels during this time.

Several characteristics also reflect increased technological control of white ware production. Pueblo III vessels typically have black organic paint over extremely white surfaces, and slipped surfaces are relatively common. Pueblo III white ware sherds also consistently exhibit a higher degree of polishing and surface finishing than earlier types. Recent experiments indicate that firing conditions necessary to obtain these characteristics require a great deal of control (Swink 1993; Toll et al. 1991), accounting for at least the specialized morphology of the trench kilns. Painted designs are commonly elaborate, highly organized, and well executed. Increasing ratios of painted to unpainted white ware sherds also indicate that a larger proportion of the total vessel surface was decorated.

In contrast to increased white ware specialization, evidence shows a decline in white ware exchange at both local and regional levels during the Pueblo III period (Blinman and Wilson 1993; Wilson 1984, 1993; Wilson and Blinman 1988). This evidence suggests that despite increased specialization, white ware production and distribution were organized at a tract or local level rather than a regional level. This areal organization may have been so efficient that it resulted in a decrease in the long-distance movement of pottery vessels. This decrease, however, was not absolute. Trace amounts of extraregional red wares were still imported, but the source changed from Tsegi Orange Ware of the Kayenta region to White Mountain Red Ware from an area farther south.

Conclusions

The production of white ware vessels appears to have been a specialized craft from its inception in the Northern San Juan region, and its organization appears to have been different from, although influenced by, the level of specialization of other wares. For the entire Basketmaker III–Pueblo III period, white ware production conformed to a household-industry model, but evidence shows both spatial and temporal variation in white ware specialization. At first, both gray and white ware production were specialized, but the degree of white ware specialization was greater. As gray wares became less specialized during the Pueblo I period, the organization of white ware production remained relatively unchanged, although the active red ware industry appears to have suppressed the volume of white ware production in the western portion of the region. A resurgence of white ware production occurred during the early Pueblo II period, probably driven by a changing role for white ware vessels within the household economy. We have no direct evidence for changes in production at the household-industry level, but Pueblo II white ware technology became increasingly refined in the use of tempers, slips, paints, and decorative styles. By the Pueblo III period, formal kiln features were used on a large scale, implying that production volume by individuals or groups of potters necessitated formal facilities. This increase in the use of formal facilities, however, may have been partly driven by technological innovations in firing regime and paint use.

Population growth and associated social changes may not have directly influenced white ware production. Indirect influences are likely, however, through the juxtaposition of potters and clays and the interplay between settlement locations, the quality of agricultural land, and fuel supplies. Factors influencing the initial low level of production specialization were the low demand for white ware vessels, the complexity of pigment selection and firing regime, and the uneven distribution of low-iron clays.

References Cited

Abel, Leland J.
1955   Pottery Types of the Southwest: Wares 5A, 10A, 10B, 12A, San Juan Red Ware, Mesa Verde Gray and White Ware, San Juan White Ware, edited by Harold S. Colton. Ceramic Series 3. Museum of Northern Arizona, Flagstaff.

Arnold, Dean E.
1975   Ceramic Ecology of the Ayacucho Basin, Peru: Implications for Prehistory. Current Anthropology 16:183–205.
1985   Ceramic Theory and Cultural Process. Cambridge University Press, Cambridge.

Balfet, Hèléne

1981 Production and Distribution of Pottery in the Maghreb. In *Production and Distribution: A Ceramic Viewpoint,* edited by Hilary Howard and Elaine L. Morris, pp. 257–269. BAR International Series 120. British Archaeological Reports, Oxford.

Blinman, Eric

1983 The Red Ware Project: Ceramic Manufacture and Exchange in the Western Mesa Verde Region. Submitted to Colorado Historical Society, Denver.

1988 *The Interpretation of Ceramic Variability: A Case Study from the Dolores Anasazi.* Unpublished Ph.D. dissertation, Department of Anthropology, Washington State University, Pullman.

1989 Potluck in the Protokiva: Ceramics and Ceremonialism in Pueblo I Villages. In *The Architecture of Social Integration in Prehistoric Pueblos,* edited by William D. Lipe and Michelle Hegmon, pp. 113–124. Occasional Papers No. 1. Crow Canyon Archaeological Center, Cortez, Colorado.

1994 Adjusting the Pueblo I Chronology: Implications for Culture Change at Dolores and in the Mesa Verde Region at Large. In *Proceedings of the Anasazi Symposium 1991,* compiled by Art Hutchinson and Jack E. Smith, pp. 51–60. Mesa Verde Museum Association, Mesa Verde, Colorado.

Blinman, Eric, and C. Dean Wilson

1988a Ceramic Data and Interpretations: The McPhee Community Cluster. In *Dolores Archaeological Program: Anasazi Communities at Dolores: McPhee Village,* compiled by A. E. Kane and C. K. Robinson, pp. 1,293–1,341. U.S. Bureau of Reclamation Engineering and Research Center, Denver.

1988b Overview of A.D. 600–800 Ceramic Production and Exchange in the Dolores Project Area. In *Dolores Archaeological Program: Supporting Studies: Additive and Reductive Technologies,* compiled by Eric Blinman, Carl J. Phagan, and Richard H. Wilshusen, pp. 395–423. U.S. Bureau of Reclamation Engineering and Research Center, Denver.

1992 Ceramic Production and Exchange in the Northern San Juan Region: A.D. 600–900. In *Ceramic Production and Distribution: An Integrated Approach,* edited by George J. Bey III and Christopher A. Pool, pp. 155–173. Westview Press, Boulder, Colorado.

1993 Ceramic Perspectives on Northern Anasazi Exchange. In *The American Southwest and Mesoamerica: Systems of Prehistoric Exchange,* edited by Jonathan E. Ericson and Timothy G. Baugh, pp. 65–94. Plenum Publishing Corporation, New York.

Blinman, Eric, C. Dean Wilson, Robert M. R. Waterworth, Mary P. Errickson, and Linda P. Hart
1984   *Additive Technologies Group Laboratory Manual*. Dolores Archaeological Program Technical Reports DAP-149. Submitted to U.S. Bureau of Reclamation, Upper Colorado Region, Salt Lake City, Contract No. 8-07-40-S0562.

Bond, Mark C.
1985   White Mesa Ceramics, 1981. In *Anasazi Subsistence and Settlement on White Mesa, San Juan County, Utah*, by William E. Davis, pp. 189–274. University Press of America, Inc., Lanham, Maryland.

Braun, David P., and Stephen Plog
1982   Evolution of "Tribal" Social Networks: Theory and Prehistoric North American Evidence. *American Antiquity* 47:504–525.

Breternitz, David A., Arthur H. Rohn, Jr., and Elizabeth A. Morris (compilers)
1974   *Prehistoric Ceramics of the Mesa Verde Region*. Ceramic Series 5. Museum of Northern Arizona, Flagstaff.

Brew, John Otis
1946   *Archaeology of Alkali Ridge, Southeastern Utah, with a Review of the Prehistory of the Mesa Verde Division of the San Juan and Some Observations on Archaeological Systematics*. Papers of the Peabody Museum of American Archaeology and Ethnology Vol. 21. Harvard University, Cambridge. (Reprinted in 1974 by Kraus Reprint Co., Millwood, New York.)

Brisbane, Mark A.
1981   Incipient Markets for Early Anglo-Saxon Ceramics: Variations in Levels and Modes of Production. In *Production and Distribution: A Ceramic Viewpoint*, edited by Hilary Howard and Elaine L. Morris, pp. 229–242. BAR International Series 120. British Archaeological Reports, Oxford.

Bronitsky, Gordon, and Robert Hamer
1986   Experiments in Ceramic Technology: The Effects of Various Tempering Materials on Impact and Thermal-Shock Resistance. *American Antiquity* 51:89–101.

Brown, Gary M., and C. Dean Wilson
1990   The Firing and Misfiring of Mesa Verde Ceramics. Poster presented at the 55th Annual Meeting of the Society for American Archaeology, Las Vegas.

Cordell, Linda S., and Fred Plog
1979   Escaping the Confines of Normative Thought: A Reevaluation of Puebloan Prehistory. *American Antiquity* 44:405–429.

Costin, Cathy Lynne
1991   Craft Specialization: Issues in Defining, Documenting, and Explaining the Organization of Production. In *Archaeological Method and Theory*,

vol. 3, edited by Michael B. Schiffer, pp. 1–56. University of Arizona Press, Tucson.

Dean, Jeffrey S.

1994   *Environmental Change and/or Human Impact: The Case of the Colorado Plateau.* Paper presented at the 1994 Southwest Symposium, Tempe, Arizona.

DeBoer, Warren R.

1985   Pots and Pans Do Not Speak, Nor Do They Lie: The Case for Occasional Reductionism. In *Decoding Prehistoric Ceramics,* edited by Ben A. Nelson, pp. 347–357. Southern Illinois University Press, Carbondale.

Earle, Timothy K.

1980   A Model of Subsistence Change. In *Modeling Change in Prehistoric Subsistence Economies,* edited by Timothy K. Earle and Andrew L. Christenson, pp. 1–29. Academic Press, New York.

Ellwood, Priscilla B.

1980   Ceramics of Durango South. In *The Durango South Project: Archaeological Salvage of Two Late Basketmaker III Sites in the Durango District,* edited by John D. Gooding, pp. 78–102. Anthropological Papers of the University of Arizona No. 34. University of Arizona Press, Tucson.

Fry, Robert E.

1980   Models of Exchange for Major Shape Classes of Lowland Maya Pottery. In *Models and Methods in Regional Exchange,* edited by Robert E. Fry, pp. 3–18. SAA Papers No. 1. Society for American Archaeology, Washington, D.C.

1981   Pottery Production-Distribution Systems in the Southern Maya Lowlands. In *Production and Distribution: A Ceramic Viewpoint,* edited by Hilary Howard and Elaine L. Morris, pp. 145–167. BAR International Series 120. British Archaeological Reports, Oxford.

Fuller, Steven L.

1984   *Late Anasazi Pottery Kilns in the Yellowjacket District, Southwestern Colorado.* CASA Papers No. 4. Complete Archaeological Service Associates, Cortez, Colorado.

1987   *Cultural Resource Inventories for the Dolores Project: The Dove Creek Canal Distribution System and Dawson Draw Reservoir.* Four Corners Archaeological Project, Report No. 7. Prepared for Cultural Resource Program, U.S. Bureau of Reclamation, Upper Colorado Region, Salt Lake City, Contract No. 4-cs-40-01650, Delivery Order No. 23. Complete Archaeological Service Associates, Cortez, Colorado.

Hayes, Alden C.

1964   *The Archeological Survey of Wetherill Mesa, Mesa Verde National Park, Colorado.* Publications in Archeology No. 7A. National Park Service, Washington, D.C.

Hayes, Alden C., and James A. Lancaster
1975   *Badger House Community, Mesa Verde National Park, Colorado.* Publications in Archeology No. 7E. National Park Service, Washington, D.C.

Helm, Claudia
1973   The Kiln Site. In *Highway U-95 Archeology: Comb Wash to Grand Flat,* edited by Gardiner F. Dalley, pp. 209–221. Department of Anthropology, University of Utah. Submitted to Utah State Department of Highways, Salt Lake City.

Hibbets, Barry N.
1984   *Excavation and Evaluation of Archeological Site 5MT8451, and a Report of Archeological Monitoring of Celsius [sic] Energy's Cutthroat No. 1 Well Site and Access Road, Montezuma County, Colorado.* LAC Report 8428. La Plata Archeological Consultants, Inc., Dolores, Colorado. Submitted to Celsius [sic] Energy Co., Rock Springs, Wyoming.

Hibbets, Barry N., and Patrick L. Harden
1982   *Archeological Monitoring of Celcius Energy Corporation's Woods Unit 1-S Well Pad and Access Road, and a Report of the Excavation and Evaluation of Site 5MT7143, Montezuma County, Colorado.* LAC Report 8205a. La Plata Archeological Consultants, Inc., Dolores, Colorado. Submitted to Celcius Energy Corp., Rock Springs, Wyoming.

Hill, David V.
1985   Pottery Making at the Ewing Site (5MT927). *Southwestern Lore* 51:19–31.

Hurst, Winston
1983   The Prehistoric Peoples of San Juan County, Utah. In *San Juan County, Utah: People, Resources, and History,* edited by Allan Kent Powell, pp. 17–44. Utah State Historical Society, Salt Lake City.
1985   Ceramics. In *Recapture Wash Archaeological Project: 1981–1983, San Juan County, Utah,* chapter 11, edited by Asa S. Nielson, Joel C. Janetski, and James D. Wilde, pp. 11-1–11-9. Technical Series 85-7. Museum of Peoples and Cultures, Brigham Young University, Provo.

Hurst, Winston, Mark Bond, and Sloan E. Emery Schwindt
1985   Piedra Black-on-white, White Mesa Variety: Formal Description of a Western Mesa Verde Anasazi Pueblo I White Ware Type. *Pottery Southwest* 12(3):1–7.

Irwin-Williams, Cynthia, and Phillip Shelley
1980   *Investigations of the Salmon Site: The Structure of Chacoan Society in the Northern Southwest.* Submitted to Funding Agencies, Portales, New Mexico.

Kane, Allen E.

1986　Prehistory of the Dolores River Valley. In *Dolores Archaeological Program: Final Synthetic Report,* compiled by David A. Breternitz, Christine K. Robinson, and G. Timothy Gross, pp. 353–435. U.S. Bureau of Reclamation, Engineering and Research Center, Denver.

Kohler, Timothy A., and Meredith Matthews

1988　Long-Term Anasazi Land Use and Forest Reduction: A Case Study from Southwest Colorado. *American Antiquity* 53:537–564.

Kuckelman, Kristin A., and James N. Morris (compilers)

1988　*Archaeological Investigations on South Canal.* Four Corners Archaeological Project, Report No. 11. Complete Archaeological Service Associates, Cortez, Colorado.

Leonhardy, Frank C., and Vickie L. Clay

1985　Bedrock Geology, Quaternary Stratigraphy, and Geomorphology. In *Dolores Archaeological Program: Studies in Environmental Archaeology,* compiled by Kenneth Lee Peterson, Vickie L. Clay, Meredith H. Matthews, and Sarah W. Neusius, pp. 131–138. U.S. Bureau of Reclamation, Engineering and Research Center, Denver.

Lucius, William A.

1981　A Resource Approach for Ceramic Analysis. Paper presented at the 46th Annual Meeting of the Society for American Archaeology, San Diego.

1982　Ceramic Analysis. In *Testing and Excavation Report, MAPCO's Rocky Mountain Liquid Hydrocarbons Pipeline, Southwest Colorado,* vol. 2, edited by Jerry E. Fetterman and Linda Honeycutt, pp. 7.1–7.40. Woodward-Clyde Consultants, San Francisco.

Lucius, William A., and David A. Breternitz

1981　The Current Status of Redwares in the Mesa Verde Region. In *Collected Papers in Honor of Erik Kellerman Reed,* edited by Albert H. Schroeder, pp. 99–111. Papers of the Archaeological Society of New Mexico No. 6. Albuquerque.

Lucius, William A., and C. Dean Wilson

1980　San Juan Redwares: A Resource Model. Paper presented at the 53rd Annual Pecos Conference, Mesa Verde National Park, Colorado.

Molenaar, C. M.

1977　Stratigraphy and Depositional History of Upper Cretaceous Rocks of the San Juan Basin Area, New Mexico and Colorado, with a Note on Economic Resources. In *Guidebook of San Juan Basin III, Northwestern New Mexico,* edited by J. E. Fassett, pp. 159-165. New Mexico Geological Society.

Nelson, Ben

1985   Reconstructing Ceramic Vessels and Their Systemic Context. In *Decoding Prehistoric Ceramics*, edited by B. A. Nelson, pp. 310–329. Southern Illinois University Press, Carbondale.

Oppelt, Norman T.

1991   *Earth, Water and Fire, The Prehistoric Pottery of Mesa Verde.* Johnson Books, Boulder, Colorado.

Orcutt, Janet D.

1987   Modeling Prehistoric Agricultural Ecology in the Dolores Area. In *Dolores Archaeological Program: Supporting Studies: Settlement and Environment*, compiled by Kenneth Lee Petersen and Janet D. Orcutt, pp. 647–677. U.S. Bureau of Reclamation, Engineering and Research Center, Denver.

Orcutt, Janet D., Eric Blinman, and Timothy A. Kohler

1990   Explanations of Population Aggregation in the Mesa Verde Region Prior to A.D. 900. In *Perspectives on Southwestern Prehistory*, edited by Paul E. Minnis and Charles L. Redman, pp. 196–212. Westview Press, Boulder, Colorado.

Peacock, D. P. S.

1982   *Pottery in the Roman World: An Ethnoarchaeological Approach.* Longman, London.

Plog, Fred

1983   Political and Economic Alliances on the Colorado Plateaus, A.D. 400–1450. In *Advances in World Archaeology*, vol. 2, edited by Fred Wendorf and Angela E. Close, pp. 289–330. Academic Press, New York.

1984   Exchange, Tribes, and Alliances: The Northern Southwest. *American Archeology* 4:217–223.

Plog, Stephen

1980   *Stylistic Variation in Prehistoric Ceramics: Design Analysis in the American Southwest.* Cambridge University Press, Cambridge.

Purcell, David E.

1993   *Pottery Kilns of the Northern San Juan Anasazi Tradition.* Unpublished M.A. thesis, Department of Anthropology, Northern Arizona University, Flagstaff.

Reed, Erik K.

1958   *Excavations in Mancos Canyon, Colorado.* Anthropological Papers No. 35. University of Utah, Salt Lake City.

Rice, Prudence M.

1980   Peten Postclassic Pottery Production and Exchange: A View From Macanche. In *Models and Methods in Regional Exchange*, edited by Robert E.

Fry, pp. 67–82. SAA Papers No. 1. Society for American Archaeology, Washington, D.C.

1984   The Archaeological Study of Specialized Pottery Production: Some Aspects of Method and Theory. In *Pots and Potters: Current Approaches in Ceramic Archaeology*, edited by Prudence M. Rice, pp. 45–54. UCLA Institute of Archaeology Monograph No. 24. University of California, Los Angeles.

1987   *Pottery Analysis: A Sourcebook.* University of Chicago Press, Chicago.

Rohn, Arthur H.

1977   *Cultural Change and Continuity on Chapin Mesa.* The Regents Press of Kansas, Lawrence.

1989   Northern San Juan Prehistory. In *Dynamics of Southwest Prehistory*, edited by Linda S. Cordell and George J. Gumerman, pp. 149–177. Smithsonian Institution Press, Washington, D.C.

Rye, Owen S.

1981   *Pottery Technology: Principles and Reconstruction.* Taraxacum Inc., Washington, D.C.

Schlanger, Sarah H.

1988   Patterns of Population Movement and Long-Term Population Growth in Southwestern Colorado. *American Antiquity* 53:773–793.

Shepard, Anna O.

1965   *Ceramics for the Archaeologist.* Publication No. 609. Carnegie Institution of Washington, Washington, D.C. (Reprinted in 1980.)

Stark, Barbara L.

1985   Archaeological Identification of Pottery Production Locations: Ethnoarchaeological and Archaeological Data in Mesoamerica. In *Decoding Prehistoric Ceramics*, edited by Ben A. Nelson, pp. 158–194. Southern Illinois University Press, Carbondale.

Sullivan, Alan P., III

1988   Prehistoric Southwestern Ceramic Manufacture: The Limitations of Current Evidence. *American Antiquity* 53:23–35.

Swink, Clint

1993   Limited Oxidation Firing of Organic Painted Pottery in Anasazi-Style Trench Kilns. *Pottery Southwest* 20:1–5.

Toll, Henry Wolcott, III

1981   Ceramic Comparisons Concerning Redistribution in Chaco Canyon, New Mexico. In *Production and Distribution: A Ceramic Viewpoint*, edited by Hilary Howard and Elaine L. Morris, pp. 83–121. BAR International Series 120. British Archaeological Reports, Oxford.

Toll, Henry Wolcott, III, Eric Blinman, and C. Dean Wilson
1992   Chaco in the Context of Ceramic Regional Systems. In *Anasazi Regional Organization and the Chaco System,* edited by David E. Doyel, pp. 147–157. Anthropological Papers No. 5. Maxwell Museum of Anthropology, Albuquerque.

Toll, Henry Wolcott, III, and Charles A. Hannaford
1989   Data Recovery Plan and Research Design for Excavations Along the La Plata Highway in the Barker Arroyo Segment. Ms. on file, Office of Archaeological Studies, Museum of New Mexico, Santa Fe.

Toll, Henry Wolcott, III, and Peter J. McKenna
1987   The Ceramography of Pueblo Alto. In *Investigations at the Pueblo Alto Complex, Chaco Canyon,* vol. 3, part 2, edited by Francis Joan Mathien and Thomas C. Windes, pp. 19–230. Publications in Archaeology No. 18F, Chaco Canyon Studies. National Park Service, Santa Fe.

Toll, Henry Wolcott, III, C. Dean Wilson, and Eric Blinman
1991   Crow Canyon Kiln Conference; or Earth, Water, Fire, and Soul Meet Oxidation, Reduction, Catalysts, and Thermocouple. *Pottery Southwest* 18(2):4–6.

Vince, A. G.
1981   The Medieval Pottery Industry in Southern England: 10th to 13th Centuries. In *Production and Distribution: A Ceramic Viewpoint,* edited by Hilary Howard and Elaine L. Morris, pp. 309–322. BAR International Series 120. British Archaeological Reports, Oxford.

Waterworth, Robert M. R., and Eric Blinman
1986   Modified Sherds, Unidirectional Abrasion, and Pottery Scrapers. *Pottery Southwest* 13(2):4–7.

Wilshusen, Richard H., and Eric Blinman
1992   Pueblo I Village Formation: A Reevaluation of Sites Recorded by Earl Morris on Ute Mountain Ute Tribal Lands. *The Kiva* 57:251–269.

Wilson, C. Dean
1984   Ceramics from Sites 5MT3777 and 5MT3778, Casa de Suenos. In *Excavations at Site 5MT3777 and Site 5MT3778, Casa de Suenos,* by M. Lee Douthit, pp. 129–139. U.S. Bureau of Land Management Technical Report, Anasazi Heritage Center, Dolores, Colorado.

1985   *Regional Exchange of San Juan Tradition Ceramics at Salmon Ruin: A Resource Approach.* Unpublished Master's thesis, Department of Anthropology, Eastern New Mexico University, Portales.

1988a   Ceramic Studies. In *Archaeological Investigations in the Bodo Canyon Area, La Plata County, Colorado,* by Steven L. Fuller, pp. 317–333. UMTRA Archaeological Report No. 25. Prepared for Jacobs Engineering Group, Inc., by Complete Archaeological Service Associates, Cortez, Colorado.

1988b   South Canal Ceramic Analysis. In *Archaeological Investigations on South Canal*, compiled by Kristin A. Kuckelman and James N. Morris, pp. 435–477. Four Corners Archaeological Project Report No. 11. Complete Archaeological Service Associates, Cortez, Colorado.

1991   Hovenweep Laterals Ceramic Analysis. In *Archaeological Excavation of the Hovenweep Lateral*, by James N. Morris. Four Corners Archaeological Project Report. Complete Archaeological Service Associates, Cortez, Colorado.

1993   Patterns of Production, Exchange, and Interaction in the Totah. Paper presented at the 5th Occasional Anasazi Symposium, San Juan College, Farmington, New Mexico.

Wilson, C. Dean, and Eric Blinman

1988   Pueblo II and Pueblo III Ceramic Patterns Within the Dolores Project Area. In *Dolores Archaeological Program: Aceramic and Late Occupations at Dolores*, compiled by G. Timothy Gross and Allen E. Kane, pp. 367–402. U.S. Bureau of Reclamation, Engineering and Research Center, Denver.

1991   Ceramic Types of the Mesa Verde Region. Handout prepared for the Colorado Council of Professional Archaeologists Ceramic Workshop, Boulder, Colorado. Ms. on file, Office of Archaeological Studies, Museum of New Mexico, Santa Fe.

1993   *Upper San Juan Region Pottery Typology*. Archaeology Notes No. 80. Office of Archaeological Studies, Museum of New Mexico, Santa Fe.

1994   Early Anasazi Ceramics and the Basketmaker Transition. In *Proceedings of the Anasazi Symposium 1991*, compiled by Art Hutchinson and Jack E. Smith, pp. 199–211. Mesa Verde Museum Association, Mesa Verde, Colorado.

Wilson, C. Dean, Vickie L. Clay, and Eric Blinman

1988   Clay Resources and Resource Use. In *Dolores Archaeological Program: Supporting Studies: Additive and Reductive Technologies*, compiled by Eric Blinman, Carl J. Phagan, and Richard H. Wilshusen, pp. 375–394. U.S. Bureau of Reclamation, Engineering and Research Center, Denver.

4

Temporal Patterns Without Temporal Variation

The Paradox of Hohokam Red Ware Ceramics

David R. Abbott and Mary-Ellen Walsh-Anduze

> All history teaches us that these questions that we think [are] the pressing ones will be transmuted before they are answered, that they will be replaced by others, and that the very process of discovery will shatter the concepts that we today use to describe our puzzlement (Oppenheimer 1954:235).

As so often happens in science, ongoing work leads to an unanticipated result, sometimes a paradox, that spawns new research by transmuting the way widely accepted facts are understood. In the Hohokam culture area, as is true in other parts of the American Southwest, ceramic variation is the backbone of chronology building. Since research began in the Hohokam area, archaeologists have sought and found patterns in the way ceramic assemblages differed from one period to the next. Researchers believed that these differences corresponded to temporal variation, which, as conceived by Hohokam archaeologists, was the result of production changes made by Hohokam potters through time (e.g., Abbott 1983; Crown 1981, 1983; Haury 1945, 1976; Masse 1982; Schroeder 1952).

The differences in Classic period red ware, the red-slipped pottery that typically makes up 10 to 30 percent of Hohokam ceramics during the interval between A.D. 1100 and 1450, have been a basis for dating Classic period sites for more than 50 years (Schroeder 1940). Surprisingly, new results indicate that temporal changes in the production of Classic period red ware were largely erratic and perhaps less significant than spatial differences in ceramic production. Nonetheless, the important temporal patterns that have been widely recognized during the last five decades of research have been reaffirmed. These results not only alter the understanding of red ware variation, but also open up new research opportunities that extend far beyond the purposes of temporal control.

The Hohokam

The Hohokam were a remarkable people of a middle-range society who continuously inhabited sedentary villages and successfully farmed their desert environment for more than a millennium. Occupying the Phoenix Basin and adjacent areas of south-central Arizona from about A.D. 1 to 1450, the Hohokam are perhaps best known for their irrigation works. They engineered and operated some of the largest and most impressive canal networks of the prehistoric New World.

In the Phoenix area, many kilometers of ditches transported water from the Salt River to fields and habitation areas spread out along the canal routes. Archaeologists divide the Phoenix-area network into four canal systems, each of which includes a set of canals with a common headgate location, and the associated settlements (fig. 4.1). Villages situated near the terminus or the middle of the canal routes were obviously dependent for water on their sister villages positioned closer to the headgates. The degree to which this cooperation conditioned other patterns of interaction among Hohokam populations is a central issue in Hohokam research. However, because direct measurements of interaction (Wilcox 1987) are lacking, this subject has been one of only intense speculation (see Ackerly 1982; Crown 1987; Doyel 1981; Gregory and Nials 1985; Nicholas and Feinman 1989; Schroeder 1953).

Red Ware Variation and Temporal Control

Since Albert Schroeder's extensive survey and test excavations in the lower Salt River valley during the late 1930s, a conventional two-type classification of red ware has served to chronologically categorize Classic period components in the Phoenix Basin. Before Schroeder's work, all

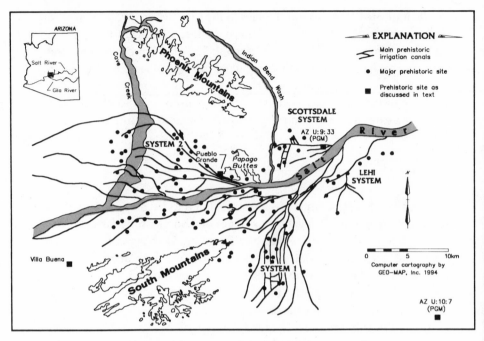

Figure 4.1 Hohokam canal systems of the lower Salt River valley.

red ware was described within a single type, Gila Red (Gladwin and Gladwin 1930). Schroeder, however, noticed important and consistent differences in the red ware from various valley locations that corresponded to the upper and lower levels of his test excavations. He codified these differences by revising the description of Gila Red and creating a new type, Salt Red. Furthermore, he designated Gila Red as a temporal diagnostic for the first part of the Classic period, the Soho phase (ca. A.D. 1100–1300), and assigned Salt Red to the following Civano phase (ca. A.D. 1300–1375).

Descriptions of Schroeder's two types are based on the presence of specific attributes of five traits: temper, surface finish, slip color, fireclouds, and fracture, although fracture is generally not considered in more recent studies, and firecloud patterns are not readily discernible on sherds. Gila Red is described as having micaceous schist temper, polishing striations, a yellow-red slip, and large and unpatterned fireclouds. Characteristic examples of Salt Red have sand temper with little or no mica, a lustrous surface without striations, an orange slip, and small and patterned fireclouds.

In retrospect it seems that Schroeder's (1952) model of red ware variation was greatly influenced by a similar model of Hohokam painted ceramics, the red-on-buff series (Gladwin et al. 1937; Haury 1976). Based on a correspondence with absolute dates, it is widely accepted that buff ware variation is subsumed under a small number of types that temporally succeeded one another. Everywhere in the Phoenix Basin, Hohokam archaeologists date their sites and components based on the temporal succession of the red-on-buff types.

Schroeder's model is basically similar: one type, Salt Red, replaced another type, Gila Red, throughout the Phoenix Basin. There are two important, but implicit, assumptions in this scheme: (1) the replacement is due to production changes made by Hohokam potters throughout the area, and (2) because Hohokam potters were so closely unified in their production techniques, a single type can account for most of the red ware variation at any one time. As an increasing number of Classic period sites have been excavated, the second assumption has been criticized, whereas the first has largely gone unchallenged. The effect has been an expansion of the red ware typology, with a continued reliance on the attributes of Gila and Salt Red as temporal indicators.

Analysts have discovered that red-slipped pottery in the Hohokam area exhibits a greater amount of variation than can be accounted for by the two traditional types (Abbott 1983:8–10; Abbott and Gregory 1988: 16–18; Cable and Gould 1988:326–327; Crown 1981:112–114; Doyel 1981; Doyel and Elson 1985; Pailes 1963:187; Weaver 1977:28). These studies have shown that numerous red ware sherds either have characteristics of both types, such as the orange slip color of Salt Red combined with the striated surface of Gila Red, or exhibit attributes uncommon to both the Gila and Salt Red types. Two new red ware types were proposed to codify much of the previously undocumented variation. Squaw Peak Red (Cable and Gould 1988) and Wingfield Red (Abbott and Gregory 1988; Doyel and Elson 1985) are defined based on the typical presence of matte finishes, thin red slips, and one of two distinctive temper types, Squaw Peak Schist and phyllite, respectively. The temper type, color, and poor surface finishes do not fit the characteristics of Gila and Salt Red.

Apart from the two new types, revisions of the red ware typology for the purpose of temporal control remained focused on the sand and micaceous schist-tempered pottery that traditionally is classified as Salt and

Gila Red, respectively. At one site after another, the apparent transition, as first described by Schroeder (1940), was definitely evident. In stratified or in otherwise dated deposits, pottery that exhibited the traits of Salt Red generally postdated ceramics with the Gila Red characteristics. However, high proportions of the sherds fell in between the two types, and two schemes were put forth to explain this variation. Just as important, both were simple revisions of Schroeder's original model, implying production changes over time to account for the variation in these ceramics.

In the first scheme, Abbott (1983:81–83) focused on the many sherds that exhibited traits of both red ware types and their place in the chronological sequence. More than 5,500 red ware sherds from nine sites were examined to determine whether there was a significant relationship between temper type and the type of surface finish as stipulated in Schroeder's typological model. Abbott found that micaceous schist-tempered sherds with striated surfaces proportionally decreased, whereas those with sand temper and those with lustrous surfaces proportionally increased through time. These proportional changes are similar to the typological changes described by Schroeder. Contrary to Schroeder's typology, however, Abbott determined that in each time interval, numerous pieces of pottery exhibited attributes of both the Salt and Gila Red types. Abbott argued for recollapsing the two types into a single type, while recognizing that proportions of some attributes changed independently and incrementally through time.

The second scheme codified the red ware variation into three temporally sequential types. The third type includes those sherds that exhibit traits of both Gila and Salt Red and is assumed to be temporally transitional between the other two types (Cable and Gould 1988:326–331; Cable and Mitchell 1989:801–807; Doyel 1974:140–141).

In both of the revisionists' models, as in Schroeder's original model, the explanation for the ceramic variation and its significance for chronological control is uniform and monotonic production changes made by red ware potters throughout the Phoenix Basin. The underlying assumption is that the potters were unified to the degree that they operated with the same set of ideas, techniques, and materials to produce similar pottery. Moreover, when changes occurred, they swept through the valley, causing similar lineal shifts in the proportions of red ware attributes at all manufacturing locations. New evidence now indicates that this assumption and principle are false. Red ware potters were not unified. Production changes, when they occurred, were not uniform. However, the temporally significant replacement of one kind of pottery by another probably did occur. This apparent paradox is the finding from a regional ceramics study associated with the recent excavations at Pueblo Grande.

Temporal Trends at Pueblo Grande

Pueblo Grande was probably the largest Hohokam village in the Phoenix area. It was centrally located in the lower Salt River valley at the headgates of Canal System 2 (fig. 4.1) and, undoubtedly, was influential in the regional settlement system during the Classic period.

Approximately 20 percent of the aboriginal village's area was slated for highway construction by the Arizona Department of Transportation, and a nearly complete excavation of this project area was completed by Soil Systems, Inc. The Hohokam occupation in the excavation area dated largely to the Classic period, which for the purposes of this paper is divided into four temporal units. Two units correspond to the later phase subdivisions of the Classic period—Civano and Polvorón. The other two, early Soho and late Soho, precede the later units and correspond to subdivisions of the Soho phase. The ceramics are grouped into four corresponding temporal sets on the basis of relative and absolute dating. The chronological analysis is described completely in the project's final report (Abbott et al. 1995).[1]

The temporal sets are characterized by substantial amounts of red ware variation. Sherds and intact vessels that can be classified as Wingfield Red, Squaw Peak Red, Gila Red, and Salt Red are present, as well as numerous pieces that could best be described as combining traits of two or more types. A comparison of attribute proportions among temporal sets showed the same temporal trend as was so often seen before in the Phoenix area. The characteristics associated with Salt Red—sand temper, an orange slip, and a lustrous surface finish—proportionally increased from one temporal unit to the next at Pueblo Grande (fig. 4.2). In addition, the identification of sherd temper in Classic period red ware (Lane 1989; Stein 1979) prompted the inclusion of this variable in the analysis; it, too, appears to be temporally related (fig. 4.3). Surprisingly, however, the results from a regional-scale analysis of the pottery demonstrate that the temporal trends, like those previously noted and assumed to have been the result of production changes *over time*, are, in fact, due to production differences *across space*.

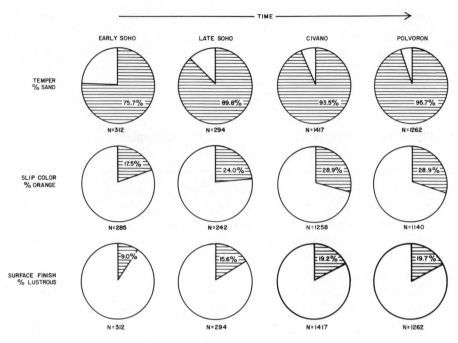

Figure 4.2 Red ware attributes by time at Pueblo Grande.

The Regional Ceramics Study

Not since Albert Schroeder's extensive survey in the late 1930s has a ceramic study been undertaken in the lower Salt River valley to match the regional-scale analysis that was performed in conjunction with the Pueblo Grande excavations. Appropriate to its scale is its emphasis—to distinguish distinct ceramic production zones in the Phoenix Basin. The diversity and geographic configuration of the bedrock and erosional sediments in the basin are ideal for ceramic sourcing. Nine spatially separated zones containing mutually distinguishable rock types and sands have been identified (fig. 4.4; Abbott and Schaller 1990, 1991; Abbott et al. 1991; Schaller and Abbott 1990).

Petrographic analysis of nearly 500 sherds from 27 sites demonstrates that 6 of these rock types were commonly procured by potters for temper (Schaller 1994). Subsequent work shows that these rock types are distinguishable in potsherds under a binocular microscope. In addition, analyses of the clay fraction in sherds, through both electron microprobe assays (Freestone 1982) and inductively coupled plasma emission (ICP) spectroscopy (Burton and Simon 1993), have shown a close association between the clay and temper types (Abbott 1994; Abbott and Schaller 1990, 1991; Abbott et al. 1991; Schaller and Abbott 1990). The association indicates that Hohokam potters relied heavily on the materials that were closest at hand. Potters used temper sources that ranged from being immediately available to as much as 10 km away from their villages. Nevertheless, their tendency to exploit the closest source makes temper an excellent indicator of production area. Six analytic zones of production have been identified, each corresponding to one of the sand types and to a different part of the Phoenix Basin.

The analysis has shown that red-slipped pottery containing phyllite (Wingfield Red) was largely produced at the western end of Canal System 2, red ware tempered with Squaw Peak Schist (Squaw Peak Red) was manufactured in the central part of Canal System 2, and, most importantly, micaceous schist-tempered red ware (Gila Red) was produced along the Gila River to the south (see fig. 4.4). In addition, the "sand" temper typically associated with Salt Red can be subdivided into four categories: (1) Camelback Granite, which is derived from the vicinity of Pueblo Grande, (2) Estrella Gneiss, which crops out on the western half of South Mountain, (3) South Mountain Granodiorite, which dominates the eastern half of South Mountain, and (4) an unidentified category whose origin(s) is (are) unknown. The unidentified category is a catch-all that probably contains several sand types, including materials from outside the study area, as well as many sherds that contained rock fragments that were too small and too few to be identified with only a binoc-

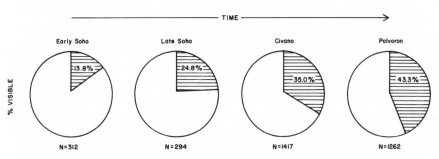

Figure 4.3 Sherd temper in red ware by time at Pueblo Grande.

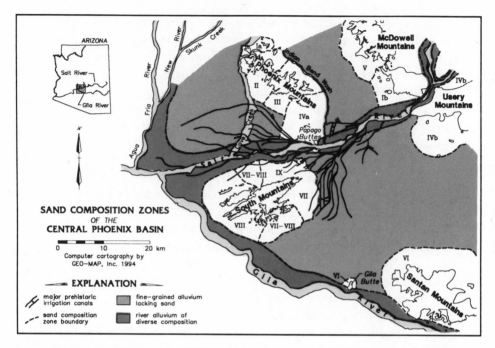

Figure 4.4 Sand composition zones of the central Phoenix Basin: Ia—basalt, Phoenix Mountains; Ib—basalt, Fountain Hills; II—phyllite; III—Squaw Peak Schist; IVa—Camelback Granite, Papago Buttes; IVb—Camelback Granite, Usery Mountains; V—quartzite; VI—micaceous schist; VII—South Mountain Granodiorite; VIII—Estrella Gneiss; VII–VIII—mixed South Mountain Granodiorite and Estrella Gneiss; IX—andesite.

ular microscope. Finally, in addition to the principal temper types, the analysts identified a subtype that is a mix of unidentified arkosic sand (the feldspar-rich sand derived from granite) and minor amounts of Squaw Peak Schist. Such a mix has formed at the boundary between the Squaw Peak Schist and Camelback Granite sand-composition zones (fig. 4.4). Pottery containing the mixed sand was probably produced near that boundary area and perhaps at Pueblo Grande, along with Camelback Granite–tempered red ware.

The production source, based on temper type, was identified for more than 3,300 red ware sherds from 74 structures and 2 stratified trash pits at Pueblo Grande. With these data, the changes in red ware characteristics over time were examined further. We documented the differences in pro-

duction of the red ware varieties by examining the pottery that was imported to Pueblo Grande during each of the Classic period intervals.
Mostly erratic, and thus probably insignificant, production changes over
time were found.

Before proceeding with that discussion, we believe it is important to
assess the effect that vessel form had on the results. Because bowls, jars,
and scoops might vary in slip color, temper, and surface finish, varying
proportions of different vessel forms could potentially explain the systematic changes in the other variables. The proportion of red ware bowls,
jars, and scoops, as determined from rim sherds, however, shows little
change over time (fig. 4.5). Further, gross measures of vessel size, obtained by measuring the orifice diameter of bowl and jar rim sherds,
change significantly over time, but not in a systematic or linear fashion
(figs. 4.6 and 4.7).[2]

It is also important to consider the vessel forms by each temper category. Although the number of rim sherds in each category is typically
small, and thus some uncertainty exists, vessel size does not seem to
change significantly over time within each temper category (table 4.1).
Therefore, the temporal trends noted below for each category probably
reflect actual production changes, rather than shifts in the kinds of vessel
forms that reached Pueblo Grande from each production area.

The strongest trend regards the presence of crushed sherd temper in
the clay body (fig. 4.8), which was added in most instances with other
temper. The analysts noted monotonic increases in sherd temper in half
of the red ware varieties and a general increase in all varieties from the
earliest to the latest ceramics. This is the kind of temporal variation that
one would expect for temper type, slip color, and surface finish if uniform

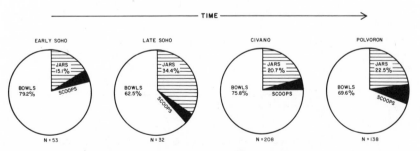

Figure 4.5 Red ware vessel forms by time at Pueblo Grande.

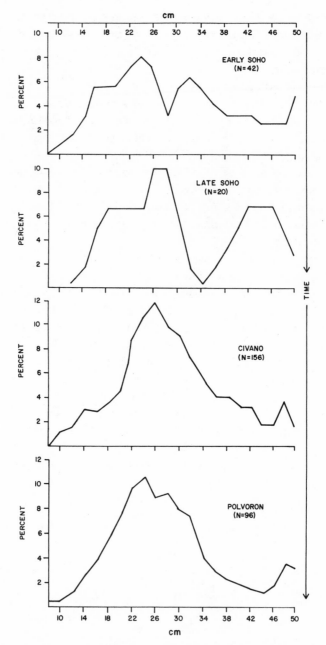

Figure 4.6 Red ware bowl orifice diameters by time at Pueblo Grande.

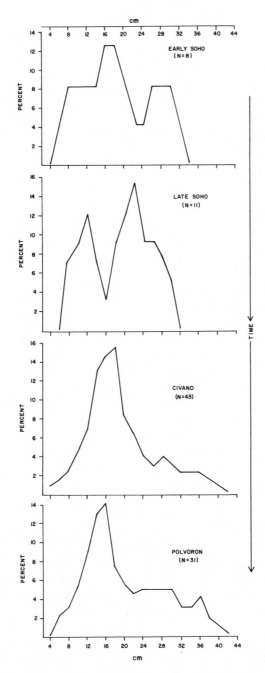

Figure 4.7 Red ware jar orifice diameters by time at Pueblo Grande.

Table 4.1 Hohokam Red Ware Orifice Diameters

Temper	Time	Bowls			Jars		
		Median	Range	N	Median	Range	N
Phyllite	Early Soho	27	6	2	30	—	1
	Late Soho	28	—	1	—	—	—
	Civano	26	—	1	—	—	—
	Polvorón	34	—	1	32	—	1
Squaw Peak Schist	Early Soho	16	—	1	16	—	1
	Late Soho	—	—	—	—	—	—
	Civano	22	12	2	24	—	1
	Polvorón	28	—	1	—	—	—
Camelback Granite	Early Soho	24	—	1	—	—	—
	Late Soho	18	—	1	24	—	1
	Civano	34	—	1	20	0	2
	Polvorón	30	12	3	19	16	4
Micaceous schist	Early Soho	44	32	7	28	—	1
	Late Soho	44	—	1	22	—	1
	Civano	31	34	10	34	—	1
	Polvorón	36	—	1	—	—	—

changes in production were the explanation for the temporal patterns previously noted. In fact, the opposite is true.

We will first consider the mix of red ware varieties at Pueblo Grande. Always dominating the assemblages are the locally made pottery (Camelback Granite and unidentified arkosic sand with Squaw Peak Schist), the variety from the South Mountain Granodiorite zone, and sherds with unidentified temper (table 4.2). Micaceous schist temper, as found in Gila Red, was also common in the earliest pottery, but its presence continuously declined to almost trace amounts by the end of the Hohokam occupation. The locally produced pottery was a relative constant over time, whereas South Mountain Granodiorite increased

Table 4.1 *Continued*

Temper	Time	Bowls			Jars		
		Median	Range	N	Median	Range	N
Estrella	Early Soho	—	—	—	—	—	—
Gneiss	Late Soho	46	26	3	20	—	1
	Civano	24	38	13	24	—	1
	Polvorón	24	14	3	—	—	—
South	Early Soho	26	38	19	10	6	3
Mountain	Late Soho	24	32	7	13	16	4
Granodiorite	Civano	28	38	76	20	30	22
	Polvorón	24	40	48	16	26	13
Arkosic sand	Early Soho	32	32	9	24	—	1
with Squaw	Late Soho	28	6	3	20	0	2
Peak Schist	Civano	36	36	16	16	12	7
	Polvorón	39	34	6	18	20	3
Unidentified	Early Soho	50	18	3	18	—	1
	Late Soho	39	14	4	19	18	2
	Civano	30	38	37	16	6	9
	Polvorón	26	34	33	20	24	10

slightly, and the red ware with unidentified temper increased steadily during the occupation.

The petrographic and clay chemistry results demonstrated that micaceous schist-tempered red ware was produced along the Gila River and not in the lower Salt River valley (Abbott 1994). Therefore, its decline in relative frequency at Pueblo Grande must be explained by changes in exchange patterns not production. The only wild card in this regard is the unidentified temper category, which possibly could have been a substitute for micaceous schist temper in the Gila River production area. This is a subject requiring further study, but for reasons discussed below this seems unlikely.

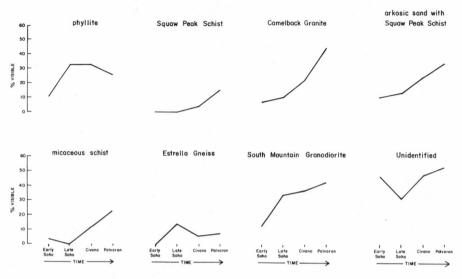

Figure 4.8 Sherd temper by time and temper type.

Temporal changes in slip color are mostly erratic (fig. 4.9). Sample size undoubtedly plays a part, but clearly these data cannot explain the temporal pattern at Pueblo Grande (fig. 4.2). The temporal pattern is explained by the relatively more frequent orange slips among the sherds in the South Mountain Granodiorite and unidentified categories (fig. 4.9) and the increase of these categories through time (table 4.2). The pattern, therefore, is probably not a result of production changes over time at Pueblo Grande; instead, increasing numbers of orange-slipped pots were probably brought to the site from elsewhere. The unidentified-temper sherds are an unknown factor in this equation because they could have been made at Pueblo Grande. They also contribute to the explanation of the surface-finish pattern.

The production changes noted for surface finish are mostly erratic, although a strong monotonic increase is apparent in the pottery from the South Mountain Granodiorite zone (fig. 4.10). The increase in lustrous surfaces at Pueblo Grande through time (fig. 4.2) can partly be explained by the production changes in this one manufacturing zone. Two other factors are equally important: (1) the increase in sherds in the unidentified category; a higher percentage of these pieces have lustrous surfaces than do most other varieties; and (2) the increase in the relative frequency of sherds tempered with South Mountain Granodiorite.

The data indicate temporal patterns at Pueblo Grande that are not the result of uniform production changes across the region; rather, these patterns are associated with production changes at specific areas and especially with changing exchange relationships. The origin(s) of the unidentified category is (are) unknown, but these ceramics generally resemble those from the South Mountain Granodiorite zone. If they are variants from that production area, then the temporal patterns at Pueblo Grande can be largely explained by exchange.

Implications for Hohokam Organization and Temporal Control

The Pueblo Grande results cast a new light on the regional data reported by Schroeder (1940) more than 50 years ago. According to Schroeder's survey of more than 100 sites, most of which were in the greater Phoenix area, Salt Red largely replaced Gila Red ceramics during the Classic period. Until now, this widespread pattern has been viewed as a uniform shift in production across the region. We interpret this pattern differently.

Table 4.2 Percentage of Temper-Type Classes by Time

Temper	Early Soho	Late Soho	Civano	Polvorón
Phyllite	6.4	3.1	1.9	1.5
Squaw Peak Schist	3.5	1.7	1.5	1.6
Camelback Granite	8.7	6.8	3.2	6.2
Micaceous schist	17.9	7.1	4.6	2.8
Estrella Gneiss	2.6	9.9	7.0	3.0
South Mountain Granodiorite	33.7	40.1	41.5	39.5
Arkosic sand with Squaw Peak Schist	15.1	10.2	10.7	11.2
Unidentified	12.2	21.1	29.7	34.3
Total N	312	294	1,417	1,262

During the early Classic period, substantial proportions of the red ware pots tempered with micaceous schist were imported to Phoenix-area villages from the Gila River area to the south. Later, most of the red ware may have been derived from an area on the eastern flanks of South Mountain. Our interpretation is based on the assumption that the pottery from various sites that Schroeder typed as Gila Red or Salt Red 50 years ago was largely produced in the Gila River valley or the South Mountain area, respectively. To test this assumption, we reexamined Schroeder's collections, which are curated at Pueblo Grande Museum.

The distribution of red ware sherds in trash mounds at three sites (fig. 4.1)—Villa Buena, AZ U:9:33(PGM), and AZ U:10:7(PGM)—was particularly important to Schroeder (1940:113–117) for revealing the temporal pattern he described. Unfortunately, only a few dozen sherds were saved from these sites; none are currently labeled as to type. The reexamination showed that the few sherds that fit the Gila Red type contained micaceous schist, and the sherds that best fit the Salt Red description contained South Mountain Granodiorite temper. There were also numerous red ware sherds that had some but not all of the traits that define Salt Red. Almost exclusively, these sherds contained temper that was unidentifiable but seemed distinct from the temper in the unidentified class

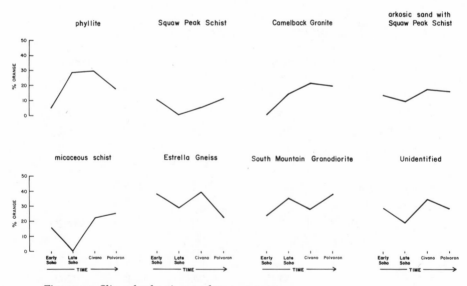

Figure 4.9 Slip color by time and temper type.

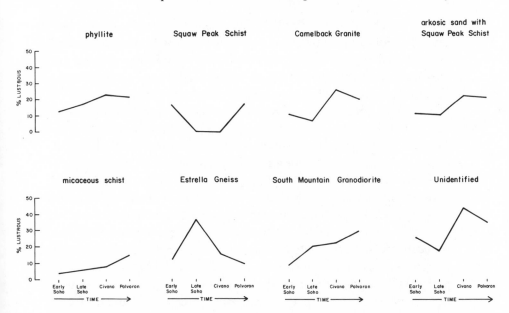

Figure 4.10 Surface finish by time and temper type.

from Pueblo Grande. Gauging from Schroeder's data tables (1940:114–116), we determined that most of the red ware sherds that were reexamined were probably typed as Salt Red. Not all of Schroeder's Salt Red, however, can be assumed to be from the South Mountain source. Nevertheless, red ware sherds containing South Mountain Granodiorite did compose a sizable portion of the Salt Red assemblages as probably typed by Schroeder, at least in the few sherds that were saved. The temporally increasing frequency of red-slipped pottery from the South Mountain area, as observed at Pueblo Grande, does seem to reflect a broad, regional exchange pattern throughout the lower Salt River valley. This inference, if correct, has important ramifications for the understanding of the social and economic lives of the Classic period Hohokam.

The results of the ceramics study indicate the large degree to which most Hohokam villages in the lower Salt River valley relied on other settlements for their red ware pottery. Red ware at Pueblo Grande during the Classic period was roughly 14 percent of the total ceramics, and their procurement represents a considerable investment in external production sources. Perhaps thousands of pots were imported to Classic period sites of the Phoenix area. Not only does the frequency of exchange indicate that Hohokam settlements were much less self-reliant for pottery production than has been long assumed (see Plog 1989:129–131), but also the directionality of the exchange demonstrates an obvious dependence by Salt River valley villages on producers in other canal systems. The Phoenix Basin populations were closely linked in ways that were independent of the cooperation required for hydraulic management, at least for the supply of pottery. Moreover, a temporal shift occurred in the scale of those dependencies. During the early Classic period, the Gila River producers were important suppliers of red ware for the Salt River communities. By the late Classic period, however, most of the red ware was being imported over shorter distances from the South Mountain area.

The results also raise the question of the organizational significance of the economic and social interaction that the exchanges represent. Important in this regard are the social contexts in which red ware pots were preferred. Red ware vessels are typically 5 to 10 times more numerous in burial contexts than in trash contexts (Abbott 1983, 1985) and have been found in abundance in at least one ceremonial precinct surrounding a platform mound (Abbott 1988). These statistics are especially true for the thick-slipped and burnished red ware now known to be from the South Mountain and Gila River production areas. Their preference, coupled with their higher production costs as compared with those for unslipped utilitarian and other red ware varieties, suggests that they were often distributed in formal social settings characterized by socially distant parties whose concerns were economic as well as social (Bohannon 1955:60; Sahlins 1972:193–196; see also Abbott 1983:109–117, 1985). The interaction between the Salt River communities and their red ware suppliers to the south may have been formalized rather than socially close.

If red ware from the Gila River and South Mountain areas was largely distributed as an economic commodity, then an interesting question arises regarding the mode of its production. According to some definitions of specialization (e.g., production above the needs of the household), red ware production for exchange may imply specialization. Specialization is a cultural trait often associated with political complexity (Peebles and Kus 1977:432; Rice 1981, 1987:188), although various kinds of specialized production are not associated with social hierarchies (Costin 1991). To explore this issue, we are analyzing the production standardization of particular vessel forms. A demonstration of red ware specialization and more complete information about the dispersement of the specialist-produced pottery would add new fuel to an already heated debate over Hohokam political organization (e.g., Doyel 1980; Gregory and Nials 1985; Haury 1976; Wilcox 1991; Wilcox and Sternberg 1983; Wood and McAllister 1980). For instance, some authors argue that the Classic period platform mounds became the residences of elites during the Civano phase (Doyel 1981; Gregory 1987; Gregory and Nials 1985; Wilcox 1987, 1991). A demonstrated abundance at the platform mounds of high-quality red ware pots produced by specialists might support the idea that socially elevated persons enjoyed greater access to status-related goods than did other people living outside the mound precincts.

Finally, we consider temporal control. The change from red ware with micaceous schist temper, a yellow-red slip, and a striated surface to red ware with "sand" temper, an orange slip, and a lustrous finish is an undeniable temporal pattern at many Phoenix-area sites. The pattern's significance for temporal control is undiminished by the results reported here, but for the sake of its utility, some fine tuning is in order. Two important implications stem from the cause of the pattern, which was not a production shift over an entire region but a shift in the way populations in that region interacted with one another. First, one should expect that the temporal differences were of a quantitative and not a qualitative nature. For instance, the mix of red ware during the late Classic period should include large proportions from the South Mountain area, but probably not to the extent that other varieties are completely excluded. Second, exchange patterns probably account for the temporal pattern; thus, the temporal differences are probably only present in the areas outside the South Mountain and Gila River supply zones. Doyel (1981:34) already noted the lack of change in one area near the Gila River. Stone (1991:2), who analyzed an early Classic period cemetery in the South Mountain area, found that the assemblage was dominated by sand-tempered red ware that fit the description of Salt Red. As these examples imply, because the chronologically significant pattern is probably due to the changing supply of red ware pottery through time, the pattern as a temporal indicator is most useful in areas beyond the supply zones.

Conclusions

Albert Schroeder's pioneering research in the late 1930s identified a broad-scale pattern of red ware variation. It has since proved useful for chronological purposes in nearly all of the research projects that involved Classic period sites in the Phoenix area. Fifty years later, the utility of Schroeder's findings remains both important and undiminished. At the same time, the underlying assumption explaining the pattern—uniform production across the region changed monotonically over time—seems to be incorrect. If this is true, then the regional pattern requires a new explanation, which we believe involves widespread patterns of interaction and exchange.

In offering this hypothesis, we try to open up new and, we hope, fruitful lines of inquiry. The circulation of plain ware, as well as red ware pottery, within the Phoenix Basin can now be traced over relatively short distances, including both within and between canal systems. Documenting these exchanges offers a new way to measure interaction between Hohokam populations directly. Organizational questions, which can largely be reduced to how interaction takes place and between whom, are now more approachable. In this regard, the study of Hohokam pottery will lead to a new and more precise understanding of Hohokam society and its development through time.

Acknowledgments

The Arizona Department of Transportation provided funding under Contract No. 87-53. Additional funding was provided by Sigma Xi Grants-in-Aid-of-Research and a Research Development Grant from the Graduate Student Association of Arizona State University. Ceramics for the petrographic, microprobe, and ICP spectroscopy analyses were provided by the Department of Anthropology and Office of Cultural Resource Management at Arizona State University, Arizona State Museum at the University of Arizona, Museum of Northern Arizona, Pueblo Grande Museum, Mesa Southwest Museum, Salt River Pima-Maricopa Indian Community, and Archaeological Consulting Services. The electron microprobe in the Department of Chemistry at Arizona State University was purchased with the aid of NSF grant EAR-8408163. Davi Saari prepared the microprobe samples. James Burton performed the ICP spectroscopy assays at the Laboratory for Archaeological Chemistry, University of Wisconsin, Madison. Holly Young and Todd Bostwick of Pueblo Grande Museum provided assistance with the Schroeder collection. The ceramic analysis was performed by Lori Ann Frye, Bong Won Kang, Mac McDonnell, Maria Martin, and

Jane Peterson. Jim Holmlund of Geo-Map, Inc. and Alison Dean prepared graphics. Tobi Taylor gave editorial help. Special thanks go to Albert Schroeder, who graciously commented on an earlier version of this paper and whose pioneering efforts and insight on Hohokam red ware inspired the present contribution.

Notes

1. The Pueblo Grande analysis is ongoing. The results presented here are expected to change, although not substantially.

2. The curves have been "corrected" or smoothed with the running average method to compensate for the difficulty of accurately measuring rim sherds. Orifice diameters are measured to the closest 2 cm and are probably accurate to ±2 cm of the encoded value. The running average method averages the percentage in each category with the percentages in the next smallest and next largest class. The plots are composed of these averaged values.

References Cited

Abbott, David R.

1983   A Technological Assessment of Ceramic Variation in the Salt-Gila Aqueduct Area: Towards a Comprehensive Documentation of Hohokam Ceramics. In *Hohokam Archaeology Along the Salt-Gila Aqueduct, Central Arizona Project, vol. VIII: Material Culture*, edited by Lynn S. Teague and Patricia L. Crown, pp. 1–117. Arizona State Museum Archaeological Series 150. University of Arizona, Tucson.

1985   Spheres of Intra-Cultural Exchange and the Ceramics of the Salt-Gila Aqueduct Project. In *Proceedings of the 1983 Hohokam Symposium*, part II, edited by Alfred E. Dittert, Jr. and Donald E. Dove, pp. 419–438. Occasional Paper No. 2. Arizona Archaeological Society, Phoenix.

1988   Form, Function, Technology, and Style in Hohokam Ceramics. In *The 1982–1984 Excavation at Las Colinas: Material Culture*, vol. 4, edited by David R. Abbott, Kim E. Beckwith, Patricia L. Crown, R. Thomas Euler, David A. Gregory, J. Ronald London, Marilyn B. Saul, Larry A. Schwalbe, and Mary Bernard-Shaw, pp. 73–198. Arizona State Museum Archaeological Series 162. University of Arizona, Tucson.

Abbott, David R. (editor)

1994   *The Pueblo Grande Project, Volume 3: Ceramics and the Production and Exchange of Pottery in the Central Phoenix Basin*. Publications in Archaeology No. 20. Soil Systems, Phoenix.

Abbott, David R., and David A. Gregory

1988   Hohokam Ceramic Wares and Types. In *The 1982–1984 Excavations at Las Colinas: Material Culture,* vol. 4, edited by David R. Abbott, Kim E. Beckwith, Patricia L. Crown, R. Thomas Euler, David A. Gregory, J. Ronald London, Marilyn B. Saul, Larry A. Schwalbe, and Mary Bernard-Shaw, pp. 5–28. Arizona State Museum Archaeological Series 162. University of Arizona, Tucson.

Abbott, David R., Douglas R. Mitchell, and Jamie A. Merewether

1995   Chronology. In *The Pueblo Grande Project: Excavations Feature Descriptions, Chronology, and Spatial Organization,* vol. 2, edited by Douglas R. Mitchell. Publications in Archaeology No. 20. Soil Systems, Phoenix, in press.

Abbott, David R., and David M. Schaller

1990   Hohokam Ceramic Exchange Within the Salt River Valley, Arizona: Results from the Hohokam Expressway Project. Poster presented at the 55th Annual Meeting of the Society for American Archaeology, Las Vegas.

1991   Electron Microprobe and Petrographic Analyses of Prehistoric Hohokam Pottery to Determine Ceramic Exchange Within the Salt River Valley, Arizona. In *Materials Issues in Art and Archaeology II,* edited by Pamela B. Vandiver, James Druzik, and George Seagan Wheeler, pp. 441–453. Symposium Proceedings 185. Materials Research Society, Pittsburgh.

Abbott, David R., David M. Schaller, and Robert I. Birnie

1991   Compositional Analysis of Hohokam Pottery from the Salt River Valley, Arizona. Paper presented at the 62nd Annual Meeting of the Southwestern Anthropological Association, Tucson.

Ackerly, Neal W.

1982   Irrigation, Water Allocation Strategies, and the Hohokam Collapse. *The Kiva* 47:91–106.

Bohannon, Paul

1955   Some Principles of Exchange and Investment Among the Tiv. *American Anthropologist* 57(1):60–70.

Burton, James H., and Arleyn W. Simon

1993   Acid Extraction as a Simple and Inexpensive Method for Compositional Characterization of Archaeological Ceramics. *American Antiquity* 58:45–59.

Cable, John S., and Ronald R. Gould

1988   The Casa Buena Ceramic Assemblage: A Study of Typological Systematics and Ceramic Change in Classic Period Assemblages. In *Excava-*

tions at Casa Buena: Changing Hohokam Land Use Along the Squaw Peak Parkway, vol. 1, edited by Jerry B. Howard, pp. 271–357. Publications in Archaeology No. 11. Soil Systems, Phoenix.

Cable, John S., and Douglas R. Mitchell
1989   Intrasite Structure, Chronology, and Community Organization of the Grand Canal Ruins. In *Archaeological Investigations at the Grand Canal Ruins: A Classic Period Site in Phoenix, Arizona*, vol. 2, edited by Douglas R. Mitchell, pp. 793–857. Publications in Archaeology No. 12. Soil Systems, Phoenix.

Costin, Cathy Lynne
1991   Craft Specialization: Issues in Defining, Documenting, and Explaining the Organization of Production. In *Archaeological Method and Theory*, vol. 3, edited by Michael B. Schiffer, pp. 1–56. University of Arizona Press, Tucson.

Crown, Patricia L.
1981   Analysis of Las Colinas Ceramics. In *The 1968 Excavations at Mound 8, Las Colinas Ruins Group, Phoenix, Arizona*, edited by Laurens C. Hammack and Alan P. Sullivan, pp. 87–169. Arizona State Museum Archaeological Series 154. University of Arizona, Tucson.
1983   Classic Period Ceramic Manufacture: Exploring Variability in the Production and Use of Hohokam Vessels. In *Hohokam Archaeology Along the Salt-Gila Aqueduct, Central Arizona Project, Vol. VIII(1): Material Culture*, edited by Lynn S. Teague and Patricia L. Crown, pp. 119–204. Arizona State Museum Archaeological Series 150. University of Arizona, Tucson.
1987   Classic Period Hohokam Settlement and Land Use in the Casa Grande Ruins Area, Arizona. *Journal of Field Archaeology* 14:147–162.

Doyel, David E.
1974   *Excavation in the Escalante Ruins Group, Southern Arizona*. Arizona State Museum Archaeological Series 37. University of Arizona, Tucson.
1980   Hohokam Social Organization and the Sedentary to Classic Transition. In *Current Issues in Hohokam Prehistory*, edited by David E. Doyel and Fred Plog, pp. 23–40. Anthropological Research Papers No. 23. Arizona State University, Tempe.
1981   *Late Hohokam Prehistory in Southern Arizona*. Contributions to Archaeology No. 2. Gila Press, Scottsdale, Arizona.

Doyel, David E., and Mark D. Elson
1985   Ceramic Analysis. In *Hohokam Settlement and Economic Systems in the Central New River Drainage, Arizona*, vol. 2, edited by David E. Doyel and Mark D. Elson, pp. 436–520. Publications in Archaeology No. 4. Soil Systems, Phoenix.

Freestone, I. C.

1982   Applications and Potential of Electron Probe Micro-analysis in Techno-
       logical and Provenance Investigations of Ancient Ceramics. *Archaeome-
       try* 24(2):99–116.

Gladwin, Harold S., Emil W. Haury, E. B. Sayles, and Nora Gladwin

1937   *Excavations at Snaketown: Material Culture.* Medallion Papers No. 25.
       Gila Pueblo, Globe, Arizona.

Gladwin, Winifred, and Harold S. Gladwin

1930   *Some Southwestern Pottery Types, Series I.* Medallion Papers No. 8. Gila
       Pueblo, Globe, Arizona.

Gregory, David A.

1987   The Morphology of Platform Mounds and the Structure of Classic Pe-
       riod Hohokam Sites. In *The Hohokam Village: Site Structure and Organi-
       zation,* edited by David E. Doyel, pp. 183–210. Southwestern and Rocky
       Mountain Division of the American Association for the Advancement
       of Science, Glenwood Springs, Colorado.

Gregory, David A., and Fred L. Nials

1985   Observations Concerning the Distribution of Classic Period Hohokam
       Platform Mounds. In *Proceedings of the 1983 Hohokam Symposium,* part I,
       edited by Alfred E. Dittert, Jr. and Donald E. Dove, pp. 373–388. Occa-
       sional Paper No. 2. Arizona Archaeological Society, Phoenix.

Haury, Emil W.

1945   *The Excavation of Los Muertos and Neighboring Ruins in the Salt River
       Valley, Southern Arizona.* Papers of the Peabody Museum of Ameri-
       can Archaeology and Ethnology Vol. 24, No. 1. Harvard University,
       Cambridge.

1976   *The Hohokam, Desert Farmers and Craftsmen: Excavations at Snaketown,
       1964–1965.* University of Arizona Press, Tucson.

Lane, Anne Marie

1989   The Grand Canal Ceramic Assemblage: Ceramic Type Descriptions. In
       *Archaeological Investigations at the Grand Canal Ruins: A Classic Period
       Site in Phoenix, Arizona,* vol. 1, edited by Douglas R. Mitchell, pp. 249–
       293. Publications in Archaeology No. 12. Soil Systems, Phoenix.

Masse, W. Bruce

1982   Hohokam Ceramic Art: Regionalism and the Imprint of Societal Change.
       In *Southwestern Ceramics: A Comparative Review,* edited by Albert H.
       Schroeder, pp. 71–105. Arizona Archaeologist No. 15. Arizona Archae-
       ological Society, Phoenix.

Nicholas, Linda, and Gary M. Feinman

1989   A Regional Perspective on Hohokam Irrigation in the Lower Salt River
       Valley, Arizona. In *The Sociopolitical Structure of Prehistoric Southwestern*

Societies, edited by Steadman Upham, Kent G. Lightfoot, and Roberta A. Jewett, pp. 199–235. Westview Press, Boulder, Colorado.

Oppenheimer, J. Robert

1954   Concluding Address at the Columbia University Bicentennial, December 26, 1954. In *Great English and American Essays,* edited by Douglass S. Mead, pp. 234–244. Rinehart, New York.

Pailes, Richard A.

1963   *An Analysis of the Fitch Site and Its Relationship to the Hohokam Classic Period.* Unpublished Master's thesis, Department of Anthropology, Arizona State University, Tempe.

Peebles, Christopher S., and Susan Kus

1977   Some Archaeological Correlates of Ranked Societies. *American Antiquity* 42:421–448.

Plog, Stephen

1989   The Sociopolitics of Exchange (and Archaeological Research) in the Northern Southwest. In *The Sociopolitical Structure of Prehistoric Southwestern Societies,* edited by Steadman Upham, Kent G. Lightfoot, and Roberta A. Jewett, pp. 129–148. Westview Press, Boulder, Colorado.

Rice, Prudence M.

1981   Evolution of Specialized Pottery Production: A Trial Model. *Current Anthropology* 22:219–240.

1987   *Pottery Analysis: A Sourcebook.* University of Chicago Press, Chicago.

Sahlins, Marshall D.

1972   *Stone Age Economics.* Aldine Publishing Co., New York.

Schaller, David M.

1994   Geographic Sources of Temper in Central Phoenix Basin Ceramics Based on Petrographic Analysis. In *The Pueblo Grande Project, Volume 3: Ceramics and the Production and Exchange of Pottery in the Central Phoenix Basin,* vol. 3, edited by David R. Abbott, pp. 17-90. Publications in Archaeology. Soil Systems, Phoenix.

Schaller, David M., and David R. Abbott

1990   Geographic Source of Hohokam Archaeological Ceramics from Phoenix, Arizona, Based on Mineralogy and Petrology. Paper presented at the 103rd Annual Meeting of the Geological Society of America, Dallas.

Schroeder, Albert H.

1940   *A Stratigraphic Survey of Pre-Spanish Trash Mounds of the Salt River Valley, Arizona.* Unpublished Master's thesis, Department of Anthropology, University of Arizona, Tucson.

1952   The Bearing of Ceramics on Developments in the Hohokam Classic Period. *Southwestern Journal of Anthropology* 8:320–335.

1953   The Bearing of Architecture on Developments in the Hohokam Classic Period. *American Antiquity* 9:174–193.

Stein, Pat H.
1979   *Archaeological Investigations Along the Salt-Gila Aqueduct.* Arizona Projects Office, U.S. Bureau of Reclamation, Phoenix.

Stone, Tammy
1991   *The Cemetery and Architectural Features of the Stadium Locus of Tempe Plaza (AZ U:9:72 ASU).* Office of Cultural Resource Management Report No. 79. Arizona State University, Tempe.

Weaver, Donald E., Jr.
1977   *Investigations Concerning the Hohokam Classic Period in the Lower Salt River Valley, Arizona.* Arizona Archaeologist No. 9. Arizona Archaeological Society, Phoenix.

Wilcox, David R.
1987   New Models of Social Structure at the Palo Parado Site. In *The Hohokam Village: Site Structure and Organization,* edited by David E. Doyel, pp. 223–248. Southwestern and Rocky Mountain Division of the American Association for the Advancement of Science, Glenwood Springs, Colorado.
1991   Hohokam Social Complexity. In *Chaco & Hohokam Prehistoric Regional Systems in the American Southwest,* edited by Patricia L. Crown and W. James Judge, pp. 253–275. School of American Research, Santa Fe.

Wilcox, David R., and Charles Sternberg
1983   *Hohokam Ballcourts and Their Interpretation.* Arizona State Museum Archaeological Series No. 160. University of Arizona, Tucson.

Wood, J. Scott, and Martin McAllister
1980   Foundation and Empire: The Colonization of the Northeastern Hohokam Periphery. In *Current Issues in Hohokam Prehistory,* edited by David E. Doyel and Fred Plog, pp. 180–200. Anthropological Research Papers No. 23. Arizona State University, Tempe.

5

The Role of Population Movement and Technology Transfer in the Manufacture of Prehistoric Southwestern Ceramics

María Nieves Zedeño

Differential distributions of prehistoric ceramics over broad areas of the American Southwest are often interpreted as the result of exchange networks of varied magnitude and complexity. Much effort has been devoted to the reconstruction of the ceramic distribution systems and their economic, social, and political implications (Bishop et al. 1988; Blinman and Wilson 1988; Braun and Plog 1982; Deutchman 1980; Douglass 1991; F. Plog 1983; S. Plog 1980; Toll 1985; Upham et al. 1981; Zedeño et al. 1993). However, current evidence of population movement throughout Southwestern prehistory (Crown 1994; Lindsay 1987; Powell 1983; Preucel 1990; Reid 1989; Wilson 1988) strongly suggests that variation in the ceramic record was the result of not only the circulation of pottery, but also the movement of people bearing knowledge on distinctive pottery technologies. This chapter reviews recent data on ceramic manufacture and circulation during the late Pueblo III period occupation of the Grasshopper region in east-central Arizona (fig. 5.1) to illustrate how population movement had a major role in the generation of highly varied assemblages.

The late Pueblo III period settlements in the mountains of east-central Arizona were occupied during a critical time in Southwestern prehistory. During the last decades of the thirteenth century, changes occurred in subsistence strategies, demographic shifts, and social reorganization in

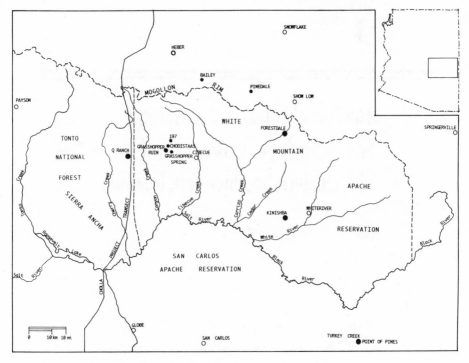

Figure 5.1 The Mogollon Mountains of east-central Arizona.

broad areas of the northern Southwest that culminated in the aggregation of ethnically diverse peoples in large pueblos (Reid 1989). The
unique character of the late Pueblo III period in the Grasshopper region
is highlighted by episodes of sudden change that resulted largely from
the migration of people from the north.

Population movement left subtle ceramic evidence that can be recognized only because exceptional conditions of archaeological recovery
and analysis are available. First and most important, there is excellent
control of temporal and contextual associations of vessel assemblages
from three excavated sites (Chodistaas, Grasshopper Spring, and AZ
P:14:197) which date to the late 1200s (Crown 1981; Montgomery and
Reid 1990). Second, the distinction between local and nonlocal vessels
from these sites—particularly Chodistaas—has been established (Zedeño
1991, 1992, 1994). Third, formation processes have been incorporated into
the archaeological analysis and interpretation of occupations at exca-

vated sites (Montgomery 1992, 1993). Fourth, information has recently been collected on the broad regional distributions of decorated and undecorated ceramics for the late Pueblo III period (Reid et al. 1995). Last, the large whole-vessel assemblage from the later Grasshopper Ruin (Ciolek-Torello 1985; Mayro et al. 1976; Triadan 1994; Whittlesey 1974) provides comparative data for evaluating changes in the manufacture and circulation of ceramics in the region. Given these conditions, it is possible to examine closely the relationships between archaeological ceramic variation, the dynamics of population movement—mobility, migration, aggregation, and ethnic coresidence—and the mechanisms of technology transfer.

The late Pueblo III period ceramic assemblages and surface collections from sites in the Grasshopper and adjacent regions generally include Cibola White Ware, Roosevelt Red Ware, White Mountain Red Ware, red plain ware, and several painted, slipped, and unpainted corrugated wares.[1] The presence of such variation in small sites that were relatively distant from large villages raises questions about where these pots were manufactured and how they were circulated into and across the mountains. Examination of the probable behaviors involved in ceramic manufacture and circulation in light of what is currently known about settlement systems and subsistence strategies may answer some of these questions.

Residential Mobility

Reconstructions of late Pueblo III period settlement and subsistence in Grasshopper and adjacent regions (Graves et al. 1982; Reid et al. 1995; Tuggle 1970; Tuggle et al. 1984; Welch 1991; Whittlesey and Reid 1982) suggest that residential mobility was a common adaptive strategy of small communities that practiced cultivation as well as hunting and gathering in mountain environments. The mountain settlement systems were commonly characterized by small hamlets of two to five rooms, which were loosely clustered around plaza-oriented focal communities of no more than 20 low-walled surface rooms that served a small, dispersed population. In this context, residential mobility may not have been a patterned or strictly seasonal activity, but rather an opportunistic strategy that allowed mountain settlers to survive times of scarcity. The duration of occupation of a small settlement likely varied within a continuum from seasonality to short-term sedentism, being dependent upon immediate resource availability.

The late Pueblo III settlement pattern in the Grasshopper region consisted of two or perhaps three settlement clusters; Longacre (1975, 1976) and Reid (1973, 1989) have estimated that only 200 rooms were built in the region during this period. In the years of the Great Drought (A.D. 1276–1299), however, population increased rather suddenly as a result of immigration from the north and higher residential stability. During the last decade of the thirteenth century, settlements became increasingly dependent upon the cultivation of corn and beans with dry farming techniques, although hunting and gathering remained a prominent component of the subsistence economy (Tuggle et al. 1984; Welch 1991). At the same time, stronger emphasis on cultivation and increased population probably restricted access to wild resources; in fact, toward the turn of the fourteenth century settlements clustered near agricultural land.

Small settlements such as Chodistaas, Grasshopper Spring, and Site 197 were abandoned by A.D. 1300, when the local population as well as immigrant groups aggregated in large masonry pueblos. Simulations of population growth (Longacre 1975, 1976) and architectural growth (Reid 1973) indicate a dramatic, tenfold increase in population density in the Grasshopper region; 2,000 rooms were built during the Pueblo IV period. This growth can only be explained by the movement of people into the region. Several lines of evidence for the multiethnic character of the Grasshopper Pueblo settlers have been presented by Crown-Robertson (1978), Ezzo (1991), Reid and Whittlesey (1982), and Whittlesey (1978), among others. Mountain communities tended to be occupied for relatively short periods of time, as indicated by the population dispersion and further abandonment of the Grasshopper and neighboring regions by A.D. 1400.

I suggest that residential mobility of the mountain communities of the late Pueblo III period affected manufacture and circulation of ceramics in two ways. First, it fostered the development of localized ceramic traditions; technological criteria were shared mainly by potters who maintained direct interaction on a regular basis. Second, it facilitated the circulation of ceramic vessels over long distances. A drastic change in this pattern of manufacture and circulation of ceramics in the Grasshopper region was brought about by the migration of people into the mountains at the end of the thirteenth century. In support of this argument, I present data on the technological and compositional variation in the whole-vessel assemblage from Chodistaas, where at least one-third of the pots were not manufactured locally.

Local Ceramic Manufacture

Local manufacture of ceramics may be conceptualized at two inclusive levels: settlement and region. In the strictest sense, local manufacture refers to the production of pottery within a given settlement. In a broader sense, regional manufacture implies ceramic production by several communities among which common resources were exploited, by-products circulated, and technological knowledge shared. In other words, ceramics may be considered local if one can reasonably demonstrate that they were manufactured within a given region.

In this analysis I use regional manufacture as a working concept for the following reasons. First, Chodistaas, Grasshopper Spring, and Site 197 lack direct evidence of on-site ceramic manufacture, namely "artifacts associated with ceramic manufacture found clustered around pottery-making and pottery-firing facilities" (Sullivan 1988:24). Although the recovery of raw materials and tools also provides good evidence for on-site manufacture (Triadan 1989), only a few tools of ambiguous function and very small amounts of pigments and clays were found at Chodistaas (Crown 1981:49) and Grasshopper Spring. Nevertheless, it is entirely possible—if not demonstrable—that both Chodistaas and Grasshopper potters made and fired their ceramics somewhere near the pueblos or even at the location of their preferred clay sources. Second, the ceramic assemblages of these sites present a similar range of variability in decorated and undecorated wares, suggesting that the communities in the region may have shared resource procurement zones and technological knowledge, and that they obtained ceramics from a common source(s). Third, late Pueblo III period sites in the region are located within a relatively homogeneous geologic setting mainly formed of sandstone and limestone deposits (Moore 1968), a situation that decreases the likelihood of successfully identifying ceramics made at each site (Bishop et al. 1982).

In the absence of direct artifact evidence for on-site ceramic manufacture, one must rely on the information carried on technological, compositional, and stylistic attributes of the assemblages under study. In this analysis, ceramic technology pertains to the knowledge about materials and the practices to manipulate them that potters used to manufacture vessels with specific physical properties and aesthetic effects (after De Atley 1991), whereas composition includes mineralogical and chemical properties of the ceramic fabric. By design styles of ceramic vessels, I refer strictly to painted patterns that were repeated in time, space, or both.

How did residential mobility affect the transfer of information on ceramic manufacture? What were the mechanisms for the transfer of stylistic and technological information? In the American Southwest, where decorated perishable items such as baskets and textiles are occasionally preserved in the archaeological record, one may observe that designs can be carried out on any medium suited to decoration and that any particular design may be transferred to pottery by inspection (Reid 1984:145). In contrast to design information, technological information is transferred within a "teaching framework" (*sensu* Schiffer and Skibo 1987:597). The adoption of a "new" ceramic technology, even by experienced craftspeople, generally entails the acquisition of an idea, the development of manipulative practice, the formation of motor habits, and most importantly, the existence of a receptive social and cultural setting (Arnold 1981; Kroeber 1963; Lechtman 1977; Schiffer and Skibo 1987; Wright 1984). Technology transfer, therefore, is often the product of face-to-face interaction among potters who produce ceramic vessels under a common mental template or shared technological knowledge (Rice 1980), whereas design is not necessarily transferred the same way.

Circulation of pots and other decorated items across geographical, social, and ethnic boundaries facilitated the spread of design styles that were readily copied or incorporated into local stylistic repertoires. Conversely, mobility of small communities may have restricted the transfer of technological knowledge to those potters who were able to interact regularly. The sharing of information on ceramic technology was probably limited to closely related communities, both geographically and socially. The prevalence of this pattern of technology transfer likely had a major bearing on the development of localized technological traditions, such as those seen in the mountains of east-central Arizona (Reid et al. 1995). It seems likely that the transfer of knowledge on pottery manufacture was also shaped by intermarriage (Graves 1981; Herbich 1987), the migration of individuals or single households (Wilson 1988), and other economic, social, and ceremonial activities involving different communities. These activities may have fostered both information transfer and material transactions.

The ceramic evidence from Chodistaas and contemporaneous sites in

Table 5.1 Corrugated Wares: Distribution of Temper Types Across
Compositional Groups (ICPS) on a Sample from Chodistaas

Ware Type	Temper Type 1	Temper Type 2	Total
GROUP 1			
Brown corrugated	10	0	10
Gray corrugated	1	0	1
Salado Red Corrugated	3	0	3
GROUP 2			
Gray corrugated	0	9	9
Painted corrugated	2	3	5
Total	16	12	28

the Grasshopper region indicates that local potters maintained a very
consistent set of technological criteria; they seldom incorporated techniques used to manufacture their nonlocal painted pots. For example, the
use of sherd temper, black mineral or organic paint, and a nonoxidizing
firing atmosphere, which was traditional to the Colorado Plateau potters,
was not incorporated in the manufacture of mountain ceramics. Compositional analyses (inductively coupled plasma emission [ICP] spectroscopy, instrumental neutron activation analysis [INAA], and binocular
examination of temper inclusions; see Zedeño 1994) of plain and corrugated vessels from Chodistaas and locally available raw materials suggest that the local repertoire included mainly diabase-tempered, brown,
indented obliterated corrugated; Salado Red Corrugated; and Salado
White-on-red (table 5.1; fig. 5.2). These analyses also show that many
sand-tempered, gray, indented corrugated and red plain pots were probably obtained from neighboring regions.

Shared technological practices were restricted to closely interacting
communities in the mountains of east-central Arizona. This confinement
is evident in the differential distributions of brown corrugated, gray corrugated, and gray-orange corrugated wares across several regions such
as, from west to east, the Q Ranch, Grasshopper, Cibecue, Forestdale, and
other regions of the eastern side of the White Mountain Apache Reserva-

tion. A recent study of the surface distribution of corrugated wares in these areas (Reid et al. 1995) shows that technological differences among demonstrably or presumably local wares can be unequivocally detected from one region to another, often within a distance of less than 50 km and sometimes within less than 15 km (table 5.2; fig. 5.1). These differences are not limited to paste attributes, but include surface treatment, vessel shape, and proportional measurements, suggesting that definite criteria characterized the manufacturing technology of each region (Zedeño 1994:69).

In contrast, the design styles of painted corrugated types found throughout the mountains of east-central Arizona, such as McDonald Painted Corrugated and Salado White-on-red, are similar to the exterior

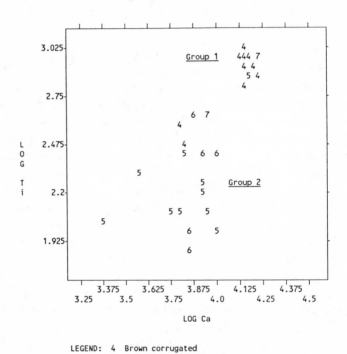

Figure 5.2 Bivariate representation of compositional groups for a sample of corrugated vessels from Chodistaas.

Table 5.2 Relative Percentages of Decorated and Undecorated Wares
from Pueblo III Period Sites by Region[a]

Ware Type	Western Region		Eastern Region	
	Q Ranch (2 sites)	Grasshopper (3 sites)	Cibecue (2 sites)	Forestdale (1 site)
UNDECORATED CERAMICS				
Brown wares	94.0	74.3	8.9	20.0
Orange-gray wares	0.0	13.0	89.0	70.0
Gray wares	1.0	3.4	1.1	9.0
Salado Red Ware	5.0	9.3	1.0	1.0
DECORATED CERAMICS				
White Mtn. Red Ware	4.0	1.0	0.0	8.0
Roosevelt Red Ware	1.0	4.5	1.0	2.0
White wares	94.0	93.5	88.0	90.0
Other	1.0	1.0	11.0	0.0

RAW DATA SOURCE: Reid et al. (1995).

[a]Percentages represent average frequencies of surface ceramics for sites with
plazas. I used percentages rather than numbers to increase comparability and to
illustrate general trends.

designs of St. Johns Polychrome bowls (see Carlson 1970) or Snowflake
Black-on-white jars (see Zedeño 1994:85). The stylistic similarities between local painted corrugated and nonlocal polished painted types suggest that mountain potters were copying designs from pots they obtained elsewhere.

Circulation of Ceramics

Residential mobility was perhaps the most common mechanism for cir-
culating pots within the mountains of east-central Arizona as well as
between the mountains and the Colorado Plateau. Frequent or even sporadic movement of social units may have stimulated the establishment of

long-distance reciprocal relationships among two or more communities. This system likely opened access to resources from different environments as well as to nonlocal goods, maintained social and political ties through marriage, and fostered community identity by transcending social and ethnolinguistic boundaries (Braun and Plog 1982; Dalton 1977; Ericson 1977; Frisbie 1982). A few pots could have been transported regularly by individuals, single families, or small communities moving in or out of the mountains. In other words, a small but recurrent flow of pottery through ties established with communities outside the region could account for the presence of nonlocal decorated ceramics in small settlements during the late 1200s.

Conversely, residential mobility in areas of low population density probably discouraged regular participation of small communities in formal trade networks. These networks apparently developed after much larger and more stable populations aggregated in large pueblos during the Pueblo IV period (Adams 1991; Triadan 1994). Competition for relatively scarce agricultural lands among local people and newcomers may have stimulated the growth of secondary economic activities, such as crafts production for exchange, to supplement household economies.

The circulation of Cibola White Ware vessels into Chodistaas, Grasshopper Spring, and Site 197 illustrates a typical form of circulation of ceramics into the mountains of east-central Arizona. Cibola White Ware (fig. 5.3) is the most abundant decorated ware in surface collections and room assemblages of sites in the Grasshopper and adjacent regions. At Chodistaas, for example, where 330 vessels were recovered from 18 excavated rooms, this ware constitutes almost 50 percent of the decorated vessels. Yet, chemical characterization and binocular examination of black-on-white vessels from the three sites and of local clays revealed that all these vessels are nonlocal (Zedeño 1994:77). Based on chemical paste composition, manufacturing technology, and data on regional geology (Moore 1968), I inferred that nonlocal Cibola White Ware was obtained from at least three sources (fig. 5.4). The pots from these sources are made of white kaolin-like clay, which is not found in the Grasshopper region or adjacent mountain regions (Moore 1968). Sand, crushed sherds, or a combination of both tempers are represented in all three sources (table 5.3). Most jars are ovoid, with high shoulders and pointy, molded bases, and were fired in a nonoxidizing atmosphere. Most Cibola White Ware sherds from the surface and room fill at the three sites share technological characteristics with the analyzed vessels, further suggesting that this ware

Figure 5.3 Pinedale Black-on-white jar from Grasshopper Pueblo.

was obtained from nonlocal sources throughout the occupation of the pueblos, during the last four decades of the thirteenth century.

Differences in the transfer of style and technology are clearly illustrated by Cibola White Ware vessels at Chodistaas, where seven design styles—Red Mesa, Puerco, Kayenta-Tusayan, Snowflake, Tularosa, Roosevelt, and Pinedale—(Crown 1981; Zedeño 1994) crosscut the three analytic sources (table 5.4). Cibola White Ware pottery that is stylistically identical to that recovered at Chodistaas can be found in many Pueblo III period sites in the Mogollon Mountains and on the Colorado Plateau. This pottery, however, presents a wider range of variation in temper techniques, vessel shapes, surface finishing, and firing. The variation is consistent not only with the distribution of different types of raw materials, but also with the sharing of technological information among closely interacting potters.

The widespread Cibola White Ware was manufactured in several regions of the Colorado Plateau. Although instances of intraregional and interregional exchange of Cibola vessels have been documented on the Colorado Plateau (Franklin 1982:929; Neily 1988:175; S. Plog 1980; Toll 1985; Wilson and Blinman 1988:366–368), evidence shows that this ware was not distributed through extensive formal trade but rather through

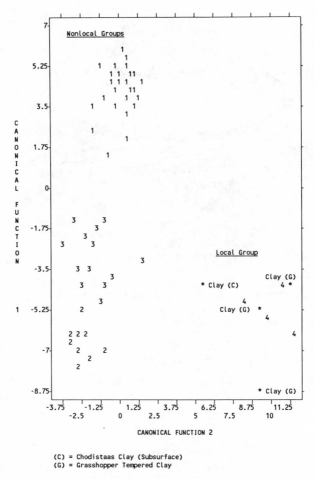

Figure 5.4 Compositional groups for Cibola White Ware vessels and clay samples from Chodistaas and Grasshopper pueblos (INAA), as defined by discriminant functions.

localized networks that typically extended into the mountains of east-central Arizona (Hantman et al. 1984; Lightfoot and Jewett 1984:57–60; Tuggle et al. 1982:28; Zedeño et al. 1993). Compositional data indicate that the relationships between mountain settlers and the communities that manufactured Cibola White Ware were maintained throughout the late Pueblo III period in the Grasshopper region and continued during the first years of occupation at Grasshopper Pueblo.

Migration and Episodic Changes in Pottery Manufacture and Circulation

In the Grasshopper and probably other regions in the mountains of east-central Arizona, detectable changes in ceramic manufacturing technology did not occur until the middle of the A.D. 1280s and, as seen at Chodistaas, they took place in a short time (Montgomery and Reid 1990).

Table 5.3 Cibola White Ware at Chodistaas and Grasshopper: Variability in Paste Color, Temper Type, and Pigment Type Across Compositional Groups (INAA)

Compositional Group	Paste Color (Munsell)	Temper (N)	Pigment (N)
NONLOCAL VESSELS			
1 (N = 12)	10YR 8/1 White	Sherd + sand (11)	Iron (7)
	10 YR 8/2 White	Sand (1)	Manganese (4)
	5 YR 8/2 Pinkish white		
2 (N = 5)	2.5Y 8/1 White	Sherd + sand (5)	Iron (1)
	5Y 8/1 White		Manganese (1)
3 (N = 8)	10YR 8/1 White	Sherd + sand (7)	Iron (6)
	10YR 6/4 Very pale		Manganese (1)
	brown	Sherd (1)	
Outliers	10 YR 8/1 White	Sherd + sand (2)	Iron (1)
(N = 2)	5Y 8/1 White		Manganese (1)
LOCAL VESSELS			
4 (N = 13)[a]	10YR 5/3 Brown	Sherd (1)	Iron (1)
	10YR 6/4 Light yellowish		Manganese (4)
	brown	Sherd + sand (3)	
	5Y 6/3 Pale olive	Diabase + sherd + opaque minerals (9)	

[a] Includes 11 vessels from Grasshopper Pueblo.

Table 5.4 Cibola White Ware at Chodistaas: Variability in Design Styles of Whole Vessels Across Compositional Groups (INAA)

	Compositional Groups					
Design Styles	1	2	3	4	Outlier	Total
Red Mesa	0	0	0	1	0	1
Puerco	1	1	1	0	0	3
Snowflake	4	0	2	0	0	6
Tularosa	8	1	5	1	1	16
Kayenta-Tusayan	1	1	1	0	0	3
Roosevelt	7	1	1	0	0	9
Pinedale	3	1	0	0	1	5
Unclassified	2	0	0	0	2	4
Total	26	5	10	2	4	47

I interpret these changes as being largely the result of population movement into the region, aggregation, and subsequent ethnic coresidence.

Perhaps the most significant change in the ceramic assemblages of mountain settlements dating to the late A.D. 1200s is the appearance of Roosevelt Red Ware. In fact, the earliest manifestations of this ware, Pinto Black-on-red (fig. 5.5) and Pinto Polychrome, are represented in several mountain regions (Crown 1994; Danson and Wallace 1956; Doyel and Haury 1976; Lange and Germick 1992). In the Grasshopper region, these types have been found in almost every late Pueblo III period site and in the room assemblages of the three excavated sites (Reid et al. 1992, 1995). Chodistaas currently provides the most complete and accurately dated early Roosevelt Red Ware assemblage. Eight Pinto Polychrome and 32 Pinto Black-on-red bowls make up 35 percent of the decorated vessels from the rooms, thus allowing detailed investigation of the provenience and timing of appearance of this ware. Montgomery and Reid (1990:95) noted that Pinto types appeared at Chodistaas rather suddenly, sometime after A.D. 1285, and replaced Cibola White Ware bowls almost completely. The overall characteristics of Pinto bowls—the presence of Pinedale designs (Crown 1981), the use of sherd temper and organic paint, and the timing and circumstances of their appearance in the

Grasshopper region—support the traditional hypothesis that Roosevelt Red Ware was adopted in the mountains of east-central Arizona as a result of the migration of people from areas north of the Mogollon Rim (Crown 1994; Fowler and Sant 1990; Gladwin and Gladwin 1934; Haury 1945; Mera 1934; Reid et al. 1992).

Preliminary INAA results of 16 Pinto bowls from Chodistaas suggest that these represent at least two sources, one of which matches local clays and local wares (Zedeño 1994:99). Bowls from the local source (13 of 16) are tempered with crushed sherds, quartz sand, or regionally available diabase sand, but have designs almost identical to those belonging to the nonlocal source. Bowls from the nonlocal source are tempered mainly with crushed sherds (table 5.5). Because of the variation in chemical composition and temper technology in early Roosevelt Red Ware, I argue that groups from the Colorado Plateau who migrated to the mountains at the end of the thirteenth century brought a few bowls with them and began to manufacture Pinto bowls with local clays. Ethnic coresidence, in turn, stimulated the adoption of a foreign ware by mountain potters. For example, variability in the temper technology of locally made Pinto bowls (crushed sherds, quartz sand, and diabase materials) indicates that these people used diverse technological practices.

Figure 5.5 Pinto Black-on-red bowl from Chodistaas Pueblo.

Table 5.5 Temper Types in Roosevelt Red Ware Bowls from Chodistaas

Bowls	Sherd	Sherd + Quartz Sand	Quartz + Quartz Sand	Diabase + Quartz Sand
Pinto Black-on-red (N = 27)	17	3	6	1
Pinto Polychrome (N = 7)	2	3	2	0
Total (N = 34)	19	6	8	1

Roosevelt Red Ware technology was not a new technology per se; it was derived from long-standing practices held by plateau potters. Nonetheless, this technology did introduce a few innovative ideas, such as the use of carbon paint, into mountain ceramic traditions. Although Roosevelt Red Ware did not require specialized production techniques (but see Crown 1994), it was not adopted until people bearing different knowledge on ceramic manufacture came together. By the fourteenth century, Roosevelt Red Ware was manufactured in almost every inhabited region of the Arizona mountains and desert basins.

Aggregation, Sedentism, and Ceramic Manufacture

Aggregation of ethnically diverse peoples in large mountain pueblos, residential stability, agricultural intensification, and the concomitant development of formal trade networks resulted in a dramatic increase in the circulation of nonlocal wares into the mountains of east-central Arizona, as well as in the production of ceramics for local consumption and exchange (Mayro et al. 1976; Triadan 1994; Whittlesey 1974). The presence of specialized manufacturing rooms at Grasshopper Ruin indicates that during the Pueblo IV period ceramic manufacture became a regular activity (Triadan 1989). Local manufacture of white wares during the Pueblo IV period is only one example of this shift toward the production of formerly imported wares.

Technological analysis of 24 black-on-white whole vessels from Grasshopper Ruin and compositional analysis (INAA, ICP spectroscopy, and binocular examination of temper inclusions) of 14 of those vessels revealed that only 6 of them (25 percent) were obtained from one of the nonlocal sources that supplied Cibola White Ware to Chodistaas. Eighteen black-on-white vessels (75 percent) were made with local clays (Zedeño 1992). This shift may have occurred during the first quarter of the fourteenth century and was probably related to the abandonment of the villages where Cibola White Ware was produced during the Pueblo III period. Subsequent migration resulted in discontinuities in the manufacture of this ware.

Local manufacture of white ware at Grasshopper was not just an attempt to replicate Cibola White Ware, as had occurred with many nonlocal polychromes. It was also an attempt to meet the demand for black-on-white pottery. Technological characteristics, such as sherd temper and nonoxidizing firing atmosphere, were used in the manufacture of local black-on-white vessels, suggesting technological influence from or perhaps manufacture by immigrant potters.

A recent analysis of late polychrome wares from Grasshopper Pueblo by Daniela Triadan (1994) provided important information regarding the local manufacture of wares that had been previously obtained from outside sources. The effect of coresidence of mountain and immigrant potters on ceramic production is evident at Grasshopper, where polychrome wares range from perfect replicas of nonlocal White Mountain Red Ware and Roosevelt Red Ware made with local clays and temper to poor imitations of these wares. Triadan (1994) identified two local and two imported sources of White Mountain Red Ware. The common use of diabase sands to temper Gila Polychrome bowls indicates that several Roosevelt Red Ware bowls were manufactured in this pueblo (Whittlesey 1974). After they aggregated at Grasshopper, potters adopted several foreign technological practices to develop a local polychrome, Grasshopper Ware, which was a crude imitation of plateau polychromes and combined Fourmile Polychrome and Gila Polychrome designs executed with carbon paint (Mayro et al. 1976; Triadan 1994). They also adopted the use of buff or cream slip to manufacture rough copies of Kinishba Polychrome.

The striking variation in technological knowledge, craftsmanship, and style evident in the decorated wares of Grasshopper Pueblo far surpasses that in ceramics from late Pueblo III period sites. This ceramic assemblage was largely a product of the heterogeneous social and ethnic makeup of large Pueblo IV period communities in east-central Arizona and of their exchange or trade relations. Future comparative analysis should focus on neighboring mountain regions, such as Point of Pines, Kinishba, or Forestdale, to broaden current perspectives on the organizational changes that brought about the expansion of pottery production for exchange and the economic impact of these processes on late prehistoric communities in the northern Southwest.

Conclusions

Data on ceramic composition and manufacturing technology from the Grasshopper region illustrate how pottery may have been circulated and production knowledge transferred through residential mobility and migration. The complex patterns of ceramic variation found in small mountain pueblos of the late Pueblo III period suggest several behavioral possibilities. First, nonlocal pots were probably obtained through networks established among relatively mobile communities; pots could have been transported regularly by people moving into or out of the mountains. Second, small social units migrating into the mountains likely brought pottery with them and also manufactured pottery with local raw materials. Third, coresidence of people bearing different knowledge on pottery making stimulated the transfer of such knowledge. As Reed (1958:7) observed, the introduction of nonlocal pots and nonlocal ceramic-manufacturing technologies into a site or region were not necessarily the consequence of extensive trade networks or mass migration. The migration of individuals or families, as well as exchange, frequent mobility, and intermarriage would have sufficed to spread pottery and techniques over wide territories.

During most of the late Pueblo III period, information on ceramic manufacture was transferred within closely interacting communities. This conclusion is based on the patterned distribution of technological variability of local corrugated wares across several mountain regions of east-central Arizona. A useful implication of this observation for interpreting ceramic variation is that technology may be a more accurate indicator of social and ethnic differences among contemporaneous groups than design style. Because ceramic technology in the American Southwest was not as readily transferred as design style, visible changes in the technological characteristics of a ceramic assemblage may signal changes in the ethnic or social makeup of a pottery-making community. Such changes are clear between ceramic assemblages of late Pueblo III period sites and those of the later Grasshopper Pueblo, where available evidence indicates multiethnic aggregation in a single community.

The dynamics of population movement are a key for understanding adaptation and organization of prehistoric communities in the Southwest. It is therefore critically important that archaeologists look for indicators of such dynamics. The study of the behaviors involved in ceramic manufacture and circulation in the Grasshopper region reveals that pottery is an extremely rich source of information for reconstructing this aspect of prehistory.

Acknowledgments

The data used in this research were collected as part of the University of Arizona Archaeological Field School at Grasshopper, directed by J. Jefferson Reid. This project was partially funded by grants from the National Science Foundation and from Agnese Lindley Foundation. Data on ceramic paste composition (INAA, ICP spectroscopy, and binocular petrography) were obtained from Ronald Bishop, Conservation Analytical Laboratory, Smithsonian Institution; James Burton, Laboratory of Archaeology, University of Wisconsin-Madison; and Beth Miksa, Department of Geosciences, University of Arizona. Ziba Ghasemi did the artwork. Patricia Crown, Barbara Mills, Barbara Montgomery, Jeff Reid, Mike Schiffer, Dani Triadan, and two anonymous reviewers provided useful comments on drafts of this paper.

Note

1. Undecorated wares from the Grasshopper region do not have formal type names, only descriptive ones.

References Cited

Adams, E. Charles
1991   *The Origin and Development of Pueblo Katsina Cult.* University of Arizona Press, Tucson.
Arnold, Dean E.
1981   A Model for the Identification of Nonlocal Ceramic Distribution: View from the Present. In *Production and Distribution: A Ceramic View Point,*

edited by Hillary Howard and Elaine Morris, pp. 31–44. BAR International Series 120. British Archaeological Reports, Oxford.

Bishop, Ronald L., Valetta Canouts, Suzanne De Atley, Alfred Qoyawayma, and C. W. Aikins

1988 The Formation of Ceramic Analytical Groups: Hopi Pottery Production and Exchange, A.D. 1300–1600. *Journal of Field Archaeology* 15:317–337.

Bishop, Ronald L., Robert L. Rands, and George R. Holley

1982 Ceramic Compositional Analysis in Archaeological Perspective. In *Advances in Archaeological Method and Theory*, vol. 5, edited by Michael B. Schiffer, pp. 276–329. Academic Press, New York.

Blinman, Eric, and C. Dean Wilson

1988 Overview of A.D. 600–800 Ceramic Production and Exchange in the Dolores Project Area. In *Dolores Archaeological Program Supporting Studies: Additive and Reductive Technologies*, compiled by Eric Blinman, Carl J. Phagan, and Richard H. Wilshusen, pp. 395–423. U.S. Bureau of Reclamation, Engineering and Research Center, Denver.

Braun, David P., and Stephen Plog

1982 Evolution of "Tribal" Social Networks: Theory and Prehistoric North American Evidence. *American Antiquity* 47(3):504–525.

Carlson, Roy L.

1970 *White Mountain Redware: A Pottery Tradition of East-Central Arizona and Western New Mexico*. Anthropological Papers of the University of Arizona No. 19. University of Arizona Press, Tucson.

Ciolek-Torello, Richard

1985 A Typology of Room Function at Grasshopper Pueblo, Arizona. *Journal of Field Archaeology* 12:41–63.

Crown, Patricia L.

1981 *Variability in Ceramic Manufacture at the Chodistaas Site, East-central Arizona*. Ph.D. dissertation, University of Arizona, Tucson. University Microfilms, Ann Arbor.

1994 *Ceramics and Ideology: Salado Polychrome Pottery*. University of New Mexico Press, Albuquerque.

Crown-Robertson, Patricia L.

1978 Migration Theory in Archaeology. Ms. on file, Arizona State Museum, Tucson.

Dalton, George

1977 Aboriginal Economies in Stateless Societies. In *Exchange Systems in Prehistory*, edited by Timothy K. Earle and Jonathon E. Ericson, pp. 191–212. Academic Press, New York.

Danson, Edward B., and Robert M. Wallace

1956   A Petrographic Study of Gila Polychrome. *American Antiquity* 22(2): 180–183.

De Atley, Suzanne P.

1991   Potter's Craft or Analyst's Tool? A Century of Ceramic Technology Studies in the American Southwest. In *Ceramic Analysis and Social Inference in American Archaeology: The Ceramic Legacy of Anna O. Shepard*, edited by Ronald L. Bishop and Frederick Lange, pp. 205–233. University of Colorado Press, Niwot.

Deutchman, Haree L.

1980   Chemical Evidence of Ceramic Exchange on Black Mesa. In *Models and Methods in Regional Exchange*, edited by Robert E. Fry, pp. 119–134. SAA Papers No. 1. Society for American Archaeology, Washington, D.C.

Douglass, Amy

1991   *Prehistoric Exchange and Sociopolitical Development in the Plateau Southwest*. Garland Publishing, Inc., New York.

Doyel, David E., and Emil W. Haury (editors)

1976   The Salado Conference. *The Kiva* 42(1).

Ericson, Jonathon E.

1977   Egalitarian Exchange Systems in California: A Preliminary View. In *Exchange Systems in Prehistory*, edited by Timothy K. Earle and Jonathon E. Ericson, pp. 109–126. Academic Press, New York.

Ezzo, Joseph

1991   *Dietary Change at Grasshopper Pueblo, Arizona: The Evidence from Bone Chemistry Analysis*. Unpublished Ph.D. dissertation, Department of Anthropology, University of Wisconsin, Madison.

Fowler, Andrew, and Mark Sant

1990   The Development of an Anasazi Redware Tradition: The Regional Implications of Showlow Redware. Paper presented at the 55th Annual Meeting of the Society for American Archaeology, Las Vegas.

Franklin, Hayward H.

1982   Ceramic Analysis of Nineteen Sites in the Bis Sa'ani Community. In *Bis Sa'ani: A Late Bonito Phase Community on Escavada Wash, Northwest New Mexico*, edited by C. D. Breternitz, D. E. Doyel, and M. P. Marshall, pp. 873–934. Prepared for the Alamito Coal Co., Tucson. Navajo Nation Papers in Anthropology Vol. 14, No. 3. Window Rock, Arizona.

Frisbie, Theodore R.

1982   The Anasazi-Mogollon Frontier? Perspectives from the Albuquerque Area or Brown vs. Gray: A Paste Case from the Albuquerque Region. In

- *Mogollon Archaeology: Proceedings of the 1980 Mogollon Conference*, edited by Patrick H. Beckett, pp. 17–23. Acoma Books, Ramona, California.

Gladwin, Winifred J., and Harold S. Gladwin
1934   *A Method for the Designation of Cultures and Their Variations.* Medallion Papers No. 15. Gila Pueblo, Globe, Arizona.

Graves, Michael W.
1981   *Ethnoarchaeology of Kalinga Ceramic Designs.* Unpublished Ph.D. dissertation, Department of Anthropology, University of Arizona, Tucson.

Graves, Michael W., William A. Longacre, and Sally J. Holbrook
1982   Aggregation and Abandonment at Grasshopper Pueblo, Arizona. *Journal of Field Archaeology* 9:193–206.

Hantman, Jeffrey L., Kent G. Lightfoot, Steadman Upham, Fred Plog, Stephen Plog, and Bruce Donaldson
1984   Cibola Whitewares, A Regional Perspective. In *Regional Analysis of Prehistoric Ceramic Variation: Contemporary Studies of the Cibola Whitewares*, edited by Alan P. Sullivan III and Jeffrey L. Hantman, pp. 17–35. Anthropological Papers No. 31. Arizona State University, Tempe.

Haury, Emil W.
1945   *The Excavation of Los Muertos and Neighboring Ruins in the Salt River Valley, Southern Arizona.* Papers of the Peabody Museum of American Archaeology and Ethnology Vol. 24, No. 1. Harvard University, Cambridge.

Herbich, Ingrid
1987   Learning Patterns, Potter Interaction, and Ceramic Style Among the Luo of Kenya. *The African Archaeological Review* 5:193–204.

Kroeber, Alfred L.
1963   *Styles and Civilizations.* Cornell University Press, Ithaca, New York.

Lange, Richard C., and Stephen Germick (editors)
1992   *Proceedings of the Second Salado Conference, Globe, AZ 1992.* Arizona Archaeological Society Occasional Paper, Phoenix.

Lechtman, Heather
1977   Style in Technology—Some Early Thoughts. In *Material Culture: Styles, Organization, and Dynamics of Technology*, edited by Heather Lechtman and Robert S. Merrill, pp.3–20. West Press, New York.

Lightfoot, Kent G., and Roberta Jewett
1984   Late Prehistoric Ceramic Distributions in East-Central Arizona: An Examination of Cibola Whiteware, White Mountain Redware, and Salado Redware. In *Regional Analysis of Prehistoric Ceramic Variation: Contemporary Studies of Cibola Whitewares*, edited by Alan P. Sullivan III and

Jeffrey L. Hantman, pp. 36–73. Anthropological Research Papers No. 31. Arizona State University, Tempe.

Lindsay, Alexander J.
1987   Anasazi Population Movements to Southeastern Arizona. *American Archaeology* 6(3):190–198.

Longacre, William A.
1975   Population Dynamics at the Grasshopper Pueblo, Arizona. *American Antiquity* 40(2):71–74.
1976   Population Dynamics at the Grasshopper Pueblo, Arizona. In *Demographic Anthropology: Quantitative Approaches*, edited by Ezra B. Zubrow, pp. 169–184. University of New Mexico Press, Albuquerque.

Mayro, Linda S., Stephanie M. Whittlesey, and J. Jefferson Reid
1976   Observations on the Salado Presence at Grasshopper Pueblo. *The Kiva* 42(1):85–94.

Mera, Harry P.
1934   *Observations on the Archaeology of the Petrified Forest National Monument.* Bulletin No. 7. Laboratory of Anthropology Technical Series, Santa Fe.

Montgomery, Barbara K.
1992   *Understanding the Formation of the Archaeological Record: Ceramic Variability at Chodistaas Pueblo, Arizona.* Unpublished Ph.D. dissertation, Department of Anthropology, University of Arizona, Tucson.
1993   Ceramic Analysis as a Tool for Discovering Processes of Pueblo Abandonment. In *Abandonment of Settlements and Regions: Ethnoarchaeological and Archaeological Approaches*, edited by Catherine M. Cameron and Steve A. Tomka, pp. 157–164. Cambridge University Press, Cambridge.

Montgomery, Barbara K., and J. Jefferson Reid
1990   An Instance of Rapid Ceramic Change. *American Antiquity* 55(1):88–97.

Moore, Richard T.
1968   *Mineral Deposits of the Fort Apache Indian Reservation, Arizona.* Bulletin No. 177. Arizona Bureau of Mines, Tucson.

Neily, Robert B.
1988   *Archaeological Investigations in the Snowflake-Mesa Redonda Area, East-Central Arizona: The Apache-Navajo South Project.* Arizona State Museum Archaeological Series 173. University of Arizona, Tucson.

Plog, Fred T.
1983   Political and Economic Alliances on the Colorado Plateau, A.D. 400–1400. In *Advances in World Archaeology* 2:289–330.

Plog, Stephen
1980   *Stylistic Variation in Prehistoric Ceramics.* Cambridge University Press, Cambridge.

Powell, Shirley
1983   *Mobility and Adaptation: The Anasazi of Black Mesa, Arizona.* Southern Illinois University Press, Carbondale.

Preucel, Robert W., Jr.
1990   *Seasonal Circulation and Dual Residence in the Pueblo Southwest.* Garland Publishing, Inc., New York.

Reed, Erik K.
1958   Comments on E. W. Haury's "Evidence at Point of Pines for a Prehistoric Migration from Northern Arizona." In *Migrations in New World Culture History,* edited by Raymond H. Thompson, pp. 7–9. University of Arizona Press, Tucson.

Reid, J. Jefferson
1973   *Growth and Response to Stress at Grasshopper Pueblo, Arizona.* Unpublished Ph.D. dissertation, Department of Anthropology, University of Arizona, Tucson.
1984   What is Black-on-White and Vague All Over? In *Regional Analysis of Prehistoric Ceramic Variation: Contemporary Studies of the Cibola Whitewares,* edited by Alan P. Sullivan III and Jeffrey L. Hantman, pp. 135–152. Anthropological Research Papers No. 31. Arizona State University, Tempe.
1989   A Grasshopper Perspective on the Mogollon of the Arizona Mountains. In *Dynamics of Southwest Prehistory,* edited by Linda S. Cordell and George J. Gumerman, pp. 65–97. Smithsonian Institution Press, Washington, D.C.

Reid, J. Jefferson, Barbara K. Montgomery, María Nieves Zedeño, and Mark A. Neupert
1992   The Origin of Roosevelt Redware. *Proceedings of the Second Salado Conference, Globe, AZ 1992,* edited by Richard C. Lange and Stephen Germick, pp. 212–215. Arizona Archaeological Society Occasional Paper, Phoenix.

Reid, J. Jefferson, John R. Welch, Barbara K. Montgomery, and María Nieves Zedeño
1995   Demographic Overview in the Late Pueblo III Period in the Mountains of East-Central Arizona. In *Pueblos in Transition: The Anasazi World, A.D. 1100–1400,* edited by Michael Adler. University of Arizona Press, Tucson, in press.

Reid, J. Jefferson, and Stephanie M. Whittlesey
1982   Households at Grasshopper Pueblo. *American Behavioral Scientist* 25(6): 687–703.

Rice, Prudence M.
1980   Peten Postclassic Pottery Production and Exchange: A View from Mancache. In *Models and Methods in Regional Exchange,* edited by Robert E.

Fry, pp. 67–82. SAA Papers No. 1. Society for American Archaeology, Washington, D.C.

Schiffer, Michael B., and James M. Skibo

1987   Theory and Experiment in the Study of Technological Change. *Current Anthropology* 28(5):595–619.

Sullivan III, Alan P.

1988   Prehistoric Southwestern Ceramic Manufacture: Limitations of Current Evidence. *American Antiquity* 53(1)23–35.

Toll III, H. Wolcott

1985   *Pottery Production, Public Architecture, and the Chaco Anasazi System.* Ph.D. dissertation, University of Colorado, Boulder. University Microfilms, Ann Arbor.

Triadan, Daniela

1989   *Defining Local Ceramic Production at Grasshopper Pueblo, Arizona.* Unpublished Master's thesis, Freie Universitat, Berlin. Ms. on file, Arizona State Museum, Tucson.

1994   White Mountain Red Ware: An Exotic Trade Item or a Local Commodity? Perspectives from the Grasshopper Region, Arizona. Paper presented at the 59th Annual Meeting of the Society for American Archaeology, Anaheim, California.

Tuggle, H. David

1970   *Prehistoric Community Relationships in East-Central Arizona.* Unpublished Ph.D. dissertation, Department of Anthropology, University of Arizona, Tucson.

Tuggle, H. David, Keith W. Kintigh, and J. Jefferson Reid

1982   Trace-Element Analysis of White Wares. In *Cholla Project Archaeology: Ceramic Studies,* vol. 5, edited by J. Jefferson Reid, pp. 22–38. Arizona State Museum Archaeological Series 161. University of Arizona, Tucson.

Tuggle, H. David, J. Jefferson Reid, and Robert C. Cole, Jr.

1984   Fourteenth Century Mogollon Agriculture in the Grasshopper Region of Arizona. In *Prehistoric Agricultural Strategies in the Southwest,* edited by Suzanne K. Fish and Paul S. Fish, pp. 101–110. Anthropological Research Papers No. 33. Arizona State University, Tempe.

Upham, Steadman, Kent G. Lightfoot, and Gary M. Feinman

1981   Explaining Socially Determined Ceramic Distributions in the Prehistoric Plateau Southwest. *American Antiquity* 46(4):822–833.

Welch, John R.

1991   From Horticulture to Agriculture in the Late Prehistory of the Grasshopper Region, Arizona. In *Mogollon V,* edited by Patrick H. Beckett, pp. 75–92. COAS Publishing, Las Cruces, New Mexico.

Whittlesey, Stephanie M.

1974   Identification of Imported Ceramics Through Functional Analysis of Attributes. *The Kiva* 40:101–112.

1978   *Status and Death at Grasshopper Pueblo: Experiments Toward an Archaeological Theory of Correlates.* Unpublished Ph.D. dissertation, Department of Anthropology, University of Arizona, Tucson.

Whittlesey, Stephanie M., and J. Jefferson Reid

1982   Cholla Project Settlement Summary. In *Cholla Project Archaeology: Introduction and Special Studies*, vol. 1, edited by J. Jefferson Reid, pp. 205–216. Arizona State Museum Archaeological Series 161. University of Arizona, Tucson.

Wilson, C. Dean

1988   An Evaluation of Individual Migration as an Explanation for the Presence of Smudged Ceramics in Dolores Project Area. In *Dolores Archaeological Program: Supporting Studies: Additive and Reductive Technologies*, compiled by Eric Blinman, Carl J. Phagan, and Richard H. Wilshusen, pp. 425–433. U.S. Bureau of Reclamation, Engineering and Research Center, Denver.

Wilson, C. Dean, and Eric Blinman

1988   Identification of Non–Mesa Verde Ceramics in Dolores Archaeological Program Collections. In *Dolores Archaeological Program: Supporting Studies: Additive and Reductive Technologies*, compiled by Eric Blinman, Carl J. Phagan, and Richard H. Wilshusen, pp. 363–371. U.S. Bureau of Reclamation, Engineering and Research Center, Denver.

Wright, Rita P.

1984   Technology and Style in Ancient Ceramics. In *Ancient Technology to Modern Science*, vol. 1, edited by W. David Kingery, pp. 5–27. The American Ceramic Society, Inc., Columbus, Ohio.

Zedeño, María Nieves

1991   *Refining Inferences of Ceramics Circulation: A Stylistic, Technological, and Compositional Analysis of Whole Vessels from Chodistaas, Arizona.* Unpublished Ph.D. dissertation, Department of Anthropology, Southern Methodist University, Dallas.

1992   Roosevelt Black-on-White Revisited. In *Proceedings of the Second Salado Conference, Globe, AZ 1992*, edited by Richard C. Lange and Stephen Germick, pp. 206–211. Arizona Archaeological Society Occasional Paper, Phoenix.

1994   *Sourcing Prehistoric Ceramics at Chodistaas Pueblo, Arizona.* Anthropological Papers of the University of Arizona No. 58. University of Arizona Press, Tucson.

Zedeño, María Nieves, James Busman, James Burton, and Barbara J. Mills
1993   Ceramic Compositional Analysis. In *Across the Colorado Plateau: Anthropological Studies for the Transwestern Pipeline Expansion Project, Vol. 16, Interpretation of Ceramic Artifacts*, by Barbara J. Mills, Christine E. Goetze, and María Nieves Zedeño, pp. 187–233. Office of Contract Archeology and Maxwell Museum of Anthropology, University of New Mexico, Albuquerque.

6

The Production of the Salado Polychromes in the American Southwest

Patricia L. Crown

The widespread distribution of the Salado polychromes in the fourteenth century in the American Southwest (Carlson 1982:224) raises questions concerning their production. In this paper, I examine the loci of production of the Salado polychromes, the distribution and use of the pottery, and the organization of production. The discussion is based on a long-term research project that included an instrumental neutron activation analysis (INAA) conducted at the Conservation Analytical Laboratory of the Smithsonian Institution and documentation of more than 750 whole Salado polychrome vessels from 80 sites (fig. 6.1). I chose the sample of whole vessels to ensure coverage of the entire spatial range of the pottery. I conclude that the Salado polychromes were manufactured in many loci and were used for many purposes, including primarily domestic serving and storage functions. The pottery was not made for use as mortuary furniture, nor was it restricted for use by any single segment of Southwestern society. Evidence indicates that the pottery was produced primarily on a household basis by nonspecialist potters, although some forms may have been produced by part-time product specialists.

Loci of Production

The INAA of 215 sherds of Gila Polychrome from 23 sites indicated the presence of a minimum of 11 analytically distinct sources for the pottery (Crown and Bishop 1987, 1991, 1994).[1] The sites are in geographically restricted areas. The results thus indicate multiple production loci that were distributed throughout the area in which the pottery was found. A larger sample of pottery would likely permit finer scale identification of analytic sources with narrower geographic distribution. The results also

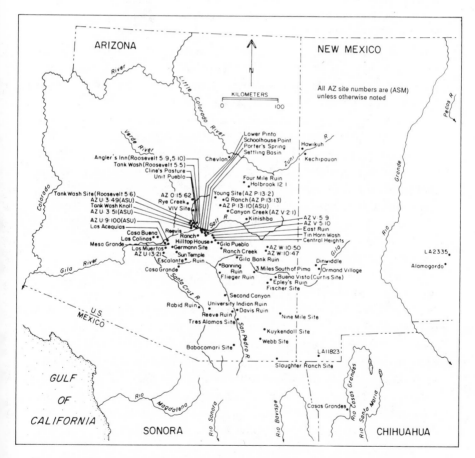

Figure 6.1 Proveniences for Salado polychrome vessels used in this study.

suggest that despite the widespread production loci, some pottery was also exchanged.

Distribution and Use

The appearance of Salado polychrome pottery at about A.D. 1275 and its rapid adoption and widespread distribution after A.D. 1300 have led many researchers to explain the pottery as a unified symbol of authority in the fourteenth century Southwest or as an item used in exchange relations among elites to secure positions of prestige (Cushing 1890; Wilcox 1987, 1995; see also Gerald 1976:68–69; Grebinger 1976; Rice 1986). Some researchers argue that the pottery signaled participation in an alliance linked through elite interaction and intermarriage (McGuire 1991; Upham 1982). Despite the appeal of such explanations, no analysis has yet identified the patterns of use, contextual association, and imagery expected if these vessels were symbols of authority or elite exchange items.

The whole vessels I examined came from varied contexts, including rooms, courtyards, inhumations, cremations, and trash (fig. 6.2). Typical forms of vessels suggest that they were used for water storage and for food storage, preparation, and serving; the contexts of recovery suggest that the vessels were initially used in household activities. Use-wear patterns indicate that the vessels were not exempt from activities that left clear abrasions and burning. Distinctive forms, such as baskets, may have had a dedicated ritual use (Kenagy 1986), but such vessels are rare. Only two vessels in my assemblage came from kivas, and two other vessels came from a cache. Most (67 percent) of the vessels used in my study were recovered from burial contexts.

The presence of abrasion on 78 percent of the 479 vessels from burials demonstrates that the pottery was not strictly produced as mortuary furniture, nor were the vessels associated with a fixed mortuary ritual (Nelson and LeBlanc 1986:5). They were found in primary and secondary cremations and flexed, extended, and multiple inhumations. Burials with Salado polychrome vessels revealed no single rule for head orientation, burial pit construction, alteration of the pottery before burial, placement of the pottery in relation to the body, or placement of the burial pit within the site.

The pottery was found with human remains from all age groups and both sexes in individual sites. However, studies of large mortuary popu-

Figure 6.2 Gila Polychrome bowl with Gila Style expedient design from the Angler's Inn Site (Roosevelt 5:10; Arizona State Museum Catalog # GP 11479).

lations indicated that Salado polychrome pottery was differentially distributed within these populations. At the Grasshopper Ruin, Whittlesey (1978:208, 210) showed that Salado polychrome vessels were more common with male adults than with either female adults or subadults. At Los Muertos, Brunson (1989:446–448) found that more subadult and male adult inhumations contained the pottery than female inhumations, whereas more female cremations contained the pottery than male cremations. Nevertheless, the widespread distribution of the pottery within sites and across contexts indicates that, although the Salado polychromes may have been more commonly associated with certain segments of the population, such patterning did not proscribe their distribution and use among other segments.

Organization of Production

The widespread manufacture, distribution, and mundane use of the Salado polychromes raises two questions: (1) Was the pottery produced by specialists or nonspecialists?; and (2) Did the organization of production change as the area in which the pottery was manufactured grew? Specialization is defined as "restriction of the production of a good by a relatively small number of individuals (compared to total output and numbers of consumers)" (Rice 1991:263). Nonspecialists were thus potters who produced for their own household use, although they may have commonly manufactured a few more vessels to distribute as gifts or to meet social obligations within or outside the residential community. For this reason, demonstration that pottery was exchanged among communities does not necessarily indicate that it was produced by specialists. As Graves (1982:339, 1991) showed, balanced reciprocal exchange among nonspecialist potters from different villages could have had a significant impact on the material record.

In contrast, specialist potters produced pottery as a supplement to or primary source of income. Specialization in pottery production represents a continuum from part-time "elementary" specialists (Balfet 1965: 163) to full-time workshops or industries. Pottery produced by part-time specialists may have remained within a village or community; thus, local production of pottery and an absence of exchange in vessels do not necessarily indicate that the pottery was produced by nonspecialists.

In addition to defining the role of individuals in pottery production, Rice (1991) argued that specialization may refer to site specialization (pottery production by specialized communities), resource specialization (restricted access and use of specific resources by potters or communities), and product specialization (production of a single form or type of vessel by potters or communities). Product specialization does not necessarily entail intensified production (Rice 1991; Stark 1985:161–163). Site specialization is known to have occurred in the prehistoric Southwest; the production of glaze-painted pottery among the Rio Grande pueblos is the best documented example (Shepard 1965). This ceramic production apparently also entailed resource specialization (Rice 1991).

Previous studies examined the organization of Salado polychrome production. Studies of Salado polychrome vessels from Grasshopper Ruin suggested that production varied with specific design styles. Although most styles were locally produced for local consumption, one style was locally produced for exchange (Mayro et al. 1976:93; see also Whittlesey 1974). A study of 24 Gila Polychrome vessels from sites excavated by the Mrs. William Boyce Thompson Expedition suggested that they were produced by specialists because of the vessels' uniform wall and rim thickness and the nestability of bowl forms (Hohmann and Kelley 1988: 225).

In recent years, archaeologists have often explored the mode of production by examining product standardization and efficiency of production (Benco 1987, 1988; Hagstrum 1985; Lindauer 1988; Longacre et al. 1988; Rice 1981, 1987, 1991; Stark, this volume). Archaeologists assume that vessels made by specialists are more standardized in form and technology than vessels made by nonspecialists (although see Hodder [1981: 231], Santley et al. [1989:111], and Stark [this volume] for some arguments against the wholesale acceptance of this assumption). Among specialist producers, greater standardization may have resulted either from fewer potters producing a given vessel form (Stark's [this volume] ratio effect) or from many potters producing highly uniform products. Researchers also assume that specialists decorated utility vessels with labor-efficient and standardized designs but decorated "luxury" goods using labor-intensive methods and elaborate designs (Hagstrum 1985:68; Rice 1981:table 1). Costin and Hagstrum (1995) argued that standardization may have resulted from the necessity of producing vessels with specific physical or social functions or from efficient manufacturing steps associated with the organization of production. They suggested that researchers separate the former intentional standardization from the latter mechanical standardization. Potters intentionally standardized their products through resource selection, vessel form, and decorative style. In contrast, mechanical standardization includes attributes such as materials selection and preparation unrelated to vessel performance characteristics, minor color variations, size variations within a size/form class, and metric attributes of vessel decoration. Archaeologists interested in gauging the organization of pottery production should therefore concentrate on the attributes of mechanical standardization.

To examine the organization of production for the Salado polychromes, I concentrated on standardization of forms and on efficiency of design execution. Standardization refers to the relative homogeneity of the vessels (Rice 1991) and should be viewed as a continuum (Arnold and Nieves 1992). Because it is a relative characteristic of groups of vessels, standardization in pottery production cannot be evaluated on a fixed scale. Following the work of previous researchers, I investigated standardization through coefficients of variation of metric attributes of vessel form. Specialist potters generally produce more standardized forms than nonspecialist potters because of their greater output, their use of more cost-effective production techniques, and the more routinized production sequence. In addition, metric attributes of vessels that are intended for exchange are partly dictated by the requirements of ease of transport (nestability) and the demands of consumers. In ethnographic situations, the degree of standardization in vessel form is partly affected by the intended market for the pottery and by the technique used to produce it (Arnold and Nieves 1992). By examining only a single type of pottery produced by a single technique (coiling, with scrape thinning), I eliminated these potential sources of variation. In practical terms, greater standardization in metric attributes will arise through measurement of vessels (which can be done with a stick or the hand), through use of a single toolkit to form and finish many vessels (e.g., a gourd scraper used in thinning multiple vessels will result in similar vessel profiles), and through the skill of the potter (Arnold and Nieves 1992).

Although there is no fixed scale for evaluating standardization in pottery production, ethnographically and historically documented assemblages provide a means of comparison for figures obtained from prehistoric assemblages. In his dissertation research, Lindauer (1988) attempted to give meaning to coefficients of variation cross-culturally by examining a wide variety of ethnographic examples of coefficients of variation for pottery produced by specialists and nonspecialists. His results suggest that pottery produced by specialists may generally be distinguished by lower coefficients of variation than pottery produced by nonspecialists. Benco (1988, 1989) also documented low coefficients of variation (all under 10 percent) for specialist potters in historical archaeological and ethnographic circumstances. Together, these results indicate that many specialist potters produce standardized vessel forms with coefficients of variation that are less than 10 percent for size variables (Benco 1988; Lindauer 1988; Longacre et al. 1988; Stark, this volume), although in some instances specialists also produce less standardized forms with coefficients of variation that are over 10 percent (table 6.1; fig. 6.3). In contrast, nonspecialists consistently produce pottery with coefficients of variation that are 10 percent or higher.

I therefore assumed that standardization of forms is indicated by coefficients of variation that are less than 10 percent for metric attributes.

Such standardization, in turn, indicates specialist production. If coefficients of variation indicate lack of standardization through figures that are greater than 10 percent, production may have entailed either specialists or nonspecialist producers, and interpretation necessitates other categories of data. Several problems, however, are associated with using prehistoric assemblages for such analyses: (1) a lack of adequate temporal control, (2) uncertainty about where the vessels were made and by how many potters, and (3) the inability to identify the emic form classes that were meaningful to the potters who produced them (Longacre et al. 1988; Stark, this volume).

Standardization

To examine Salado polychrome standardization, I controlled time by dividing the assemblage into the three types, Pinto, Gila, and Tonto. Use of these typological categories is not ideal because their production overlapped in time and they were not produced for equal lengths of time. Although Pinto Polychrome apparently preceded Gila Polychrome, Gila and Tonto Polychromes appear to overlap in their temporal distribution: Tonto Polychrome was produced for a shorter period of time at the end of the Gila Polychrome production interval. Pinto Polychrome was manufactured for approximately 25 years, Gila Polychrome for approximately 150 years, and Tonto Polychrome for 50 to 100 years.

Form categories combined morphological characteristics with size variation. Five morphological forms were represented in sufficient amounts for this study, including: incurved bowls, recurved bowls, outcurved bowls, straight-walled bowls, and jars. These morphological classes were further subdivided into small, medium, and large sizes based on groupings apparent in scattergrams of heights and maximum diameters for each morphological class.[2] Coefficients of variation for the heights and maximum diameters of the combined form and type categories were then calculated for individual site assemblages (table 6.2). I only presented the figures for sites with at least 10 vessels in each category; unfortunately, few sites produced samples of this size. When no sites produced 10 vessels of a particular type-form category, I included the figures for all vessels of that type and form from all sites. Because the INAA indicated widescale production loci, I assumed that the site-specific figures were more reliable indicators of mode of production than the combined type figures.

Table 6.1 Coefficients of Variation for Ceramics Made by Specialist and
Nonspecialist Potters Among Ethnographic Groups

Height	Maximum Diameter	Orifice	Group	Form
SPECIALISTS				
0.07	0.04	0.05	Paradijon	small-medium cooking
0.06	0.03	0.04	Paradijon	medium cooking
0.05	0.04	0.05	Paradijon	medium-large cooking
0.17	0.11	0.13	Paradijon	small flower pots
0.11	0.10	0.12	Paradijon	medium flower pots
0.11	0.08	0.11	Paradijon	large flower pots
0.10	0.07	0.09	Paradijon	extra large flower pots
	0.15	0.18	Amphlett Isl.[a]	small household cooking
	0.08	0.10	Amphlett Isl.	ceremonial cooking
	0.06	0.06	Amphlett Isl.	ceremonial cooking
	0.18	0.21	Amphlett Isl.	large household cooking
	0.15	0.11	Sacoj Grande	medium cooking
	0.06	0.06	Sacoj Grande	medium cooking
	0.07	0.12	Sacojito	medium water
	0.05	0.09	Sacojito	large water
	0.02	0.09	Durazno	small water
	0.03	0.05	Durazno	medium-large water
	0.05	0.02	Durazno	medium-large water

The coefficients of variation for all categories of small vessels from individual sites are higher than 10 percent, indicating a relative lack of standardization. The figures for the medium and large vessels are generally lower than those for the small vessels and include some figures that are less than 10 percent, indicating that the small Salado vessels generally exhibit greater variation in metric attributes than their large counterparts. These data indicate that the small forms are less standardized than the larger forms and were more likely produced by nonspecialist potters.

Support for this interpretation comes from the designs on some of the vessels. Nine small vessels from eight sites have designs painted by indi-

Table 6.1 *Continued*

Height	Maximum Diameter	Orifice	Group	Form
	0.14	0.12	Ticul	plant pot
	0.06	0.04	Ticul	decorative vessel
	0.18	0.11	Ticul	small food bowl
NONSPECIALISTS				
0.14	0.12	0.12	Kalinga	medium vegetable
0.11	0.10	0.13	Kalinga	medium rice
	0.13	0.15	Goodenough Isl.	small cooking
	0.12	0.14	Goodenough Isl.	small cooking
	0.12	0.12	Goodenough Isl.	small cooking
	0.16	0.21	Shipibo-Conibo	small cooking
	0.22	0.24	Shipibo-Conibo	medium cooking
	0.12	0.15	Shipibo-Conibo	large cooking
	0.16	0.19	Shipibo-Conibo	water
	0.18	0.22	Shipibo-Conibo	water
	0.18	0.21	Shipibo-Conibo	water

SOURCES: Arnold and Nieves (1992:table 2), Lindauer (1988:table 6), Longacre et al. (1988: tables 1, 2), and Stark (this volume).

[a]Although the Amphlett Island potters are classified as specialists, the potters produce only about six vessels per month (Stark, this volume).

viduals with poorly developed motor skills, probably children. All of these vessels show evidence of use after manufacture. The presence of such vessels decorated in what appears to have been a learning context and then used before disposal indicates that production of Salado polychrome vessels was not restricted to a single competency class within these sites and that beginners' efforts were not discarded to maintain a level of quality and competition.

As stated previously, the larger vessels are generally more standardized than the small vessels and include some coefficients of variation that are below 10 percent. However, only one site assemblage (the VIV Site in

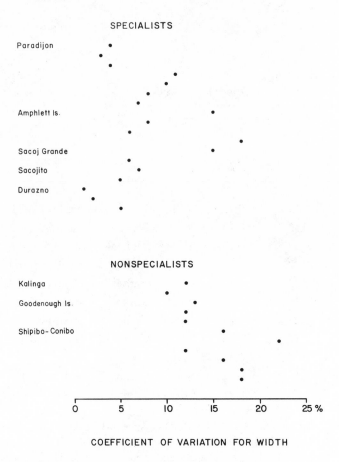

Figure 6.3 Coefficients of variation for maximum diameters (widths) of vessels produced by specialist and nonspecialist potters.

central Arizona) produced a category of vessels (large Tonto Polychrome jars) with coefficients of variation that are below 10 percent for both heights and maximum diameters. Table 6.3 and figure 6.4 illustrate the coefficients of variation obtained when all Gila and Tonto Polychrome vessels over 315 mm in maximum diameter were considered as a single group. The combined figures for 13 Gila and Tonto Polychrome jars over 315 mm in maximum diameter from the VIV Site produced coefficients

Table 6.2 Sample Means, Standard Deviations, and Coefficients of Variation for Salado Polychrome Form-Type Categories

Type & Site	Height Mean	S.D.	C.V.	Maximum Diameter Mean	S.D.	C.V.	N	No. of sites
SMALL BOWLS (maximum diameter 1–240 mm) n = 387								
Incurved Bowls								
Pinto	80.91	18.17	0.22	165.00	38.36	0.23	11	8
Gila	90.15	12.94	0.14	181.94	28.66	0.16	127	30
Angler's Inn	87.48	13.05	0.15	172.48	27.28	0.16	25	1
Gila Pueblo	91.69	11.94	0.13	182.44	25.23	0.14	32	1
Four Mile	89.18	14.74	0.17	201.64	30.92	0.15	11	1
Recurved Bowls								
Gila	102.42	36.53	0.36	175.64	35.51	0.20	33	20
Outcurved Bowls								
Pinto	78.50	9.50	0.12	181.08	21.86	0.12	12	7
Gila	74.93	18.12	0.24	163.95	38.81	0.24	41	13
Angler's Inn	74.14	9.38	0.13	171.79	24.27	0.14	14	1
Straight-Walled Bowls								
Pinto	80.06	16.58	0.21	174.00	40.24	0.23	16	8
Gila	85.30	14.53	0.17	167.95	34.68	0.20	97	27
Angler's Inn	84.74	12.06	0.14	163.07	30.72	0.19	27	1
Gila Pueblo	88.70	13.54	0.15	180.74	30.49	0.17	23	1
SMALL JARS (maximum diameter 1–314 mm) n = 121								
Gila	140.14	28.79	0.21	174.52	43.27	0.25	92	23
Gila Pueblo	143.38	26.75	0.19	168.34	28.74	0.17	32	1
Tonto	151.00	28.36	0.19	194.39	52.67	0.27	28	13
MEDIUM BOWLS (maximum diameter over 240 mm) n = 105								
Incurved Bowls (maximum diameter 240–314 mm)								
Gila	128.25	14.85	0.12	269.53	20.83	0.08	40	14
Recurved Bowls (maximum diameter 240–314 mm)								
Gila	143.24	16.24	0.11	285.84	20.02	0.07	25	11

Table 6.2 *Continued*

Type & Site	Height			Maximum Diameter			N	No. of sites
	Mean	S.D.	C.V.	Mean	S.D.	C.V.		
Straight-Walled Bowls (maximum diameter over 240 mm)								
Gila	132.53	12.12	0.09	277.93	19.64	0.07	15	9
LARGE BOWLS (maximum diameter over 315 mm) n = 45								
Incurved Bowls								
Gila	172.00	15.30	0.09	327.90	9.24	0.03	10	8
Recurved Bowls								
Gila	176.84	28.55	0.19	344.84	21.73	0.06	19	9
Tonto	180.77	20.80	0.12	374.08	27.69	0.07	13	8
LARGE JARS (maximum diameter over 315 mm) n = 79								
Gila	257.67	31.67	0.12	363.78	24.60	0.07	27	13
Tonto	259.08	33.81	0.13	402.35	42.63	0.11	51	14
Kuykendall	265.57	31.63	0.12	413.38	46.25	0.11	21	1
VIV	243.10	20.44	0.08	391.40	27.57	0.07	10	1

of variation of 8 percent for both height and maximum diameter (table 6.3). These jars came from six different, noncontiguous rooms at the site. Examination of other vessel attributes, including red slip color, temper, and presence or absence of a break in encircling lifelines revealed a narrow range of variability in these attributes, suggesting that the vessels were made by few, or highly standardized, potters.

I obtained similar results for the Dinwiddie Site in southwestern New Mexico. Six very large recurved bowls over 315 mm in maximum diameter produced coefficients of variation of 5 percent for height and 8 percent for maximum diameter (table 6.3). The Dinwiddie Site bowls came from the floors of four separate, noncontiguous rooms. Five of the six bowls are smudged, constituting all but one of the smudged bowls in the entire assemblage. The six bowls show consistent temper, slip color, and lifeline location, which also suggests a standardized manufacturing regime.

If the form-type categories created for this analysis are behaviorally meaningful, then small vessel categories are not standardized in form, and some large vessel categories from some sites are standardized. However, the lack of standardization among the small vessel categories may be partly due to differences in the samples of vessels. First, the contexts that produced each of these size categories differ: 84 percent of small vessels (under 240 mm in maximum diameter) came from burials, whereas 89 percent of large vessels (over 315 mm in maximum diameter) came from nonburial contexts, primarily rooms and courtyards. Of the medium vessels, 58 percent came from burials, and 42 percent came from rooms. The large vessels from nonburial contexts were primarily left in place when the sites were abandoned, and thus, might have been produced over a shorter period of time and by fewer potters than the groups of vessels found in burials at the same sites. Second, the small vessels are more portable and more likely to have been exchanged than the large vessels. This attribute may have led more potters to contribute to the pool of small vessels.

Despite these possible differences in the samples, the coefficients of variation for the large vessels from the Dinwiddie and VIV sites do suggest production by specialists. Additional factors suggest that this produc-

Table 6.3 Sample Means, Standard Deviations, and Coefficients of Variation for Large Salado Polychrome Vessels over 315 mm in Maximum Diameter, with Gila and Tonto Polychrome Vessels Combined

	Height			Maximum Diameter				No. of
Type & Site	Mean	S.D.	C.V.	Mean	S.D.	C.V.	N	sites
Incurved bowls	166.31	18.21	0.11	333.38	20.09	0.06	13	9
Recurved bowls	176.84	28.55	0.16	356.72	28.00	0.08	32	17
Kuykendall	163.86	22.46	0.14	333.57	15.10	0.05	7	1
Dinwiddie	165.83	7.78	0.05	375.17	31.13	0.08	6	1
Jars	265.11	34.55	0.13	386.99	41.43	0.11	82	21
Kuykendall	252.18	37.60	0.15	390.35	48.12	0.12	33	1
VIV	244.08	19.71	0.08	383.23	31.42	0.08	13	1

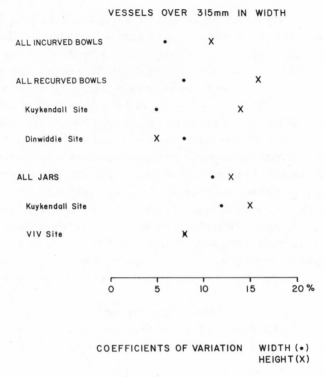

VESSELS OVER 315mm IN WIDTH

COEFFICIENTS OF VARIATION   WIDTH (•)
                              HEIGHT (X)

Figure 6.4 Coefficients of variation for maximum diameters (widths) and heights of vessels over 315 mm in width.

tion entailed product specialization by a few skilled potters without intensification. Although there is no evidence that the distribution of these large vessels was restricted, the demand for them was apparently not great. Only 45 large bowls (over 315 mm in diameter) from 15 sites are included in the assemblage of 778 vessels (6 percent of the assemblage). The 79 large jars represent 10 percent of the assemblage, but they were widely distributed at 23 sites. I have argued elsewhere that these large vessels were used in community feasting (bowls) and communal storage (jars) (Crown 1994:203). Low demand would suggest the need for fewer potters to produce such vessels.

Time may also have been a factor in the production of large vessels. DeBoer and Lathrap (1979:120) timed the manufacture of several vessel forms among the Shipibo-Conibo and found that large jars took 4.5 times longer to produce than small jars.[3] Fewer potters may have been willing to invest their time in the production of these forms.

Finally, fewer potters would have had the skills necessary to make the very large vessels than to make the smaller forms. Support for this interpretation comes from the quality of design artistry on the vessels. In ranking the quality of painting on the vessels on a scale of 1 to 5, where 1 was the best and 5 the worst execution, I found that only 4 percent of the vessels over 315 mm in maximum diameter were ranked above 3, whereas 12 percent of the smaller vessels were ranked above 3. This suggests that children and less skilled potters did not attempt to produce the difficult larger forms.

Although the low coefficients of variation for large recurved bowls from the Dinwiddie Site and large jars from the VIV Site suggest specialist production, I did not find comparably low figures for large vessel forms from other sites. At the Kuykendall Site, 7 recurved bowls and 33 jars comparable in size to those from Dinwiddie and VIV had coefficients of variation that were considerably higher (table 6.3). Because the Kuykendall vessels came from comparable contexts (nonburials) and are of comparable size, function, and quality, it is likely that the difference lies in the number of potters who produced the vessels at each of these sites.

I therefore suggest that the standardization of some vessel forms from some sites is due to a smaller pool of potters who were capable of producing these low-demand forms at particular sites. Such product specialization does not imply economic intensification.

Efficiency in Decoration

The lack of standardization in small vessel forms leaves unresolved the issue of mode of production, particularly because of the possible sampling problems noted. Further investigation of this issue requires examination of another dimension of specialized production. Researchers have suggested that mass production of utilitarian wares with low value and wide distribution was accompanied by standardized and cost-effective design execution, whereas specialization in the production of "luxury" wares with high value, special function, and low or restricted distribution entailed labor-intensive methods (Hagstrum 1985; Rice 1987). By evaluating the energy expenditure of Salado polychrome designs, I could further assess the degree to which cost-effective measures influenced production. Unfortunately, like standardization, efficiency is a relative concept.

In relative terms, only 1 of 12 decorative styles on the Salado polychrome vessels—the Gila Style—can be considered cost effective. Gila Style vessels have expedient designs executed with wide brushes and minimal brush strokes (e.g., the vessel in fig. 6.2). These designs are highly redundant; identical designs were found on vessels from many different sites. Gila Style designs contrast with other design styles on the Salado polychromes, which are generally characterized by more complex motifs that incorporate hatching, ticking, and other labor-intensive patterns. Gila Style designs were thus both efficiently executed and highly standardized. Of all of the Salado polychrome design styles, only these designs are likely to have been produced by specialists who were concerned with efficient execution. If the subset of vessels with Gila Style designs have standardized vessel forms, a stronger case could be made for their production by specialists.

Gila Style designs were painted on 12 percent of the vessels in my sample; almost all (91 percent) are Gila Polychrome, and almost all (92 percent) fit into the small size class. However, once these vessels are divided into the form classes, the sample sizes are quite low. Nevertheless, the coefficients of variation for the Gila Style small vessels are in all but one case quite close to the figures for the assemblage as a whole (table 6.4 and fig. 6.5), indicating that the forms were no more standardized than most of the assemblage and that the pots were probably not produced by specialists.

The single exception is a group of seven straight-walled bowls from the Angler's Inn Site with coefficients of variation that are below 10 percent. This small sample of vessels with both standardized forms and cost-efficient designs may indicate that specialists produced one form of Salado polychrome vessels at one site. Examination of nonplastic inclusions, paint types, and the presence of a break in the lifeline indicates six distinct combinations of attributes, which may signify that six different potters produced these seven vessels with standardized dimensions. Unfortunately, the small sample size makes any interpretation tentative.

By contrast, the large vessels with standardized forms from the Dinwiddie and VIV sites exhibit varied and labor-intensive designs, painted with small brushes and many brush strokes. These vessels were too widely distributed within these sites to have been strictly elite wares, but they were probably valued, special-function vessels that required skills

Table 6.4 Sample Means, Standard Deviations, and Coefficients of Variation for Small Salado Polychrome Vessels with Gila Style Design

Type & Site	Height			Maximum Diameter			N	No. of Sites
	Mean	S.D.	C.V.	Mean	S.D.	C.V.		
Incurved bowls	86.13	10.81	0.13	170.65	25.27	0.15	31	14
Angler's Inn	86.67	13.80	0.15	172.11	31.27	0.18	9	1
Recurved bowls	87.88	19.68	0.22	152.75	33.42	0.22	8	5
Outcurved bowls	73.50	15.31	0.21	151.40	19.97	0.13	10	5
Straight-walled bowls	81.10	12.64	0.16	154.90	26.09	0.17	20	10
Angler's Inn	86.71	7.78	0.09	165.71	10.05	0.06	7	1

possessed by few potters. At these two sites, only highly skilled potters may have manufactured certain complex vessel forms, perhaps for special purposes, as a form of product specialization (Rice 1991).

Conclusions

Salado polychrome pottery was produced in many locales over a broad area of the American Southwest. Despite the wide production area, current evidence indicates some pottery exchange. The use and distribution of vessels within sites suggest that the pots were not symbols of authority or items of exchange among elites. The vessels were used for food processing, serving, and storage and were ultimately abandoned in households, courtyards, or kivas or placed in burials, caches, or trash after use. The vessels were not associated with any single burial ritual. The distribution of vessels in burials was not restricted to any single age or sex group, although the patterns do suggest that the vessels were more commonly associated with adults of a single sex in some burial populations.

The unstandardized forms and labor-intensive designs of most Salado polychrome vessels are most consistent with the argument for nonspecialist production. However, the nature and sizes of the samples make it

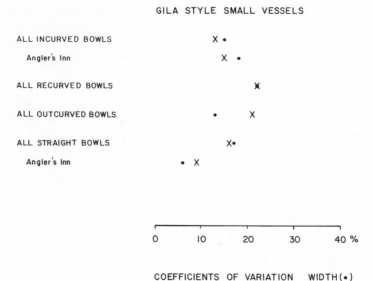

GILA STYLE SMALL VESSELS

ALL INCURVED BOWLS

Angler's Inn

ALL RECURVED BOWLS

ALL OUTCURVED BOWLS

ALL STRAIGHT BOWLS

Angler's Inn

0   10   20   30   40 %

COEFFICIENTS OF VARIATION   WIDTH(•)
                              HEIGHT (X)

Figure 6.5 Coefficients of variation for maximum diameters (widths) and heights of small vessels with Gila Style designs.

impossible to demonstrate nonspecialist production conclusively. The presence of vessels decorated by unskilled individuals indicates that the potters who made Salado polychrome vessels varied greatly in their skill and apparent output.

Small vessels with standardized forms and efficient, standardized designs suggest possible mass production of one form of Salado polychrome vessel at a single site. At two sites, large vessels with standardized forms and complex designs suggest possible production by a few potters. Although such "product specialization" may have occurred at these sites, the absence of high volumes of these large vessels and the presence of labor-intensive, nonrepetitive designs on these vessels suggest that this specialization did not occur in an atmosphere of craft production intensification. Rather, fewer, more highly skilled potters produced these difficult shapes, probably as part-time "elementary" specialists (Balfet 1965).

One implication of this research is that ceramic specialization in these middle-range societies may have begun with production of low-demand forms that required unusual skill to manufacture. Such an interpretation potentially challenges assumptions based on Balfet's (1965) conclusion that ceramic specialization began among disenfranchised women. Instead, the research presented here suggests that highly skilled potters may have produced a few difficult forms above the needs of the household as one path toward specialized production.

Interestingly, the coefficients of variation for all Salado polychrome vessels are generally smaller than those obtained for contemporaneous cooking jars from Grasshopper Pueblo (Longacre et al. 1988:table 3), earlier Sedentary period Hohokam Red-on-buff vessels from cremations at Snaketown (Lindauer 1988:table 12), and the other assemblages discussed in this volume (Hegmon et al.; Mills). Although one can argue that standardization should not be compared from one population to another (Arnold and Nieves 1992) and that the forms, functions, and relative time depth represented by the various assemblages are not comparable, the greater standardization of the Salado polychrome vessels may indicate that they were produced by a smaller pool of potters than the other types.

The organization of production of the Salado polychromes does not appear to have altered substantially over time as the areal extent of production increased. Comparisons of coefficients of variation for the general temporal sequence of Pinto, Gila, and Tonto vessels reveal variable trends in the relative standardization of vessel forms, i.e., an inconsistent temporal pattern. However, the possible examples of specialized production noted above all entail the fourteenth-century Gila or Tonto Polychrome vessels. Although most Salado polychrome vessel production probably remained in the hands of nonspecialist household producers throughout this period, other means of organizing production may have been added after A.D. 1300.

I conclude that Salado polychrome vessels were produced in many places, for many purposes, by individuals with highly variable skills, factors that suggest the presence of multiple levels in the organization of production within individual sites. In this case, the analytic construct "type" subsumes visually similar products of highly varied origin.

Acknowledgments

The research described here was completed with funding from the American Philosophical Foundation, Southern Methodist University, and the Smithsonian Institution. Charles Sternberg drafted Figure 6.1. The specimen in Figure 6.2 is published courtesy of the Arizona State Museum, University of Arizona. I am grateful to Nancy Benco, Melissa Hagstrum, Owen Lindauer, Carla Sinopoli, and an anonymous reviewer for providing insightful comments on earlier drafts of this paper. I particularly wish to thank the University of New Mexico Press for permission to use material from *Ceramics and Ideology: Salado Polychrome Pottery* (Crown 1994).

Notes

1. Many smaller scale studies (primarily of Gila and Tonto Polychromes) have demonstrated local production through petrographic, X-ray fluorescence, and X-ray diffraction analyses. I do not review all of these studies here, but the interested reader is referred to Crown and Bishop (1991) for a complete listing of these projects. Two recent research projects demonstrate that the Pinto Polychrome vessels recovered at specific sites are both manufactured locally and exchanged from other areas (White 1993; Zedeño 1991, this volume), although the magnitude of the local production vs. the exchange is impossible to gauge on the basis of the small samples investigated.

2. Scattergrams of vessel height and maximum diameter for each bowl class showed breaks at the same location: heights of 115 mm and widths of 240 mm. In addition, scattergrams for incurved bowls and recurved bowls showed breaks at maximum diameters of 315 mm. For the jar class, a break was apparent at a height of 200 mm and a width of 315 mm. These categories provide a means for subdividing this large assemblage into potentially more meaningful classes.

3. DeBoer and Lathrap (1979) indicated that small ollas required seven production steps and 195 minutes to manufacture, whereas large jars took nine production steps and 895 minutes.

References Cited

Arnold, Dean, and Alvaro L. Nieves

1992   Factors Affecting Ceramic Standardization. In *Ceramic Production and Distribution: An Integrated Approach*, edited by George J. Bey III and Christopher A. Pool, pp. 93–113. Westview Press, Boulder, Colorado.

Balfet, Hélène

1965   Ethnological Observations in North Africa and Archaeological Interpretation. In *Ceramics and Man*, edited by Frederick R. Matson, pp. 161–177. Viking Fund Publications in Anthropology No. 41. Aldine Publishing Co., Chicago.

Benco, Nancy L.

1987   *The Early Medieval Pottery Industry at al-Basra, Morocco.* BAR International Series 341. British Archaeological Reports, Oxford.

1988   Morphological Standardization: An Approach to the Study of Craft Specialization. In *A Pot for All Reasons: Ceramic Ecology Revisited,* edited by Charles C. Kolb and Louanna M. Lackey, pp. 57–72. Temple University, Philadelphia.

1989   Material Correlates of Specialized Pottery Production: An Ethnoarchaeological Example from Morocco. Paper presented at the 88th Annual Meeting of the American Anthropological Association, Washington, D.C.

Brunson, Judy L.

1989   *The Social Organization of the Los Muertos Hohokam: A Reanalysis of Cushing's Hemenway Expedition Data.* Unpublished Ph.D. dissertation, Department of Anthropology, Arizona State University, Tempe.

Carlson, Roy L.

1982   The Polychrome Complexes. In *Southwestern Ceramics: A Comparative Review,* edited by Albert H. Schroeder, pp. 210–234. The Arizona Archaeologist No. 15. Arizona Archaeological Society, Phoenix.

Costin, Cathy L., and Melissa B. Hagstrum

1995   Standardization, Labor Investment, Skill and the Organization of Ceramic Production in Late Pre-Hispanic Highland Peru. *American Antiquity,* in press.

Crown, Patricia L.

1994   *Ceramics and Ideology: Salado Polychrome Pottery.* University of New Mexico Press, Albuquerque.

Crown, Patricia L., and Ronald L. Bishop

1987   The Manufacture of the Salado Polychromes. *Pottery Southwest* 14(4): 1–4.

1991   Manufacture of Gila Polychrome in the Greater American Southwest: An Instrumental Neutron Activation Analysis. In *Excavation and Surface Collection of Homolovi II Ruin,* edited by E. Charles Adams and Kelley A. Hays, pp. 49–56. Anthropological Papers of the University of Arizona No. 55. University of Arizona Press, Tucson.

1994   The Question of Source. In *Ceramics and the Ideology: Salado Polychrome Pottery,* by Patricia L. Crown, pp. 21–35. University of New Mexico Press, Albuquerque.

Cushing, Frank H.

1890   Preliminary Notes on the Origin, Working Hypothesis and Preliminary Researches of the Hemenway Southwestern Archaeological Expedition. In *Congres International des Americanistes, Compte-rendu de la*

Septieme Session, pp. 151–194. International Congress of Americanists, Berlin.

DeBoer, Warren R., and Donald W. Lathrap
1979   The Making and Breaking of Shipibo-Conibo Ceramics. In *Ethnoarchaeology,* edited by Carol Kramer, pp. 102–138. Columbia University Press, New York.

Gerald, Rex E.
1976   A Conceptual Framework for Evaluating Salado and Salado-Related Material in the El Paso Area. *The Kiva* 42:65–70.

Graves, Michael W.
1982   Breaking Down Ceramic Design Variation: Testing Modes of White Mountain Redware Design Style Development. *Journal of Anthropological Archaeology* 1(4):305–354.
1991   Pottery Production and Distribution Among the Kalinga: A Study of Household and Regional Organization and Differentiation. In *Ceramic Ethnoarchaeology,* edited by William A. Longacre, pp. 112–143. University of Arizona Press, Tucson.

Grebinger, Paul
1976   Salado—Perspectives from the Middle Santa Cruz Valley. *The Kiva* 42:39–46.

Hagstrum, Melissa
1985   Measuring Prehistoric Ceramic Craft Specialization: A Test Case in the American Southwest. *Journal of Field Archaeology* 12:65–75.

Hodder, Ian
1981   Comments of Rice's Paper. *Current Anthropology* 22(3):231–232.

Hohmann, John W., and Linda B. Kelley
1988   *Erich F. Schmidt's Investigations of Salado Sites in Central Arizona.* Bulletin No. 56. Museum of Northern Arizona, Flagstaff.

Kenagy, Susan
1986   *Ritual Pueblo Ceramics: Symbolic Stylistic Behavior as a Medium of Information Exchange.* Ph.D. dissertation, Department of Art History, University of New Mexico, Albuquerque.

Lindauer, Owen
1988   *A Study of Vessel Form and Painted Designs to Explore Regional Interaction of the Sedentary Period Hohokam.* Unpublished Ph.D. dissertation, Department of Anthropology, Arizona State University, Tempe.

Longacre, William A., Kenneth L. Kvamme, and Masashi Kobayashi
1988   Southwestern Pottery Standardization: An Ethnoarchaeological View from the Philippines. *The Kiva* 53:101–112.

McGuire, Randall H.

1991   On the Outside Looking In: The Concept of Periphery in Hohokam Archaeology. In *Exploring the Hohokam: Prehistoric Desert Dwellers of the Southwest*, edited by George J. Gumerman, pp. 347–382. University of New Mexico Press, Albuquerque.

Mayro, Linda L., Stephanie M. Whittlesey, and J. Jefferson Reid

1976   Observations on the Salado Presence at Grasshopper Pueblo. *The Kiva* 42:85–94.

Nelson, Ben A., and Steven A. LeBlanc

1986   *Short-term Sedentism in the American Southwest.* University of New Mexico Press, Albuquerque.

Rice, Glen E.

1986   Working Hypotheses for the Study of Hohokam Community Complexes. Paper presented at the Spring 1986 Meeting of the Arizona Archaeological Council, Phoenix.

Rice, Prudence M.

1981   Evolution of Specialized Pottery Production: A Trial Model. *Current Anthropology* 22:219–240.

1987   *Pottery Analysis, A Sourcebook.* University of Chicago Press, Chicago.

1991   Specialization, Standardization, and Diversity: A Retrospective. In *The Ceramic Legacy of Anna O. Shepard*, edited by Ronald L. Bishop and Frederick W. Lange, pp. 257–279. University Press of Colorado, Niwot, Colorado.

Santley, Robert S., Phillip J. Arnold III, and Christopher A. Pool

1989   The Ceramics Production System at Matacapan, Veracruz, Mexico. *Journal of Field Archaeology* 16:107–132.

Shepard, Anna O.

1965   Rio Grande Glaze-Paint Pottery: A Test of Petrographic Analysis. In *Ceramics and Man*, edited by Frederick R. Matson, pp. 62–87. Viking Fund Publications in Anthropology 41. Aldine Publishing Co., Chicago.

Stark, Barbara L.

1985   Archaeological Identification of Pottery Production Locations: Ethnoarchaeological and Archaeological Data in Mesoamerica. In *Decoding Prehistoric Ceramics*, edited by Ben A. Nelson, pp. 158–194. Southern Illinois University, Carbondale.

Upham, Steadman

1982   *Polities and Power: An Economic and Political History of the Western Pueblo.* Academic Press, New York.

White, Diane E.

1993   *Pinto Polychrome Origin and Distribution, Indicator of Interaction and Trade, in East-Central Arizona.* Unpublished M.A. thesis, Department of Anthropology, Arizona State University, Tempe.

Whittlesey, Stephanie M.

1974   Identification of Imported Ceramics Through Functional Analysis of Attributes. *The Kiva* 40(1–2):101–112.

1978   *Status and Death at Grasshopper Pueblo.* Unpublished Ph.D. dissertation, Department of Anthropology, University of Arizona, Tucson.

Wilcox, David R.

1987   *Frank Midvale's Investigations of the Site of La Ciudad.* Anthropological Field Studies No. 16. Arizona State University, Tempe.

1995   A Processual Model of Charles C. Di Peso's Babocomari Site and Related Systems. In *The Gran Chichimeca: Essays on the Archaeology and Ethnohistory of Northern Mesoamerica,* edited by Jonathon E. Reyman, pp. 281–319. Avebury, Aldershot, England.

Zedeño, María Nieves

1991   *Refining Inferences of Ceramic Circulation: A Stylistic, Technological, and Compositional Analysis of Whole Vessels from Chodistaas, Arizona.* Unpublished Ph.D. dissertation, Department of Anthropology, Southern Methodist University, Dallas.

7

Changing Patterns of Pottery Manufacture and Trade in the Northern Rio Grande Region

Judith A. Habicht-Mauche

Unlike materials that do not vary in composition as they are transformed into human resources (e.g., lithics), ceramic materials are inherently malleable. This plasticity is evident not only in their physical composition and form, but also in how their production, distribution, and use map onto changing cultural landscapes. As a result, ceramic materials have the potential to yield compelling and detailed information about transformations in these landscapes. The following study presents evidence for a major shift in the organization of ceramic production and distribution in the northern Rio Grande Valley of New Mexico, within the context of changing economic and social relations in the region during the fourteenth century.

The development of a widespread network of craft and resource specialization and long-distance trade is often cited as one of the defining hallmarks of the early Classic period (A.D. 1300–1450) in the northern Rio Grande region (Snow 1981). Specialization in this context is defined by the related processes of differentiation of production by district (i.e., "community specialization") and the "commodification" of specific socially valued objects, such as glaze-painted pottery. In turn, these processes have been interpreted as reflecting the emergence of a broad regional system of socio-political and economic integration (Wilcox

1981). Unfortunately, little work has been done to define either the exact structure of these economic transactions or the nature of the emerging social relationships that both sustained and were sustained by them. To address these issues, I conducted a detailed study to record evidence for changing patterns of pottery manufacture and trade at the early Classic period site of Arroyo Hondo (LA 12), New Mexico (Habicht-Mauche 1993).

The adobe ruins of Arroyo Hondo Pueblo (LA 12) are located along the eastern flank of the Sangre de Cristo Mountains, just south of the modern city of Santa Fe (fig. 7.1). The site was the subject of a multiyear, interdisciplinary excavation project directed by Douglas Schwartz of the School of American Research during the early 1970s (Schwartz 1986; Schwartz and Lang 1973). The researchers' objective was to study processes of demographic expansion, settlement aggregation, and regional integration in the northern Rio Grande Valley during the fourteenth century by examining the life history of a single community.

Tree-ring dates from the site indicate that Arroyo Hondo was founded shortly after A.D. 1300. The settlement grew rapidly until, by the 1330s, it consisted of more than 1,000 rooms arranged in 24 multistory room blocks enclosing nine plazas, making it one of the largest pueblo communities in the northern Rio Grande at the time (fig. 7.2). By 1345, however, an episode of increased variability and unpredictability in seasonal precipitation led to the virtual abandonment of the site for nearly a generation (Lang and Harris 1984; Rose et al. 1981; Schwartz 1986). In the 1370s a second, smaller village was constructed over part of the first (fig. 7.3). This second component village consisted of 200 single-story rooms arranged in nine room blocks around three plazas. Much of the second component village burned in the 1420s, and by the end of that decade, the site appears to have been permanently abandoned.

The decorated ceramic assemblage from Arroyo Hondo was dominated by black-on-white painted pottery throughout both occupations (table 7.1). Seriational studies, however, indicate that during the height of the second component occupation, glaze-painted pottery may have accounted for as much as 35 percent of the decorated ceramics (Lang 1993). The increased popularity of glaze-painted ceramics at Arroyo Hondo is a reflection of broader regional changes in the organization and structure of pottery manufacture and trade that took place throughout the northern Rio Grande during the second half of the fourteenth century.

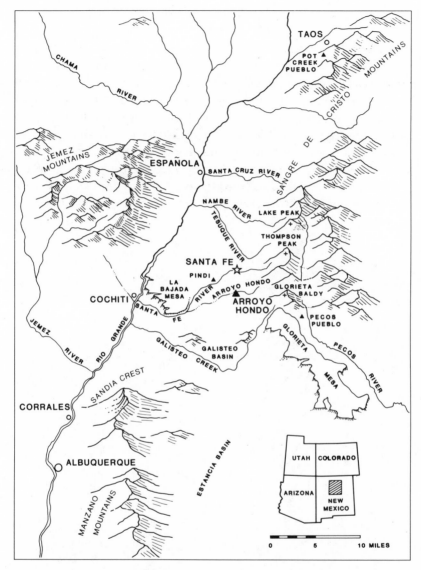

Figure 7.1 Location of Arroyo Hondo Pueblo in the northern Rio Grande region.

Methods of Analysis

To examine these fundamental changes in local ceramic manufacture and regional trade in greater detail, I performed a series of mineralogical and chemical analyses on a sample of decorated pottery from Arroyo Hondo Pueblo. Petrography was the primary method of mineralogical analysis. Using a low-power stereo microscope, I sorted sherds from each of the major pottery types into discrete categories based on recognizable differences in paste composition and texture. For each of the decorated types, I selected one sherd from each of the major paste categories for petrographic analysis and then analyzed standard thin sections with a polarizing microscope. Based on these petrographic data, I reexamined each

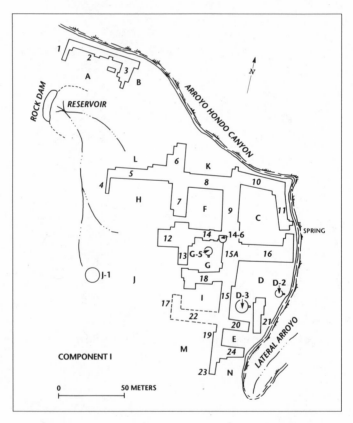

Figure 7.2 Schematic plan of Arroyo Hondo Pueblo, Component I.

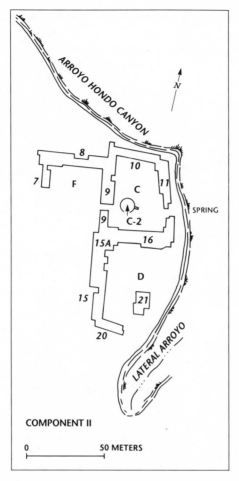

Figure 7.3 Schematic plan of Arroyo Hondo Pueblo, Component II.

sherd in the sample using a low-power stereo microscope to form the more inclusive temper categories summarized in the pie charts (see figs. 7.5a, 7.7a, 7.8a, 7.9a, 7.10a, and 7.12a).

Bart Olinger of Los Alamos National Laboratory conducted a chemical analysis, using X-ray fluorescence (XRF), on a sample of 15 sherds from each of the major decorated ceramic types at the site (Olinger 1993). Polished sections rather than powdered samples were used for this analysis because they were easier and less expensive to prepare and largely

Table 7.1 Frequency of Decorated Pottery Types from Arroyo Hondo Pueblo

Type	Component I		Component II	
	N	%	N	%
Indeterminate white ware	702	8.6	962	10.0
Santa Fe B/W: Santa Fe Variety	1,429	17.5	1,723	18.0
Santa Fe B/W: Pindi Variety	1,033	12.7	415	4.3
Wiyo B/W	1,475	18.1	1,925	20.1
Abiquiú B/W	12	0.1	151	1.6
Galisteo B/W	1,169	14.3	1,288	13.5
Rowe B/W: Poge and Arroyo Hondo Varieties	1,973	24.2	1,519	15.9
Misc. imported white wares	17	0.1	11	0.1
Indeterminate early Glaze Red	225	2.8	1,139	11.9
Glaze A Red	64	0.8	293	2.9
Glaze B Red	4	0	45	0.5
Misc. imported red wares	18	0.2	18	0.2
Glaze A Yellow	32	0.4	95	1.0
Glaze B Yellow	2	0	0	0
Misc. imported yellow wares	0	0	1	0
Total	8,155	100.0	9,585	100.0

nondestructive to the original specimen. Techniques such as XRF are bulk analyses: the chemical signature they produce combines all the compositional elements of a ceramic, including clay, temper, slip, and paint. It is impossible, therefore, to determine from the chemical data alone which aspect of the signature is due to which component. In this case, however, the accompanying petrographic studies provided a mineralogical and geologic context in which to interpret the chemical data.

The scatter plots (see figs. 7.5b, 7.7b, 7.8b, 7.9b, 7.10b, and 7.12b) record the chemical signature, as a function of the percentage X-ray counts of iron (Fe), strontium (Sr), and zirconium (Zr)[1], for sherds within each paste category and pottery type. These values represent the relative frequency of X-ray counts detected for each element and not actual compositional ratios. As a result, these data are largely qualitative in nature and should be analyzed as such. Interpretation of the chemical data is based on previous studies in the area (Olinger 1987a,b) that showed that ceramics known to have been produced locally with the same materials tend to give a tight, homogeneous X-ray signature, whereas ceramics from a wide variety of sources that used different raw materials tend to give a relatively diffuse, heterogeneous signature.

The goals of these compositional analyses were to identify the origin of manufacture of the decorated pottery recovered from the site and to trace the nature and extent of Arroyo Hondo's trade relationships with other towns and districts in the northern Rio Grande. By comparing data from the early (Component I, ca. A.D. 1300–1350) and late (Component II, ca. A.D. 1370–1420) construction phases at the site, I could trace temporal changes in the structure and pattern of these regional relationships.

Pottery Manufacture and Trade at Arroyo Hondo

The oldest deposits at Arroyo Hondo Pueblo are characterized by a high percentage of Santa Fe Black-on-white pottery. Throughout much of the thirteenth century, Santa Fe Black-on-white was the dominant decorated ceramic type on sites stretching from the Taos Valley to areas south of Albuquerque and from the Jemez Mountains on the west to the eastern slopes of the Sangre de Cristo Mountains (fig. 7.4). As a type, Santa Fe Black-on-white is characterized by broad, regional, stylistic uniformity (i.e., similarity in specific motifs and overall design structure), contrasting with a high degree of local compositional and technological variation. Warren (1976), for example, identified at least 35 distinct temper varieties for Santa Fe Black-on-white. Her findings indicated that throughout the northern Rio Grande, potters produced these ceramic vessels using locally available resources while adhering to widely accepted regional canons of ceramic style.

All of the Santa Fe Black-on-white vessels found at Arroyo Hondo probably reached the town as a result of trade with neighboring communities to the north. Most of the pottery was made from silty sedimentary clays that are scattered throughout the Tesuque Formation of the Española Basin (fig. 7.5a). Furthermore, about half the samples tested were tempered with a very fine, white, volcanic ash that is also interbedded in this

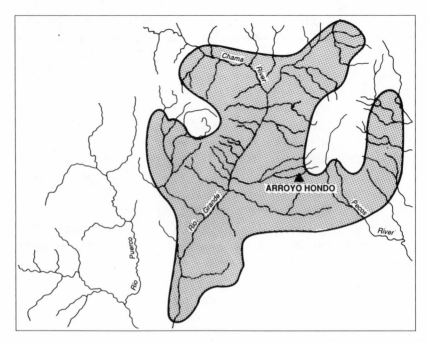

Figure 7.4 Distribution of Santa Fe Black-on-white pottery during the thirteenth century.

formation (Galusha and Blick 1971; Spiegel and Baldwin 1963). Tewa potters in the area continued to use this same basic suite of raw materials into the historical era (Guthe 1925).

The XRF results indicate that most of the Santa Fe Black-on-white sherds sampled from Arroyo Hondo fall within a single analytic cluster (fig. 7.5b). Petrographic analyses suggest that the relatively crude XRF technique used in this study may not have been sensitive enough to detect subtle differences among distinct, yet geologically similar, sources of clay and temper from locations throughout the Española Basin, thus masking potentially significant variability within the type. Three to five additional analytic sources, however, may be distinguishable on the XRF plot. These secondary sources appear to have been more important during the first component (solid points on plot) and are characterized by generally higher strontium counts but exhibit a diverse range of zirconium counts.

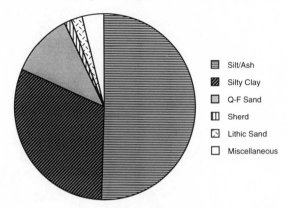

**Arroyo Hondo (LA 12)-Santa Fe B/W
Temper Categories**

Silt/Ash
Silty Clay
Q-F Sand
Sherd
Lithic Sand
Miscellaneous

Figure 7.5a Santa Fe Black-on-white temper categories.

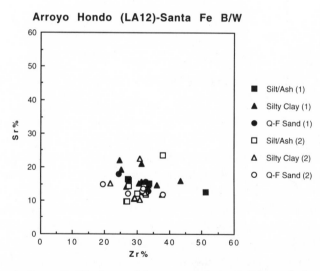

Arroyo Hondo (LA12)-Santa Fe B/W

Silt/Ash (1)
Silty Clay (1)
Q-F Sand (1)
Silt/Ash (2)
Silty Clay (2)
Q-F Sand (2)

Figure 7.5b Santa Fe Black-on-white xRF analysis. Solid symbols represent sherds from Component I contexts; open symbols represent sherds from Component II contexts.

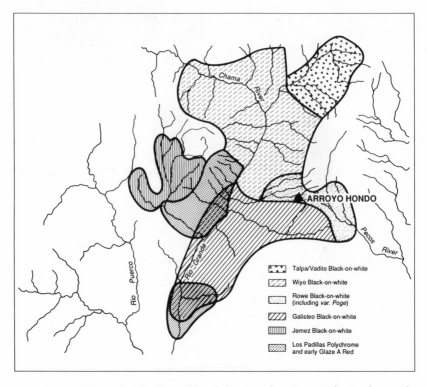

Figure 7.6 Primary distribution of local decorated pottery styles in the northern Rio Grande region, ca. A.D. 1300.

Around the turn of the fourteenth century, there appears to have been a rapid proliferation of local black-on-white pottery styles throughout the northern Rio Grande (fig. 7.6). This pattern is clearly reflected at Arroyo Hondo where, after ca. A.D. 1310, the frequency of Santa Fe Black-on-white dropped precipitously in favor of a variety of both local and imported black-on-white pottery types (Lang 1993).

The mineralogical and chemical data, in conjunction with regional distributional studies, indicate that two minor varieties of black-on-white pottery were produced locally at or near Arroyo Hondo Pueblo. Making up 24 percent of the Component I and 16 percent of the Component II decorated assemblage, Rowe Black-on-white: Poge Variety is the characteristic local pottery type at Arroyo Hondo. The distribution of Rowe Black-on-white and its variants is limited primarily to a crescent that extends from the upper Pecos River, around the southern and western flanks of the Sangre de Cristo Mountains and up the Santa Fe River, to the vicinity of Santa Fe. The Poge Variety is distinguished from the classic variety of Rowe Black-on-white by the use of lithic sand or a mixture of lithic sand and sherd as temper (fig. 7.7a). The sources of this lithic sand were probably any of several local stream beds that carry erosional materials from the Precambrian formations of the Sangre de Cristo Mountains to the piedmont surrounding Arroyo Hondo. The relatively tight X-ray signature for Rowe Black-on-white: Poge Variety from Arroyo Hondo also suggests local production by potters who used geologically similar sources of raw materials (fig. 7.7b).

For a brief period during the middle of the fourteenth century, potters at Arroyo Hondo produced a local variant of the ash-tempered pottery of their neighbors in the Española-Chama district to the north. Santa Fe Black-on-white: Pindi Variety accounts for as much as 35 percent of the decorated pottery assemblage from Arroyo Hondo dating to the 1330s, but is found in only trace quantities in the Component II assemblage (Lang 1993). Pindi Variety pottery was tempered with coarse pumiceous ash from deposits that outcrop along the upper wall of Arroyo Hondo canyon, adjacent to the pueblo (fig. 7.8a). Distinct analytic sources are not distinguishable on the XRF plot, which supports the mineralogical evidence for local production (fig. 7.8b).

The spatial distribution of Santa Fe Black-on-white: Pindi Variety parallels that of Rowe Black-on-white: Poge Variety (fig. 7.6). Both varieties are not commonly found outside the Santa Fe area, suggesting that they were produced primarily for local consumption and were not exchanged in large quantities with other pueblos in the region.

The two most common imported white wares at Arroyo Hondo are Wiyo Black-on-white and Galisteo Black-on-white. Wiyo Black-on-white makes up 18 percent and 20 percent of the Component I and Component II decorated assemblages, respectively. This pottery type is characterized by fine-textured pastes tempered with volcanic ash, which may have been obtained from any of the numerous lenses that dissect the Tesuque Formation north of Santa Fe (fig. 7.9a). The diffuse X-ray signature of Wiyo pottery from Arroyo Hondo suggests that potters produced these vessels using a wide variety of analytic sources of raw materials from within the Española-Chama district of New Mexico (fig. 7.9b). A similar chemical signature characterizes the secondary analytic categories recorded for Santa Fe Black-on-white (fig. 7.5b), suggesting that this signature may be

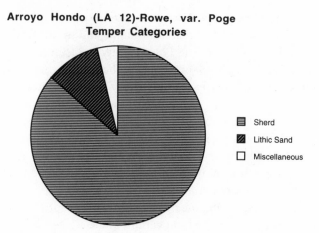

Figure 7.7a Rowe Black-on-white: Poge Variety temper categories.

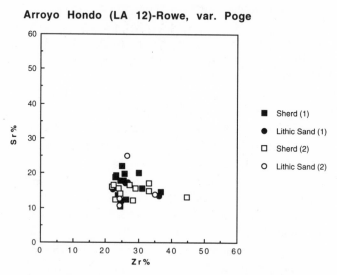

Figure 7.7b Rowe Black-on-white: Poge Variety XRF analysis.

Arroyo Hondo (LA 12)-Santa Fe, var. Pindi

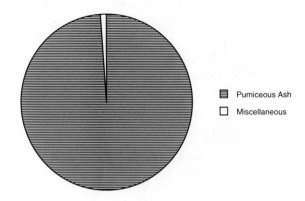

Figure 7.8a Santa Fe Black-on-white: Pindi Variety temper categories.

Arroyo Hondo (LA 12)-Santa Fe, var. Pindi

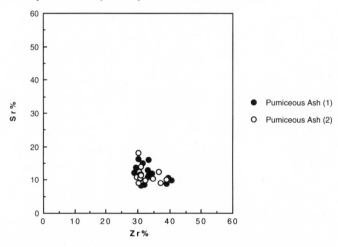

Figure 7.8b Santa Fe Black-on-white: Pindi Variety XRF analysis.

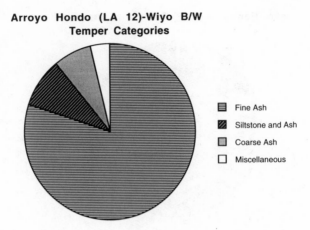

Figure 7.9a Wiyo Black-on-white temper categories.

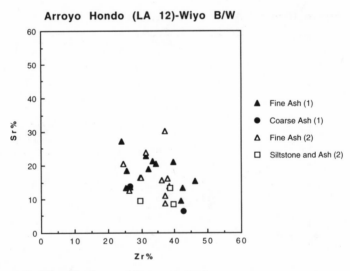

Figure 7.9b Wiyo Black-on-white xRF analysis.

associated with those areas of the Española-Chama district where Wiyo Black-on-white became the dominant decorated ceramic type after A.D. 1300. The diffuse signature for Wiyo pottery also suggests that no single analytic source dominated the production or trade of these vessels throughout the northern Rio Grande Valley.

Galisteo Black-on-white pottery reached its peak of popularity at Arroyo Hondo during the 1320s and 1330s when, in some contexts, it accounted for as much as 60 percent of the decorated pottery (Lang 1993). The classic variety of Galisteo Black-on-white pottery is characterized by the addition of crushed sherd as temper (fig. 7.10a). Unfortunately, sherd temper is of little help in sourcing ceramic materials mineralogically because pottery crushed for temper can be of either local or imported origin. The known distribution of the type, however, suggests that production was centered in the Galisteo Basin, south of Arroyo Hondo (fig. 7.1). The highly distinct, light gray to white pastes that characterize Galisteo Black-on-white sherds from Arroyo Hondo are diagnostic of the light-firing Cretaceous clays of the Galisteo Basin, also indicating that this region is the most likely source for most of this material (Kidder and Shepard 1936). As with Wiyo Black-on-white pottery, the diffuse X-ray signature of Galisteo Black-on-white ceramics from Arroyo Hondo suggests that this pottery was produced at several analytically distinct sources within the Galisteo Basin (fig. 7.10b).

Red-slipped, glaze-painted pottery was first produced in the Rio Grande Valley at sites near Albuquerque around the turn of the fourteenth century (fig. 7.6). These early glazes are characteristically tempered with dark crushed sherd containing lithic fragments of mica schist (Shepard 1942). Schist-tempered sherd characterizes less than 1 percent of all the glaze-on-red pottery analyzed from Arroyo Hondo (fig. 7.12a). Many of these sherds represent very early transitional glaze ware types (i.e., Los Padillas Glaze-on-red) that reveal strong stylistic ties to western glazes, such as Heshotauthla Polychrome from the Acoma-Laguna area.

In general, glaze-painted pottery was not widely distributed in the northern Rio Grande until around A.D. 1340 to 1350, when it suddenly became a common imported ware on sites throughout much of the region. At this time, production of glaze-painted ceramics also seems to have expanded beyond the Albuquerque district (fig. 7.11) to areas such as the Santo Domingo and Galisteo basins (Shepard 1942). At Arroyo Hondo, glaze ware was not present in significant quantities until after A.D. 1340, or toward the very end of the Component I occupation. The ware dramat-

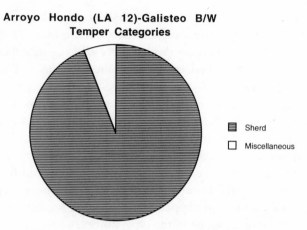

Figure 7.10a Galisteo Black-on-white temper categories.

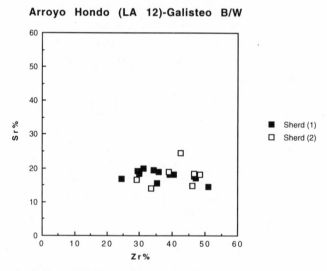

Figure 7.10b Galisteo Black-on-white xrf analysis.

ically increased in popularity at the beginning of the second component and peaked around the turn of the fifteenth century, at which time it may have represented more than 35 percent of the decorated ceramic assemblage (Lang 1993). Imported and local white wares, however, continued to dominate the assemblage until the site was abandoned in the 1420s.

Two major geologic sources of glaze-painted ceramics are represented at Arroyo Hondo (fig. 7.12a). Forty-three percent of the Glaze A Red sherds from the site are tempered with one of a variety of intermediate volcanic rocks that are diagnostic of glaze-painted pottery produced in the Galisteo Basin (Shepard 1942; Warren 1970, 1976, 1981). More than 50 percent of the sherds are tempered with fine crystalline basalt or basalt-tempered sherd, most likely from Santa Ana Mesa, near San Felipe Pueblo (Warren 1976, 1979) in the Santo Domingo district south of Cochiti (fig. 7.1). These results corroborate previous petrographic studies (e.g., Shepard 1942; Warren 1970) that demonstrated that these two districts

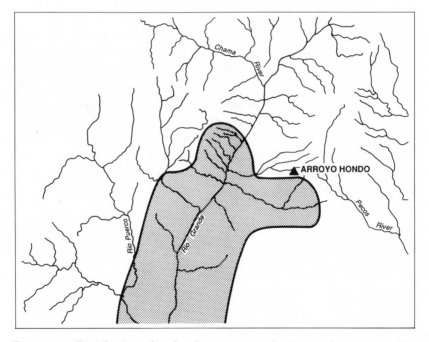

Figure 7.11 Distribution of early glaze ware production in the northern Rio Grande region, ca. A.D. 1350–1450.

dominated the production and trade of early glazes throughout the northern Rio Grande.

The XRF plot of Glaze A Red pottery from Arroyo Hondo shows a striking pattern (fig. 7.12b). Three distinct clusters are clearly distinguishable on the scatter plot. Each of these analytic sources correlates with one of the three archaeological districts (i.e., Albuquerque, Santo Domingo, and Galisteo) identified petrographically as major production areas for early glaze-painted pottery. Within each analytic cluster, the chemical signature appears to be relatively homogeneous, in contrast to the overall diffuse signatures that characterize the imported white wares from the site (compare figs. 7.9b, 7.10b, and 7.12b). This pattern may indicate a greater degree of standardization in resource selection and use within each district than was recorded for the imported white wares. However, it may also be simply an artifact of the inability of the XRF analysis to distinguish between closely related geologic sources of raw materials.

In either case, the glaze ware data do seem to reflect a fundamental shift in ceramic production and trade in the northern Rio Grande. As noted above, the inhabitants of Arroyo Hondo appear to have gotten most of their earlier black-on-white decorated pottery from either local potters or through trade with their immediate neighbors in the Española and Galisteo districts. In contrast, the predominance of glaze-painted pottery from the more distant Santo Domingo district, found in later contexts at Arroyo Hondo, suggests that the size and scope of ceramic trade networks expanded dramatically after A.D. 1350. The chemical data also suggest that, unlike the black-on-white pottery, highly localized glaze-painted pottery styles were not produced in each archaeological district. Instead, very similar early glaze ware vessels were made at only a few villages within two or three districts and then traded in large quantities over broad areas of the region.

Interpretation

The seriational and compositional data summarized above indicate that most of the decorated pottery from both occupational components at Arroyo Hondo was imported to the site from other areas in the northern Rio Grande (fig. 7.13). Changes in the relative frequencies of imported decorated ceramic types and their sources of manufacture, recorded at Arroyo Hondo, reflect broader structural changes in the organization of economic

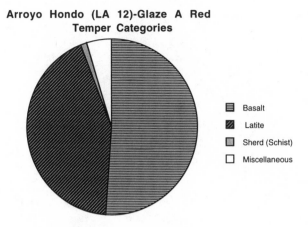

Figure 7.12a Glaze A Red temper categories.

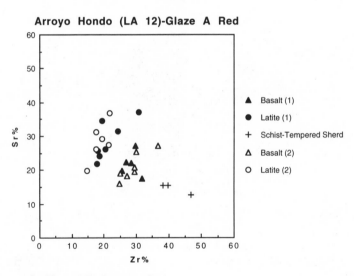

Figure 7.12b Glaze A Red XRF analysis.

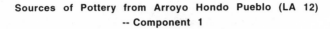

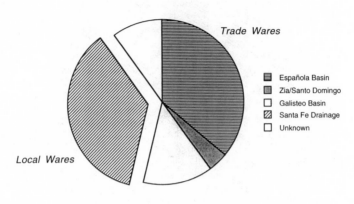

Figure 7.13 Sources of decorated pottery from Arroyo Hondo Pueblo.

and social relations throughout the northern Rio Grande during the fourteenth century.

During the preceding century, northern Rio Grande settlement had
been characterized by small dispersed communities located in a variety
of topographic settings. To compensate for spatial, seasonal, and annual
variability in the distribution of wild resources and the productivity of
farmland, each group needed to maintain access to a broad range of
diverse territory. It would have been extremely difficult, if not impossi-

ble, for such small, unconsolidated communities to establish and maintain exclusive-use rights to areas far from their main settlements (Anschuetz 1987:154). Instead, a fairly broad, open network of social relations among communities would have been essential to ensure that groups had mutual access to neighboring foraging territories and to information about the availability and distribution of food resources outside their home ranges. The widespread distribution of Santa Fe Black-on-white pottery throughout the northern Rio Grande during much of the thirteenth century may be a reflection of just such a network.

Around the turn of the fourteenth century, distinct local variants of the generic black-on-white ceramic style replaced the ubiquitous Santa Fe Black-on-white throughout the northern Rio Grande. Many of these new pottery types share several traits that are generally believed to have been derived from a common Mesa Verde style (Douglass 1985; Lambert 1954; Lang 1982; Mera 1935; Stubbs and Stallings 1953; Sundt 1987; Wendorf and Reed 1955). Traits diagnostic of this style include thick, polished, and crackled slips; rounded or flattened rims; rim ticking; paneled-band design layouts; a preference for solid design elements; the use of secondary design elements, such as dots, dashes, and ticks; and the use of sherd and crushed rock tempers (Douglass 1985; Lang 1982: 178). The appearance of this style in the northern Rio Grande is generally cited as evidence for the arrival of Mesa Verde immigrants (Lang 1982; Wendorf and Reed 1955). However, the adoption, modification, and spread of the several variants of this style may have resulted more from the dynamics of intergroup relations within the northern Rio Grande Valley than from the mere arrival of immigrants.

Immigrants from the Northern San Juan region may have been drawn to the northern Rio Grande Valley by the promise of potentially rich farmland along permanent rivers and streams. However, a large influx of population into the area would have placed increasing stress on limited agricultural resources. Around the turn of the fourteenth century, there was a dramatic shift in settlement patterns in the northern Rio Grande. Many smaller sites, especially those in more marginal upland locations, were abandoned in favor of large aggregated communities, such as Arroyo Hondo, located on land of relatively high agricultural potential along permanent drainages. This shift can be interpreted as a direct result of continued population expansion in the region and the concomitant competition for limited arable land and natural resources (Cordell et al. 1984; Hunter-Anderson 1979).

The agricultural productivity of these well-watered lowland sites could have been intensified through the construction and maintenance of water diversion and conservation facilities or through the more efficient organization of the increased labor pool from these large aggregated settlements (e.g., Stone et al. 1990). Aggregation may have also promoted and facilitated the development of more formalized systems of food sharing, land tenure, and territorial boundary maintenance (Hunter-Anderson 1979; Kohler 1989).

Increased territorial circumscription, however, would have intensified competition and conflict between communities by limiting people's access to widely dispersed and scattered resources. The presence of conflict among the Classic period residents of the northern Rio Grande is reflected in the depiction of shield-and weapon-bearing figures in the rock art of the time (e.g., Adams 1991; Schaafsma 1990) and in the defensive layout of many villages and settlement clusters (Mera 1934; Peckham 1984). Further evidence of the endemic nature of intergroup conflict among the Eastern Pueblos is the central focus on war themes in their mythology and the traditionally high status of "war chiefs" and warrior societies in many Rio Grande communities. War and warrior society symbolism are also common themes in northern Rio Grande kiva murals dated to the Classic period (Adams 1991).

Aggregated settlements would have provided inhabitants with greater security and protection against raids, and the abandoned upland areas may have acted as buffer zones that physically separated competing local groups. Settlement during the early Classic period was characterized by the presence of discrete clusters of large aggregated villages within each of the major tributary drainages along the northern Rio Grande and Upper Pecos rivers. These settlement clusters probably represent emerging ethnic alliances, bound by loose networks of kinship ties and reciprocal social and ritual obligations. Such ties would have promoted cooperation among allied settlements in the face of competition and conflict with neighboring groups. Intergroup competition would have also fostered an increasing emphasis on social and territorial boundary maintenance as a means of strengthening group identity and structuring intergroup relations.

Thus, the northern Rio Grande region during the early fourteenth century appears to have been characterized by a fragmentation of the cultural landscape that reflected the emergence of several larger and more consolidated local ethnic alliances. The presence of these new social groups was marked by the sudden appearance of a plethora of highly localized, black-on-white ceramic styles throughout the region. The manufacturing area for each of these local styles (fig. 7.6) corresponds, more or less, with the boundaries of cultural provinces or districts, identified archaeologically on the basis of similarities in other aspects of material culture, architecture, and settlement pattern, which also became apparent at that time.

The frequency and distribution of these various pottery styles at Arroyo Hondo and other contemporaneous sites indicate that large quantities of decorated ceramics were exchanged between villages within districts, as well as between neighboring villages in adjacent districts. There is little evidence, however, of extensive, regularized, long-distance trade. Although some large towns, such as Arroyo Hondo, appear to have produced few of their own black-on-white ceramics, no data indicate that any one village or district ever controlled or dominated trade in these wares. Black-on-white pottery appears to have been produced largely for local consumption or changed hands as part of fairly generalized exchanges between closely neighboring communities.

There is also little evidence for craft specialization, i.e., the standardization of production and decoration of these various black-on-white types. For example, the two most common imported white ware types at Arroyo Hondo—Galisteo Black-on-white and Wiyo Black-on-white—are both characterized by a high degree of variability in vessel form and size, surface treatment, content and complexity of decoration, and overall quality of workmanship. This same lack of standardization has been recorded for imported Santa Fe–Wiyo vessels recovered from the nearby site of Pindi Pueblo (Hagstrum 1985).

Around A.D. 1300 a new style of pottery, featuring vitrified glaze-painted decorations on a red-slipped background, began to be produced in the Albuquerque district of the northern Rio Grande region. The wide variety of technical skill and decoration that characterize these early glazes suggests an era of experimentation with a new and unfamiliar technology (Snow 1976:B179). By the middle decades of the century, however, the production of Glaze A Red pottery became highly standardized, reaching a level of craftsmanship that far surpassed that of the preceding white ware tradition in the area (Kidder and Shepard 1936; Lambert 1954).

Also at about that time, glaze ware ceramics achieved widespread popularity throughout the northern Rio Grande region (Kidder and Shepard 1936; Mera 1940; Shepard 1942; Stubbs and Stallings 1953).

Along with the Albuquerque district, the Santo Domingo and Galisteo districts emerged as important early centers for the production and trade of this new pottery type (Shepard 1942; Warren 1969, 1976, 1979; fig. 7.11). This trend is reflected in the Glaze A Red assemblage from Arroyo Hondo, which is dominated by basalt- and latite-tempered pottery from the Santo Domingo and Galisteo districts, respectively (fig. 7.12a).

Glaze technology is very complex and requires special resources, such as lead, that are extremely limited in their distribution. Centers of production and trade probably developed in those areas where potters controlled access to both the new technology and the necessary resources. Not only was production of early glaze-painted pottery limited to a small number of districts, but fewer villages within each district may have been involved in ceramic production and trade. This trend toward increasing community specialization may be reflected in the widespread distribution of a few exotic temper types, as well as in an apparent increase in the mineralogical and chemical homogeneity that characterizes each temper category.

Unfortunately, archaeologists do not yet possess the necessary micro-provenience data that would allow them to pinpoint actual production centers within districts or to analyze the actual organization of production, i.e., the division of labor and resources among individuals or groups within these communities (Rice 1984). The limited production and widespread trade of the early glazes do, however, appear to represent a shift in the basic mode of ceramic production in the northern Rio Grande from the level of "household production," largely for local domestic consumption, to that of a "household industry," with pottery being produced as a commodity specifically for trade (Rice 1987:184).

Despite the widespread popularity of glaze ware ceramics, local black-on-white types continued to be produced in several areas in the northern Rio Grande. In general, these Classic period black-on-white ceramics were produced for local consumption and were not traded extensively beyond their home districts. The biscuit wares produced after A.D. 1370 in the Española-Chama district, however, are a notable exception to this general pattern. Both Abiquiú and Bandelier Black-on-white reflect a level of standardization and efficiency of production and design that is generally associated with more specialized modes of production (Hagstrum 1985; Kidder and Shepard 1936; Snow 1976:B177). There also appears to have been a trend toward community specialization in the biscuit ware area, similar to that suggested for the glaze wares. Biscuit wares were also traded widely throughout the northern Rio Grande, although in not nearly as great a quantity as the contemporaneous glaze wares (e.g., Kidder and Amsden 1931).

Regional ceramic trade was part of a broader network of social and economic interaction that linked the various districts of the northern Rio Grande Valley during the late fourteenth century. This new regional system probably emerged in response to the increasing fragmentation of the cultural landscape during the first half of the century. The development of this regional network would have stabilized intergroup relations and reduced competition and conflict by ameliorating the negative effects that decreasing seasonal mobility and increasing territoriality had on the subsistence base of local communities. In particular, the ceremonial network and reciprocal social obligations that sustained these economic transactions would have helped to forge important interdependent links among individuals, communities, and ethnic groups. In times of crop failure, food shortage, or other local crisis, these networks would have provided an established structural context through which communities and individuals could have gained access to the more abundant resources of other districts (Ford 1972; Snow 1981).

The stability and interdependence of such nonhierarchical alliances are often sustained through a process of complementarity and reciprocity (Barth 1969; Braun and Plog 1982; Sahlins 1968). In particular, the exchange of localized resources is typically a central feature of such interactions. If resources are fairly homogeneous throughout a given region, then complementarity may be established through role differentiation and the subsequent exchange of specialized goods and services.

Archaeological evidence for the emergence of such a complementary network of regional integration and economic interdependence is reflected in the widespread distribution of locally circumscribed raw materials and exotic goods obtained in trade with groups living outside the northern Rio Grande. Historical, ethnographic, and archaeological evidence suggest that some districts also may have specialized in the production of certain craft items, such as basketry, textiles, leather goods, or pottery (Snow 1981; Wilcox 1984). The restricted production and widespread distribution recorded for the early Rio Grande glazes probably signal the development of such a system of regional integration during the late fourteenth century.

This regional system of production and exchange can be thought of as a form of craft specialization in the sense that it involved regulation of the manufacture, distribution, and use of some material by a particular group within a society via certain socially instituted mechanisms (Rice 1984). This type of specialization was defined by two general processes of intensification. First, in the process of community specialization (Rice 1991), as noted above, each district focused on the exploitation or production of specific raw materials or craft items. This process would have fostered a sense of complementarity and interdependence among diverse communities. Second, in the process of commodification, materials that had previously been produced primarily for local domestic consumption were produced in increasingly large quantities specifically for trade between communities. *Commodities* are defined here as "objects of value," with value being constituted within specific social and economic interactions (Appadurai 1986). Both of these processes are interrelated and appear to have occurred simultaneously in the northern Rio Grande around the middle of the fourteenth century.

Similar large-scale regional networks in the Southwest have been interpreted as being controlled by the village leadership or a specific group of elite individuals (e.g., Lightfoot 1984; Upham 1982). Such a model does not fit the data from the northern Rio Grande for several reasons. Most of the materials exchanged between districts were relatively utilitarian craft products and raw materials whose distribution does not appear to have been limited to any particular segment of society. Also, there is no archaeological evidence at Arroyo Hondo, or at the other large early Classic period pueblos in the northern Rio Grande, of wealth accumulation, architectural differentiation, or the other status differences one would generally associate with the control of valuable commodities within a ranked or stratified society. Furthermore, no evidence of centralized workshops or storage facilities have been identified from any of these sites.

Craft production, although increasingly commoditized, appears to have remained largely a household industry under the control of individual artisans and their families. The continuing control of the basic means of production by independent family units within an economic system characterized by increasing complementarity and interdependence on a regional scale is a diagnostic feature of tribal systems of social integration (Habicht-Mauche et al. 1987; Sahlins 1968; Service 1971).

Conclusions

The fourteenth century was marked by fundamental changes in the structure and scale of northern Rio Grande society. The early Classic period was characterized by a dramatic rise in local population, settlement aggregation into large clustered villages, increasing differentiation of local, competing ethnic groups, and finally, the emergence of a regional tribal system of social and economic integration. These fundamental transformations in the cultural landscape of the northern Rio Grande region can be traced in the changing patterns of ceramic manufacture and trade, as recorded at large Classic period sites, such as Arroyo Hondo.

Toward the end of the fourteenth century, the earlier pattern of ceramic distribution in the northern Rio Grande, characterized by widespread production and local exchange, was replaced by one characterized by a few specialized production centers and trade over increasingly large distances. The role of decorated pottery shifted from that of a domestic craft produced largely for local consumption to that of a specialized economic commodity. The proliferation of local ceramic styles that marked the emergence of competing ethnic groups during the early fourteenth century was superseded by the end of the century, when a uniform ceramic style developed. The distribution of this style signaled the incorporation of these groups into a highly integrated economic system that formed the basis of a regional tribal alliance.

Acknowledgments

The research presented in this paper was generously sponsored by the School of American Research in Santa Fe. I would especially like to thank Dr. Douglas Schwartz, the school's president, for his personal support and encouragement. My lab assistants, Tony Thibodeau and Cary Virtue, also made important contributions to the completion of this project. I conducted the petrographic analyses while I was a guest scientist with the Geology and Geochemistry Group at Los Alamos National Laboratory in New Mexico. Dr. Scott Baldridge was extremely helpful in making the arrangements for this affiliation and provided many important insights into the geology of the northern Rio Grande Valley. Dr. Bart Olinger, also of Los Alamos National Laboratory, conducted the XRF analysis. Figures 7.1, 7.2, 7.3, 7.4, 7.6, and 7.11 were drawn by Katrina Lasko and appear by permission of the School of American Research Press in Santa

Fe. The present version of this paper benefited from the insightful comments of Patricia Crown, Melissa Hagstrum, Diane Gifford-Gonzalez, and several anonymous reviewers. I did not always take their advice, but I am grateful for all their thoughtful criticisms and suggestions.

Note

1. $Sr\% = (Sr/[Fe+Zr+Sr]) \times 100; Zr\% = (Zr/[Fe+Zr+Sr]) \times 100$

References Cited

Adams, E. Charles
1991   *The Origins and Development of the Pueblo Katsina Cult.* University of Arizona Press, Tucson.

Anschuetz, Kurt F.
1987   Pueblo III Subsistence, Settlement, and Territoriality in the Northern Rio Grande: The Albuquerque Frontier. In *Secrets of the City: Papers on Albuquerque Area Archaeology,* edited by A. V. Poore and John Montgomery, pp. 148–164. Papers of the Anthropological Society of New Mexico No. 13. Ancient City Press, Santa Fe.

Appadurai, A.
1986   Introduction: Commodities and the Politics of Value. In *The Social Life of Things: Commodities in Cultural Perspective,* edited by A. Appadurai, pp. 3–63. Cambridge University Press, Cambridge.

Barth, Frederick
1969   Introduction. In *Ethnic Groups and Boundaries: The Social Organization of Cultural Difference,* edited by Frederick Barth, pp. 9–38. Little, Brown, and Co., Boston.

Braun, David P., and Stephen Plog
1982   Evolution of "Tribal" Social Networks: Theory and Prehistoric North American Evidence. *American Antiquity* 47(3):504–525.

Cordell, Linda S., Amy C. Earls, and Martha R. Binford
1984   Subsistence Systems in the Mountainous Settings of the Rio Grande Valley. In *Prehistoric Agricultural Strategies in the Southwest,* edited by Suzanne K. Fish and Paul R. Fish, pp. 233–241. Anthropological Research Papers No. 33. Arizona State University, Tempe.

Douglass, Amy A.
1985   The Pottery of Rowe Ruin: A Stylistic Analysis of the Black-on-White Ceramics. Paper presented at the 50th Annual Meeting of the Society for American Archaeology, Denver.

Ford, Richard I.
1972   Barter, Gift, or Violence: An Analysis of Tewa Intertribal Exchange. In
        Social Exchange and Interaction, edited by Edwin N. Wilmsen, pp. 21–45.
        Anthropological Papers No. 46. Museum of Anthropology, University
        of Michigan, Ann Arbor.

Galusha, Ted, and John C. Blick
1971   *Stratigraphy of the Santa Fe Group, New Mexico*. Bulletin of the American
        Museum of Natural History Vol. 144, No. 1. New York.

Guthe, Carl E.
1925   *Pueblo Pottery Making: A Study at the Village of San Ildefonso*. Phillips
        Academy, Andover, and Yale University Press, New Haven.

Habicht-Mauche, Judith A.
1993   *The Pottery from Arroyo Hondo Pueblo, New Mexico: Tribalization and Trade
        in the Northern Rio Grande*. Arroyo Hondo Archaeological Series Vol. 8.
        School of American Research Press, Santa Fe.

Habicht-Mauche, Judith A., John Hoopes, and Michael Geselowitz
1987   Where's the Chief?: The Archaeology of Complex Tribes. Paper pre-
        sented at the 52nd Annual Meeting of the Society for American Ar-
        chaeology, Toronto.

Hagstrum, Melissa B.
1985   Measuring Prehistoric Ceramic Craft Specialization: A Test Case in the
        American Southwest. *Journal of Field Archaeology* 12(1):65–75.

Hunter-Anderson, Rosalind
1979   Explaining Residential Aggregation in the Northern Rio Grande: A
        Competition Reduction Model. In *Archaeological Investigations in Cochiti
        Reservoir, New Mexico*, vol. 4, edited by Jan V. Biella and Richard C.
        Chapman, pp. 169–175. Office of Contract Archeology, University of
        New Mexico, Albuquerque.

Kidder, Alfred V., and Charles A. Amsden
1931   *The Pottery of Pecos: The Dull-Paint Wares*, vol. 1. Papers of the South
        West Expedition No. 5. Phillips Academy, Andover, and Yale Univer-
        sity Press, New Haven.

Kidder, Alfred V., and Anna O. Shepard
1936   *The Pottery of Pecos: The Glaze-Paint, Culinary, and Other Wares*, vol. 2.
        Papers of the South West Expedition No. 7. Phillips Academy, An-
        dover, and Yale University Press, New Haven.

Kohler, Timothy A.
1989   *Bandelier Archaeological Excavation Project: Research Design and Summer
        1988 Sampling*. Reports of Investigations No. 61. Department of An-
        thropology, Washington State University, Pullman.

Lambert, Marjorie F.

1954   *Paa-ko: Archaeological Chronicle of an Indian Village in North Central New Mexico.* School of American Research Monograph No. 19. University of New Mexico Press, Albuquerque.

Lang, Richard W.

1982   Transformation in White Ware Pottery of the Northern Rio Grande. In *Southwestern Ceramics: A Comparative Review,* edited by Albert H. Schroeder, pp. 153–200. The Arizona Archaeologist, vol. 15. Phoenix.

1993   Analysis and Seriation of Stratigraphic Ceramic Samples from Arroyo Hondo Pueblo. In *The Pottery from Arroyo Hondo Pueblo, New Mexico: Tribalization and Trade in the Northern Rio Grande,* by Judith A. Habicht-Mauche, pp. 166–181. Arroyo Hondo Archaeological Series, vol. 8. School of American Research Press, Santa Fe.

Lang, Richard W., and Arthur H. Harris

1984   *The Faunal Remains from Arroyo Hondo Pueblo, New Mexico: A Study in Short-Term Subsistence Change.* Arroyo Hondo Archaeological Series, vol. 5. School of American Research Press, Santa Fe.

Lightfoot, Kent G.

1984   *Prehistoric Political Dynamics: A Case Study from the American Southwest.* Northern Illinois University Press, De Kalb.

Mera, Harry P.

1934   *A Survey of the Biscuit Ware Area in Northern New Mexico.* Technical Series Bulletin No. 6. Laboratory of Anthropology, Santa Fe.

1935   *Ceramic Clues to the Prehistory of North Central New Mexico.* Technical Series Bulletin No. 8. Laboratory of Anthropology, Santa Fe.

1940   *Population Changes in the Rio Grande Glaze-Paint Area.* Technical Series Bulletin No. 11. Laboratory of Anthropology, Santa Fe.

Olinger, Bart

1987a   Pottery Studies Using X-Ray Fluorescence. Part 1: An Introduction, Nambe Pueblo as an Example. *Pottery Southwest* 14(1):1–5.

1987b   Pottery Studies Using X-Ray Fluorescence. Part 2: Evidence for Prehistoric Reoccupation of the Pajarito Plateau. *Pottery Southwest* 14(2):2–5.

1993   Appendix C. Summary of X-Ray Fluorescence Analysis. In *The Pottery from Arroyo Hondo Pueblo, New Mexico: Tribalization and Trade in the Northern Rio Grande,* by Judith A. Habicht-Mauche, pp. 157–163. Arroyo Hondo Archaeological Series Vol. 8. School of American Research Press, Santa Fe.

Peckham, Stewart

1984   The Anasazi Culture of the Northern Rio Grande Rift. In *Rio Grande Rift: Northern New Mexico,* edited by W. S. Baldridge, P. W. Dickerson,

R. E. Riecker, and J. Zidek, pp. 275–281. Guidebook, 35th Field Conference. New Mexico Geological Society.

Rice, Prudence M.

1984   The Archaeological Study of Specialized Pottery Production: Some Aspects of Method and Theory. In *Pots and Potters: Current Approaches in Ceramic Archaeology*, edited by Prudence M. Rice, pp. 45–54. UCLA Institute of Archaeology Monograph No. 24. University of California, Los Angeles.

1987   *Pottery Analysis: A Sourcebook*. University of Chicago Press, Chicago.

1991   Specialization, Standardization, and Diversity: A Retrospective. In *The Ceramic Legacy of Anna O. Shepard*, edited by Ronald L. Bishop and Frederick W. Lange, pp. 257–279. University Press of Colorado, Niwot.

Rose, Martin R., Jeffrey S. Dean, and William J. Robinson

1981   *The Past Climate of Arroyo Hondo, New Mexico, Reconstructed from Tree Rings*. Arroyo Hondo Archaeological Series Vol. 4. School of American Research Press, Santa Fe.

Sahlins, Marshall D.

1968   *Tribesmen*. Prentice-Hall, Englewood Cliffs, New Jersey.

Schaafsma, Polly

1990   War Imagery and Magic: Petroglyphs at Comanche Gap, Galisteo Basin, New Mexico. Paper presented at the 55th Annual Meeting of the Society for American Archaeology, Las Vegas.

Schwartz, Douglas W.

1986   Foreword. In *Food, Diet, and Population at Prehistoric Arroyo Hondo Pueblo, New Mexico*, by W. Wetterstrom. Arroyo Hondo Archaeological Series Vol. 6. School of American Research Press, Santa Fe.

Schwartz, Douglas W., and Richard W. Lang

1973   *Archaeological Investigations at the Arroyo Hondo Site: Third Field Report— 1972*. School of American Research Press, Santa Fe.

Service, Elman R.

1971   *Primitive Social Organization*. 2nd ed. Random House, New York.

Shepard, Anna O.

1942   *Rio Grande Glaze Paint Ware: A Study Illustrating the Place of Ceramic Technological Analysis in Archaeological Research*. Carnegie Institution of Washington Publication No. 528. Washington, D.C.

Snow, David H.

1976   Summary. In *The Ceramics and Mineral Resources of LA 70 and the Cochiti Area*, by A. H. Warren. In *Archaeological Excavations at Pueblo del Encierro, LA 70, Cochiti Dam Salvage Project, Cochiti, New Mexico, Final*

Report: 1964–1965 Field Seasons, section B, edited by David H. Snow. Laboratory of Anthropology Notes No. 78. Museum of New Mexico, Santa Fe.

1981   Protohistoric Rio Grande Economics: A Review of Trends. In *The Proto-historic Period in the North American Southwest, A.D. 1450–1700,* edited by David R. Wilcox and W. Bruce Masse, pp. 354–377. Research Papers No. 24. Arizona State University, Tempe.

Spiegal, Zane, and Brewster Baldwin

1963   *Geology and Water Resources of the Santa Fe Area, New Mexico.* U.S. Geological Survey Water-Supply Paper No. 1525. U.S. Government Printing Office, Washington, D.C.

Stone, Glenn D., Robert McC. Netting, and M. Priscilla Stone

1990   Seasonality, Labor Scheduling, and Agricultural Intensification in the Nigerian Savanna. *American Anthropologist* 92(1):7–23.

Stubbs, Stanley A., and W. S. Stallings, Jr.

1953   *The Excavation of Pindi Pueblo, New Mexico.* Monographs of the School of American Research No. 18. Santa Fe.

Sundt, William M.

1987   Pottery of Central New Mexico and Its Role as Key to Both Time and Space. In *Secrets of a City: Papers on Albuquerque Area Archaeology,* edited by A. V. Poore and John Montgomery, pp.116–147. Papers of the Archaeological Society of New Mexico No. 13. Ancient City Press, Santa Fe.

Upham, Steadman

1982   *Polities and Power: An Economic and Political History of the Western Pueblo.* Academic Press, New York.

Warren, A. Helene

1969   Tonque: One Pueblo's Glaze Pottery Industry Dominated Middle Rio Grande Commerce. *El Palacio* 76(2):36–42.

1970   Notes on the Manufacture and Trade of Rio Grande Glazes. *The Artifact* 8(4):1–7.

1976   The Ceramics and Mineral Resources of LA70 and the Cochiti Area. In *Archaeological Excavations at Pueblo del Encierro, LA 70, Cochiti Dam Salvage Project, Cochiti, New Mexico, Final Report: 1964–1965 Field Seasons,* section B, edited by David H. Snow. Laboratory of Anthropology Notes No. 78. Museum of New Mexico, Santa Fe.

1979   The Glaze Paint Wares of the Upper Middle Rio Grande. In *Archaeological Investigations in Cochiti Reservoir, New Mexico,* vol. 4, edited by Jan V. Biella and Richard C. Chapman. Office of Contract Archaeology, Department of Anthropology, University of New Mexico, Albuquerque.

1981   A Petrographic Study of the Pottery. In *Contributions to Gran Quivira Archaeology*, edited by Alden C. Hayes. Publications in Archaeology No. 17. National Park Service, Washington, D.C.

Wendorf, Fred, and Erik K. Reed
1955   An Alternative Reconstruction of Northern Rio Grande Prehistory. *El Palacio* 62(5–6):131–173.

Wilcox, David R.
1981   Changing Perspectives on the Protohistoric Pueblos, A.D. 1450–1700. In *The Protohistoric Period in the North American Southwest, A.D. 1450–1700*, edited by David R. Wilcox and W. Bruce Masse, pp. 378–409. Anthropological Research Papers No. 24. Arizona State University, Tempe.

1984   Multi-Ethnic Division of Labor in the Protohistoric Southwest. In *Collected Papers in Honor of Harry L. Haddock*, edited by Nancy L. Fox, pp. 141–154. Papers of the Archaeological Society of New Mexico No. 9. Ancient City Press, Santa Fe.

8

The Organization of Protohistoric Zuni Ceramic Production

Barbara J. Mills

In this chapter, I summarize previous interpretations of late prehistoric and early historical Zuni socio-economic organization, and I test these with variables of ceramic production. I use compositional and morphological data collected from the two decorated wares of the Proto-historic period at Zuni—Matsaki Buff Ware and Zuni Glaze Ware—to track changes in the organization of ceramic production across the period of initial European contact. The results of these analyses indicate the presence of changes between the pre- and post-Contact decorated assemblages. These changes, however, are not in the direction one would expect, given previous models for protohistoric Zuni economic organization. Instead, European impact on the organization of Zuni ceramic production appears to have resulted in little change in spatial, morphological, and technological variation during the period of initial contact in the sixteenth century. This changed in the seventeenth century when one ware, Zuni Glaze Ware, was produced under more restricted conditions that may represent a shift toward greater specialization in production. Both compositional and morphological data contribute to the understanding of the organization of production, but with varying results.

Protohistoric Zuni Settlement and Economic Organization

The Zuni region of west-central New Mexico and east-central Arizona has an archaeological sequence extending from ca. 6000 B.C. to the present. As in other areas of the Colorado Plateau, settlement patterns in the Zuni area underwent considerable change through time, from small, dispersed sites to larger, aggregated settlements during the late prehistoric period. This transition took place in the mid-A.D. 1200s in the Zuni area (Ferguson and Hart 1985; Ferguson and Mills 1982; Kintigh 1985; LeBlanc 1989; Watson et al. 1980; Woodbury 1956, 1979). From A.D. 1275 to 1450, several large sites were occupied, some of which had hundreds of rooms. Although large, each of these late prehistoric pueblos was probably occupied for only about 50 years (Kintigh 1985).

During the mid-fifteenth century, a new pattern of settlement stability emerged: durations of site occupation were at least twice as long as in previous periods (Kintigh 1990). This stable residential pattern continued throughout the Protohistoric period—the fifteenth through the seventeenth centuries—a period that includes initial European contact with the pueblos of the Southwest.

Nine Zuni villages are known to have been occupied between the mid-fifteenth and mid-seventeenth centuries (Kintigh 1990). When the first Europeans entered the Southwest in the mid-sixteenth century, searching for the fabled "Cities of Cibola," they reported six occupied villages. The work of several historians have resulted in the concordance of these names with their modern Zuni equivalents: Hawikku,[1] Kechiba:wa, Kwa'kin'a, Halona:wa (present-day Zuni Pueblo), Mats'a:kya, and Kyaki:ma (Bandelier 1892; Ferguson 1981; Hodge 1926, 1937). Another site, Binna:wa, was apparently abandoned in the early sixteenth century, just before the first Europeans entered the area. In addition, at least two other sites, Chalo:wa and Ah:kya:ya, are thought to have been occupied during the sixteenth century, based on recently collected archaeological evidence (Anyon 1992; Kintigh 1990). All nine sites were abandoned for habitation purposes by the Pueblo Revolt of 1680, when most of the tribe retreated to the top of Dowa Yallanne—a major consolidation into one village that has continued to the present time.

One of the most salient features of the sites of the Protohistoric period is their segregated spatial distribution (fig. 8.1). There is an eastern cluster of five sites around and south of present-day Zuni Pueblo and a western

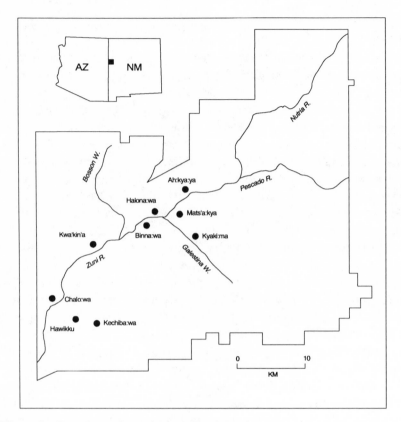

Figure 8.1 Locations of protohistoric Zuni sites.

cluster of three sites in the southwestern corner of the Zuni Indian Reservation. The four largest sites (Mats'a:kya, Hawikku, Kyaki:ma, and Kechiba:wa) are equally divided between the two clusters. Only one relatively small site, Kwa'kin'a, is located in the 20 km separating the two clusters. The spatial pattern is at least partially conditioned by the presence of permanent water; the Zuni River currently runs underground in the area between the two clusters during most of the year.

Considerable controversy surrounds the interpretation of the level of socio-economic complexity in protohistoric Puebloan society, including the Zuni area. Two major views persist. Some researchers see few differences between ethnographic descriptions of relatively egalitarian nineteenth- and twentieth-century Zuni society and the existing archaeological and ethnohistoric data on fifteenth- through seventeenth-century Zuni society. According to this view, protohistoric Zuni social structure was unstratified, authority was uncentralized, population was in the few thousands, and the scale of production was relatively simple and unspecialized (e.g., Riley 1987).

Other researchers have suggested that the organization of protohistoric Zuni society was very different from that of the nineteenth and twentieth centuries. According to this view, the pre-Contact western pueblos (including Zuni) were socially stratified, had a centralized political structure, and were governed by an elite that controlled the production and distribution of certain goods (Upham 1982:32). Demographic changes produced by the introduction of European diseases are seen as a major factor in the change to the more egalitarian social structures documented by anthropologists in the nineteenth and twentieth centuries.

Although there is little doubt that Europeans brought infectious diseases to the New World, the absolute effects for populations in the Southwest are not well known. The effects have been interpreted as "catastrophic" for eastern North American populations (Ramenofsky 1987:173) and "drastic, extensive, and fundamental" for the Rio Grande pueblos (Lycett 1989:119). Direct evidence from Zuni itself is lacking because of continuous occupation at the Contact period sites. However, based on a combination of ethnohistoric and archaeological data, Kintigh (1990:270–271) suggested that there was a period of post-Contact depopulation, but that it was probably not as extensive as Upham's (1982) reconstruction.

A major stumbling block to the resolution of this controversy is the dearth of new research on Protohistoric period sites in the Zuni area. One observer, speaking of the entire Southwest, has commented that the currently available data on the Protohistoric period are elusive enough to support opposing interpretations with the same evidence (Doelle 1990:227). This observation is as valid for the Zuni area as it is for any other area of the Southwest. It is clear that if the controversy about protohistoric Zuni is to be resolved, new questions must be asked of new data.

One question that has not yet been addressed with new data is the economic organization of protohistoric Zuni society. Because the production, use, and distribution of goods form an important part of many arguments about the nature of protohistoric society, an in-depth study of Zuni economic organization is warranted. Here, I focus on one aspect of economic organization—ceramic production. I contrast differences between pre- and post-Contact ceramic assemblages to address questions about the social context of production.

Standardization and Specialization

The methods used to measure change in economic organization are based upon linkages between the organization of production and the measurement of variability in ceramic assemblages. I particularly draw upon ideas about linking increases in standardization of ceramic vessels with the interpretation of changes in productive specialization. Specialization is defined here as differences in production along a continuum of the producer-consumer ratio rather than as modes of full- vs. part-time producers. *Specialization* in ceramic production is itself not directly measured but is inferred from other attributes that can be directly measured.

Two of the most frequently cited indicators of ceramic specialization are standardization (or reduction in diversity) in the selection and preparation of ceramic raw materials and standardization in the finished products (e.g., Costin 1991; Costin and Hagstrum 1995; Hagstrum 1985; Longacre et al. 1988; Rice 1981, 1991; Sinopoli 1988; Stein and Blackman 1993; see also Stark, this volume). Ethnoarchaeological research tends to support the linkage between specialization and standardization, but researchers have offered important caveats. First, Rice (1991) pointed out that there is no decontextualized measure of standardization. It is a relative concept that can only be defined by comparison of cases. Second, Longacre et al. (1988) recognized that similar functional classes should be analyzed to control for differences in standardization across shape and size classes. Third, Stark (this volume) has pointed out that the underlying variable of changes in standardization is the ratio of producers to consumers; any change in the relative number of producers to consumers will produce changes in measures of standardization.

With these caveats in mind, I use the concept of standardization as a bridge between the analysis of ceramic artifacts and interpretations about the relative degree of productive specialization. I define *standardization* as a reduction in variation, which can be identified through greater homogeneity in the materials used or in morphological attributes of the finished products. In this chapter, the concept of standardization is applied to pre- and post-Contact Zuni ceramic assemblages. I address the first of the above problems by using temporal variation to compare relative standardization in ceramic production. I address the second problem by controlling for functional classes on the basis of attributes of vessel form. I have not controlled for the third problem, known as the "ratio effect" (Stark, this volume), in the analysis. This effect is, in fact, the independent variable of interest for measuring the organization of production: the ratio of producers to consumers.

The Database

Archaeological excavations have been conducted at only three of the nine Zuni sites occupied between A.D. 1450 and 1680: Hawikku, Kechiba:wa, and Halona:wa. Because of the depth of more recent historical deposits at the latter site (Ferguson and Mills 1982; Spier 1917), the character of the pre-Revolt occupation is unknown. The results of excavations at Kechiba:wa, conducted between 1919 and 1923 by Cambridge University, were only preliminarily reported (Bushnell 1955; Hodge 1920a, 1924a). Excavations at the site of Hawikku, conducted by Frederick Webb Hodge between 1917 and 1923, are better documented than the work at Kechiba:wa (Hodge 1918a, 1918b, 1920b, 1921a, 1921b, 1922, 1924b, 1924c, 1939, 1952; Smith et al. 1966). Thus, nearly all excavation data from protohistoric Zuni sites are from the western cluster alone.

In this chapter, I combined data collected from the analysis of surface, subsurface, and geologic samples. Ceramics were collected from surface proveniences at all protohistoric Zuni sites except for Halona:wa and Ah:kya:ya. The subsurface collection used in this study includes all whole, decorated vessels excavated from the site of Hawikku by Frederick Webb Hodge (curated by the National Museum of the American Indian) and those excavated from the site of Kechiba:wa by Louis Clarke (curated by Cambridge University). Geologic samples were collected from clay-bearing formations in the western portion of the Zuni Indian Reservation surrounding each protohistoric site.

Chronological Control

Relative chronological control of protohistoric Zuni ceramics is possible through the use of formal and stylistic attributes of the two major painted wares produced at Zuni during the fifteenth through seven-

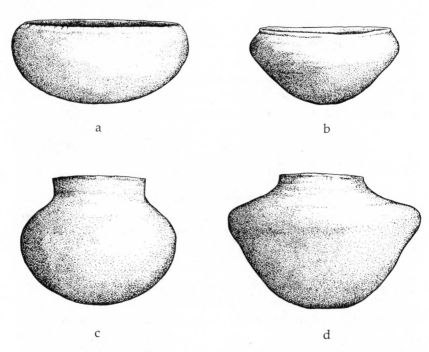

Figure 8.2 Major form classes for protohistoric Zuni ceramics: (a) hemispherical bowl, (b) shouldered bowl, (c) globular jar, and (d) shouldered jar.

teenth centuries: Zuni Glaze Ware and Matsaki Buff Ware. Based on Hodge's initial work at Hawikku and Richard and Nathalie Woodbury's synthesis (Woodbury and Woodbury 1966), early and late types of glaze ware may be differentiated by paint, slip, vessel form, and field of decoration. Application of the chronological classification of glaze ware vessel forms and decorative fields to buff ware vessels allows a similar division of the buff ware into early and late vessels.

Early Zuni Glaze Ware types are largely white-slipped (Pinnawa Glaze-on-white, Pinnawa Red-on-white[2], and Kechipauan Polychrome), whereas late Zuni Glaze Ware vessels are slipped red, or red and white (Hawikuh Black-on-red and Hawikuh Polychrome). Hodge was the first to recognize a temporal gap in the production of early and late glaze ware ceramics from the Zuni area. His stratigraphic and burial assemblage data both support a period during which no glaze ware types were made, followed by a revival of glaze ware production in the historical period. Hodge's burial data further suggest that the late Zuni Glaze Ware types of Hawikuh Black-on-red and Hawikuh Polychrome were strongly associated with objects of European manufacture; the types were probably made after the missionization of Zuni in 1629 (Hodge 1966:148). The absence of glaze-painted ceramics and Matsaki Buff Ware at sites dating to the Pueblo Revolt supports an end date of 1680 for both technological traditions (Woodbury and Woodbury 1966).

Vessel form is a reliable attribute for separating early from late glaze ware ceramics in the Zuni area. Early Zuni Glaze Ware bowls are hemispherical (fig. 8.2a), whereas late Zuni Glaze Ware bowls are shouldered (fig. 8.2b). Early glaze ware jars are globular and have cylindrical necks (fig. 8.2c). Late glaze ware jars are strongly shouldered (fig. 8.2d). The association of early and late Zuni Glaze Ware types with vessel form is very strong (tables 8.1 and 8.2), allowing one to use either paint and slip combinations or vessel form to identify chronologically significant differences within the glaze-painted whole-vessel assemblage.

Morphological changes between early and late Zuni Glaze Ware vessels are paralleled by changes in the design structure. The focus of decoration on early bowls is the vessel interior, whereas later bowls also include an exterior band. Early, globular jars are typically only decorated around the maximum diameter, whereas later, strongly shouldered jars have a design field that extends to the rim itself. Additional confirmation of the temporal significance of these differences is present in certain design elements. For example, the roman cross is only present on shouldered jars, suggesting a post-1540 date for these vessels.

The other major painted ware produced at Zuni during the Protohistoric period is Matsaki Buff Ware. In fact, Matsaki Buff Ware was pro-

Table 8.1 Relationship Between Early and Late Glaze
Wares and Bowl Form

Ware	Hemispherical Bowl	Shouldered Bowl	Total
Early glaze	61	5	66
Late glaze	7	118	125
Total	68	123	191

Fisher's exact test prob < 0.0001; phi $= 0.862$

Table 8.2 Relationship Between Early and Late Glaze
Wares and Jar Form

Ware	Globular Jar	Shouldered Jar	Total
Early glaze	31	3	34
Late glaze	1	67	68
Total	32	70	102

Fisher's exact test prob $<$ 0.001; phi $=$ 0.911

duced in greater quantities than the glaze wares, as evidenced by its high
proportion in surface (Kintigh 1985) and subsurface assemblages (Smith
et al. 1966). The same changes in vessel forms, fields of decoration, and
use of design attributes found on glaze ware vessels are present on Matsaki Buff Ware vessels, supporting a similar ability to divide vessels into
early and late periods. Previous evidence supported continuous manufacture of Matsaki Buff Ware throughout the entire Protohistoric period
(Kintigh 1985; Woodbury and Woodbury 1966). Current evidence suggests that the change in vessel forms took place sometime in the sixteenth
century.

Standardization in Raw Material Procurement

I assessed standardization in raw material procurement by looking at the
variety of clay sources exploited. Forty-eight clay samples collected from
the area of protohistoric Zuni settlement provided data for evaluating
changes in raw material procurement (fig. 8.3; several samples that were
taken close together are indicated as one sample location). Fortunately,
geologic diversity is high in the Zuni area. Folding, faulting, uplift, and
erosion have created elevational changes from northeast to southwest
that provide a relatively patterned distribution of exposed surface deposits (fig. 8.4; Ferguson and Hart 1985; U.S. Bureau of Indian Affairs
1981). Besides alluvial deposits, two formations contain most of the clay
resources in the area of protohistoric settlement: the Cretaceous Dakota
Sandstone and the Triassic Chinle Formation. I heavily sampled both of

these formations to understand inter- and intra-source compositional variation.

The distribution of protohistoric sites relative to the Chinle Formation indicates that potters at all sites would have had access to Chinle clays (fig. 8.5). On the other hand, the Dakota Sandstone would have been much more accessible to potters who resided within the eastern cluster of sites. Potters from the western cluster would have had to travel 12 km to reach the closest outcrop of the Dakota Sandstone. Based on Arnold's cross-cultural analyses, which showed that potters rarely travel even 7 or 8 km to obtain clays (Arnold 1985), it seems unlikely that potters in the western cluster used Dakota Sandstone clays.

The compositions of the Dakota and Chinle clays are mineralogically distinct. X-ray diffraction results indicate that the Chinle clays tend to contain higher proportions of smectites, whereas the Dakota Sandstone

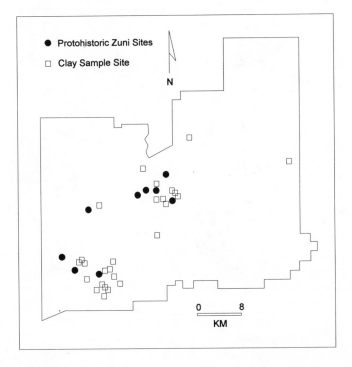

Figure 8.3 Distribution of clay samples relative to locations of protohistoric sites.

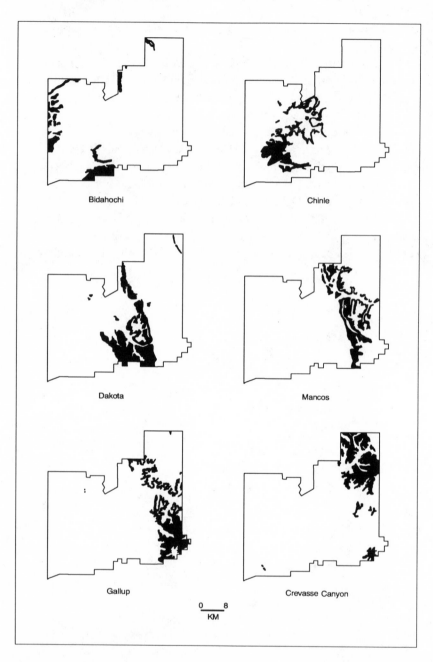

Figure 8.4 Major clay-bearing geologic formations on the Zuni Indian Reservation.

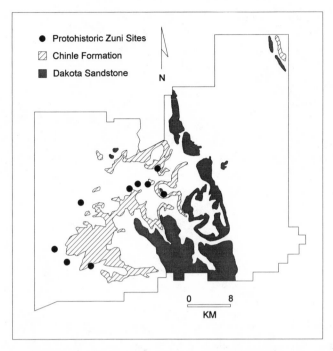

Figure 8.5 Distribution of Chinle Formation and Dakota Sandstone relative to locations of protohistoric sites.

samples are proportionally higher in kaolinitic clays (Parnell 1990; Roderick Parnell, personal communication 1991). Because these mineralogical differences disappear upon firing at temperatures above 500°C to 600°C, further analyses were needed to identify differences in raw material sources in fired ceramics.

Chemical analyses of clay samples from the Zuni area were conducted in collaboration with Frank Walker of the Department of Chemistry, Northern Arizona University. The samples came from two formations, the Chinle and Dakota. The Chinle Formation was subdivided into two groups: the first was from an exposure of the Rock Point Member just north of present-day Zuni Pueblo; the second was from an area near Ojo Caliente Springs that appears to be a spring-related redeposition of Chinle-derived clays. From each of these three deposits, nine samples were analyzed. I chose the nine samples, which came from horizontally and vertically adjacent areas, to determine the amount of within-source variation.

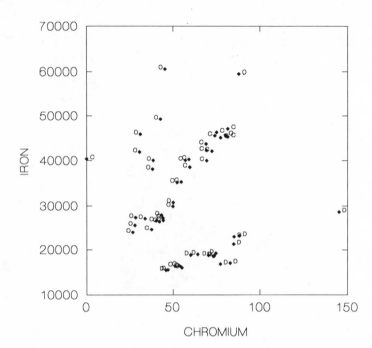

Figure 8.6 Plot of concentrations of chromium and iron for clay samples based on atomic absorption data.

Two different techniques of chemical characterization were used on the clay samples: flame atomic absorption spectroscopy (FAAS) and graphite furnace atomic absorption spectroscopy (GFAAS). Walker (1992) presented a more detailed discussion of the analytic techniques and standards. Two separate analysis runs were conducted on each of 27 samples to ensure accuracy of the results. The results of statistical analyses of the atomic absorption data indicated that the four elements of manganese, chromium, cobalt, and iron could be used to discriminate samples from the three major deposits at the 99-percent confidence level (Walker 1992:fig. 4). Iron is one of the most important discriminating elements among the Dakota and the two different Chinle sources, as shown in a plot of samples using iron and chromium analyses (fig. 8.6; both analyses conducted on each sample are plotted). The Dakota Sandstone clays are very low in iron, whereas the Chinle clays from both sources are generally higher in iron. All but one sample of the redeposited Chinle clays (indicated with an *O* in fig. 8.6) are lower in chromium than the nonrede-posited Chinle clays (indicated with a *C* in fig. 8.6).

Because iron is such a strong discriminator of clays from the Dakota Sandstone and the Chinle Formation, clay oxidation analysis on a larger sample size can be used to find general trends in the iron content of raw clays and fired pottery; iron is measurable both by chemical analysis and by visual differences in fired colors. Both the raw clays and the sherd samples were fired to a constant temperature of 1,000°C, which effectively eliminated the influence of differences in firing conditions on the paste color of sherds (Rice 1987; Shepard 1939, 1953).

The fired colors of raw clays of different members of the Chinle Formation provide excellent contrast with raw clays of the Dakota Sandstone. Table 8.3 uses a method of grouping the Munsell color designations into analytic groups for source discrimination (Mills 1987; Toll et al. 1980; Windes 1977); the Dakota Sandstone is shown in the center column of the table (labeled "Kd"). Clays of this formation can be clearly distinguished from the Chinle Formation clays, as well as from the smaller number of samples of alluvial clays in the Zuni River Valley. The Dakota Sandstone is the only source of clays that oxidize to white or buff color groups. In addition, only two samples from the Dakota Sandstone fired yellowish red or red. By contrast, most of the Chinle Formation clays fired red and, to a lesser extent, yellowish red.

I applied these general color trends of raw clays to sherd samples to evaluate differences between and within wares in raw material selection (table 8.4). Differences between Matsaki Buff Ware (first column) and the Zuni Glaze Ware types (second and third columns) clearly indicate that the glaze ware types are made from fewer sources than the buff ware. Differences between the early and late glazes are minimal, suggesting that the same restriction in clay selection was present during both time periods. To test the hypothesis that glaze ware vessels were produced from a more restricted range of raw material sources, I analyzed 46 early and late Zuni Glaze Ware sherds for the four elements of iron, chromium, cobalt, and manganese using the same GFAAS and FAAS methods I used for the raw clays. Walker's (1992) discriminant function analysis resulted in all but one of the 45 glaze ware sherds being assigned to the Dakota Sandstone group of clays.

I draw three conclusions from the analyses of raw materials and their selection for different wares. First, the differences among the raw clays

Table 8.3 Frequencies of Oxidized Color Groups by Geologic Formation for Zuni-Area Clays

Color Group[a]	Formation[b]					Total
	Ŧcp	Ŧcr	Ŧcs	Kd	Qal	
White	0	0	0	4	0	4
Buff (1, 2)	0	0	0	1	0	1
Buff (3)	0	0	0	3	0	3
Yellow-red (4)	2	0	0	1	0	3
Yellow-red (5)	2	0	2	0	0	4
Red (6)	17	11	1	1	2	32
Total	21	11	3	10	2	47

[a]Color groups follow those published by Windes (1977), Toll et al. (1980), and Mills (1987).

[b]Symbols for geologic formations are as follows: Ŧcp = Triassic Chinle Formation, Petrified Forest Member; Ŧcr = Triassic Chinle Formation, Rock Point Member; Ŧcs = Triassic Chinle Formation, unidenfied spring-related redeposition; Kd = Cretaceous Dakota Sandstone; Qal = Quarternary alluvium.

are strong enough to be detected through chemical and mineralogical methods. Because iron is such a strong discriminating element, even clay oxidation analysis may be used with a relatively high degree of confidence. Second, there appears to have been more variability between glaze ware samples and Matsaki Buff Ware samples than between early and late Zuni Glaze Ware samples, suggesting that although the selection of resources changed, this pattern is not monotonic. At least in terms of the dimension of spatial concentration of production, early and late Zuni Glaze Ware types were produced under more "specialized" (i.e., more restricted) conditions than Matsaki Buff Ware. Third, if glaze ware production had been spatially restricted, it was more likely made in the eastern cluster than in the western cluster because of the proximity of the Dakota Sandstone buff-firing clays to the eastern end of the protohistoric Zuni settlement distribution. It is ironic, but possible, that the two late glaze ware types of Hawikuh Black-on-red and Hawikuh Polychrome were not made at the site of Hawikku, which is part of the western settlement cluster.

Standardization in Whole Vessel Sizes

The second method of looking at standardization is through the analysis of whole vessel metric data. I examined all whole vessels excavated from the sites of Hawikku and Kechiba:wa in the collections of the National Museum of the American Indian (Smithsonian Institution) and the Cambridge University Museum of Archaeology and Anthropology. I recorded metric and nonmetric data on Matsaki Buff Ware and Zuni Glaze Ware vessels, which represent most of the decorated assemblages recovered from these two sites. The analyses of metric standardization rely on the variables of rim diameter and height, which are exterior vessel measurements (to the nearest 0.1 cm).

The relative measure of standardization used in this analysis is the coefficient of variation (the standard deviation divided by the mean). The coefficient of variation is a commonly used statistic to describe the dispersion of values around a particular location (such as the mean) when one cannot assume that the means of two or more samples are the same. Summary statistics for bowl and jar forms were broken down by early and late shape classes and by ware (table 8.5).

I also analyzed metric data on the Zuni whole vessels to check for the presence of modality that could indicate subclasses in vessel size. I

Table 8.4 Color Groups of Matsaki Buff Ware and Glaze Polychromes

	Ware			
Color Group	Buff	Early Glaze	Late Glaze	Total
Buff (1, 2)	29	13	27	69
Buff (3)	63	12	23	98
Yellow-red (4)	16	1	2	19
Yellow-red (5)	74	2	8	84
Red (6)	28	2	2	32
Red (7)	21	1	0	22
Total	231	31	62	324

NOTE: Several cells have fewer than five cases. Pearson chi-square $= 55.655$; $d = 10$; $p < 0.001$; phi $= 0.414$.

Table 8.5 Summary Statistics for Protohistoric Zuni Vessel Classes

Vessel Class & Variable	N	Mean	S.D.	C.V.
Buff ware hemispherical bowls				
Rim diameter	149	22.50	5.16	22.9
Height	143	10.43	2.70	25.5
Early glaze ware hemispherical bowls				
Rim diameter	57	20.40	4.07	20.0
Height	56	9.55	2.15	22.5
Buff ware shouldered bowls				
Rim diameter	290	23.26	4.82	20.7
Height	282	11.87	3.20	26.9
Late glaze ware shouldered bowls				
Rim diameter	115	24.93	5.69	22.8
Height	111	12.61	3.42	27.1
Early buff ware globular jars				
Rim diameter	76	13.64	1.96	14.3
Height	71	16.52	3.63	22.0
Early glaze ware globular jars				
Rim diameter	31	14.79	2.44	16.5
Height	25	20.41	3.63	17.8
Late buff ware shouldered jars				
Rim diameter	151	14.87	2.63	17.7
Height	132	19.40	4.68	24.1
Late glaze ware shouldered jars				
Rim diameter	66	15.48	1.06	6.9
Height	51	21.75	2.39	11.0

generated plots of vessel height by rim diameters and individual variable histograms for the four general form classes of hemispherical bowls, shouldered bowls, globular jars, and shouldered jars (figs. 8.7 through 8.10). Of the four general form classes, only shouldered bowls (fig. 8.8) and globular jars (fig. 8.9) have well-defined modes. Ideally, volume would be the best measure of size. In the absence of volumetric data, rim diameter and height are the most highly correlated single dimensions for determining vessel size of bowls and jars, respectively (Mills 1989). Therefore, I used rim diameter to differentiate size subclasses within the shouldered bowl category and height to differentiate size subclasses within the globular jar category. Because subclasses are only present in two of the four general form classes, the general form classes are discussed first, followed by the discussion of size subclasses.

Rather than showing a strong decreasing or increasing trend, most of the coefficients of variation for the general form classes look remarkably similar. The exception is the late Zuni Glaze Ware shouldered jar class. The coefficients of variation for both rim diameter and height are less than one-half the values for most other classes of vessels. Using a test of significance for the difference between two coefficients of variation (Sokal and Rohlf 1981:149–150), I found that the contrast of these vessels with the other vessel classes is significant at the 0.05 level. Thus, the metric measure of standardization suggests greater specialization in only the shouldered glaze ware jars.

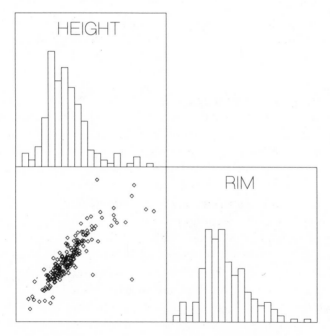

Figure 8.7 Plot of height by rim diameter for hemispherical bowls (early glaze and buff wares).

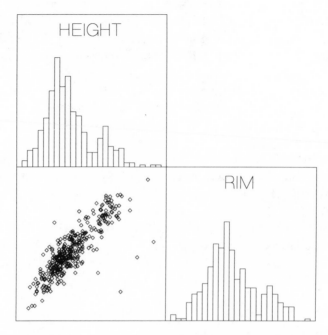

Figure 8.8 Plot of height by rim diameter for shouldered bowls (late glaze and buff wares).

The data using the size subclasses (table 8.6) show that the coefficients of variation for the late Zuni Glaze Ware jars do not differ from those for the shouldered bowls and globular jars. In addition, when one looks more closely at the range of vessel sizes for the late Zuni Glaze Ware jars, it becomes apparent that this category includes a much narrower size range than the other general form subclasses in the sample; the former category contains no subclasses because production was limited to relatively large jars. Thus, the strong contrast in coefficients of variation between the late glaze ware jars and the other general form categories disappears when these jars are compared to the subclasses of the categories—another example of the problem in applying the coefficient of variation to unequal classes, as Longacre et al. (1988) described.

In fact, one of the strongest patterns evident in the metric data on the whole vessels is one of increasing size through time accompanied by a reduction in the size range. This pattern is present for both bowl and jar forms (table 8.5). Kruskall-Wallis one-way analyses of variance of rim

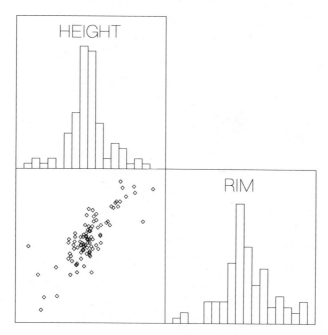

Figure 8.9 Plot of height by rim diameter for globular jars (early glaze and buff wares).

diameters and heights both indicate that size significantly varies through the chronological series of vessel-form/surface-treatment classes (table 8.7).

Conclusions

The results of the analyses suggest that the organization of production was not static during the period before and after initial European contact; the expression of these changes, however, differs when the organization of production is broken up into different dimensions. Compositional and morphological data each contribute to the understanding of change and stability in ceramic production through time, with varying results. Compositional variation informs on the spatial concentration of production, whereas morphological variation provides a basis for discussing production intensity.

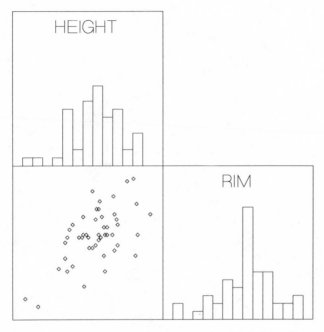

Figure 8.10 Plot of height by rim diameter for shouldered jars (late glaze and buff wares).

Based on the compositional analyses, the sample of early Zuni Glaze Ware vessels of the late fourteenth and early fifteenth centuries indicates that they were produced from relatively few sources. Early Zuni Glaze Ware types overlap in time with the production of the more numerous vessels of Matsaki Buff Ware. By the time the first Europeans reached Zuni, however, Matsaki Buff Ware was the major, if not only, decorated ware made at the protohistoric villages. Matsaki Buff Ware was clearly made from a wider variety of sources than the early Zuni Glaze Ware vessels, suggesting that production of the former was widespread. In the seventeenth century, late Zuni Glaze Ware types replaced the Matsaki Buff Ware, and again fewer sources were used. The spatial concentration of production, therefore, changed from restricted to unrestricted and then back to more restricted sources.

The use of fewer sources (or even a single source) for the production of both early and late Zuni Glaze Ware vessels suggests that selection may have been based on the technological requirements of glaze ware production. In fact, the highly kaolinitic Dakota Sandstone clays chosen for the production of the glaze ware vessels tend to have lower thermal expansion properties and can be fired at higher temperatures than many of the other clays in the Zuni area, particularly those near the protohistoric villages. Thus, in the Zuni case, changes in the selection of clay sources, one dimension of the organization of production, is strongly tied to technological considerations.

Changes in standardization in raw material sources are not coterminous with changes in size standardization through time. I found little difference among the chronologically significant form classes. The only significant change disappeared when size subclasses were considered, suggesting that producers possessed a similar level of skill throughout the period from the mid-fifteenth through late seventeenth centuries. These results suggest that late Zuni Glaze Ware vessels were probably produced in fewer locations, but the ratio of producers to consumers did not significantly change.

Fewer villages were occupied in the seventeenth century than at the time of first European contact, and demographic reconstructions indicate that the Zuni population was reduced as an effect of European diseases. Settlement aggregation could have caused the reduction in raw material sources *if* those sources were all available near sites where the finished vessels were produced. This is not the case with the sites occupied when the late Zuni Glaze Ware ceramics were made. Only a few of the seventeenth-century villages are located directly near the Dakota Sandstone, which was the source of clays for glaze ware vessel production. The distance between the two sites, Hawikku and Kechiba:wa, and this source and catchment area is farther than the distance that potters will generally travel to procure raw clays (Arnold 1985). Potters who lived in villages in the eastern cluster (e.g., the sites of Mats'a:kya and Halona:wa) either produced the glaze ware vessels for exchange with sites in the western cluster, or the Zuni case is an exception to the clay procurement distances that Arnold compiled using cross-cultural data. Changes in transportation introduced by the Spanish may have been a factor in the use of more distant sources for the production of late glaze ware vessels.

The absence of changes in size standardization suggests that despite demographic flux, production standardization remained at the same level. The exact nature of this level of production cannot be absolutely determined because standardization has no decontextualized measure (Rice 1991). However, the variability among contemporaneous vessel

Table 8.6 Summary Statistics for Protohistoric Zuni Vessel Subclasses

Vessel Class & Variable	N	Mean	S.D.	C.V.
Small buff ware shouldered bowls (<28.1-cm rim diameter)				
Rim diameter	241	21.59	3.24	15.0
Height	236	10.93	2.43	22.2
Small glaze ware shouldered bowls (<28.1-cm rim diameter)				
Rim diameter	86	22.29	3.73	16.7
Height	84	11.27	2.71	24.1
Large buff ware shouldered bowls (>28.1-cm rim diameter)				
Rim diameter	49	31.49	2.05	6.5
Height	46	16.70	2.11	12.7
Large glaze ware shouldered bowls (>28.1-cm rim diameter)				
Rim diameter	29	32.76	2.17	6.6
Height	27	16.75	1.56	9.3
Small buff ware globular jars (<12.0-cm height)				
Rim diameter	11	12.76	3.65	28.6
Height	6	8.78	2.14	24.4
Small glaze ware globular jars (<12.0-cm height)				
Rim diameter	6	13.92	4.14	29.8
Height	—	—	—	—
Medium buff ware globular jars (12- to 20-cm height)				
Rim diameter	58	13.48	1.25	9.3
Height	58	16.46	1.60	9.7
Medium glaze ware globular jars (12- to 20-cm height)				
Rim diameter	16	13.83	0.93	6.7
Height	16	18.15	1.13	6.2

Table 8.6 *Continued*

Vessel Class & Variable	N	Mean	S.D.	C.V.
Large buff ware globular jars (>20.0-cm height)				
Rim diameter	7	16.33	0.86	5.3
Height	7	23.71	2.30	9.7
Large glaze ware globular jars (>20.0-cm height)				
Rim diameter	9	17.10	1.22	7.2
Height	9	24.43	2.96	12.1

classes in size standardization and the similar ranges for both pre- and post-Contact vessel classes suggest a level of production that is consistent with household-based production in other contexts.

One of the strongest patterns in the metric data is the trend toward increasing bowl and jar sizes through time. Late glaze ware bowls and jars are generally larger than Matsaki Buff Ware or early Zuni Glaze Ware vessels. As Snow (1982) observed for the Rio Grande area, the introduction of wheat flour and domesticated animals into the Puebloan diet was paralleled by changes in bowl form and increasing sizes of bowls and dry storage jars. A similar explanation may hold true for the increasing sizes of bowls at Zuni during the early historical period. These trends would not, however, explain the parallel changes in sizes of late glaze ware jars, which were most likely used for water storage.

European influence on the reintroduction of glaze ware technology at Zuni may also be suggested for the Protohistoric period. Although glaze ware vessels were continuously made in some parts of the Rio Grande area, there is a temporal gap between the early and late glaze ware types at Zuni. When reintroduced, the application and firing technology of glaze paints at Zuni resulted in runny glazes that were more similar to the Rio Grande Glaze Ware than to early Zuni Glaze Ware. Exactly how this technology was reintroduced to the Zuni area is unknown. However, associated European artifacts from the site of Hawikku (Hodge 1966:148)

Table 8.7 Results of Kruskall-Wallis One-Way ANOVA
for Bowl and Jar Metrics Through Chronological Classes

Form	Attribute	K-W Statistic	Prob.
Bowls[a]	Rim diameter	37.552	<0.001
	Height	67.762	<0.001
Jars[b]	Rim diameter	38.305	<0.001
	Height	59.883	<0.001

[a]Classes include early glaze ware hemispherical bowls, Matsaki
Buff Ware hemispherical bowls, Matsaki Buff Ware shouldered bowls, and late glaze ware shouldered bowls.
[b]Classes include early glaze ware globular jars, Matsaki Buff
Ware globular jars, Matsaki Buff Ware shouldered jars, and
late glaze ware shouldered jars.

show that it occurred at about the same time that a mission was established at Zuni in the early seventeenth century.

Compositional and morphological variables for investigating the organization of production do not change at the same rate or in the same
direction. The data discussed here, therefore, do not support either of the
polar positions on protohistoric pueblo economic organization that are
proposed in the archaeological literature. Instead, a more complex model
that considers the technological requirements of glaze ware production
and changes in the economic conditions associated with European contact is a more parsimonious way of looking at the organization of production at Zuni during the Protohistoric period.

Acknowledgments

I would like to thank Roger Anyon of the Zuni Archaeology Program for his
help in facilitating surface collections from the protohistoric Zuni sites. Eulalia
Wierdsma and Mary Jane Lenz of the National Museum of the American

Indian (Smithsonian Institution) and Christopher Chippindale of the Cambridge University Museum of Archaeology and Anthropology provided extensive assistance in accessing the Hawikku and Kechiba:wa site collections, respectively. Research grants from the National Science Foundation Anthropology Program, the National Endowment for the Humanities Travel to Collections Program, Northern Arizona University, and the American Anthropological Association (Wray Grant Program) all contributed to the research reported here. Rod Parnell of the Department of Geology, Northern Arizona University, graciously allowed access to his lab for preparing the clays for X-ray diffraction analysis and made preliminary interpretations of the data. I would particularly like to thank James Vint for his help in preparing the X-ray diffraction samples and entering much of the data on the whole vessels. Christine Goetze conducted the time-consuming clay oxidation analysis, Susan Hall assisted in data collection at the National Museum of the American Indian, and Ziba Ghassemi drew Figure 8.2. Keith Kintigh, T. J. Ferguson, Carla Sinopoli, and an anonymous reviewer provided very helpful comments, for which I am most grateful.

Notes

1. The conventions of transliteration of Zuni place names follows those used by the Zuni Archaeology Program. Ceramic type names follow those previously used in the literature.

2. The pigment used on Pinnawa Red-on-white is not a glaze, but the type is included here because it is technologically the same as Pinnawa Glaze-on-white and Kechipauan Polychrome in all other respects.

References Cited

Anyon, Roger
1992   The Late Prehistoric and Early Historic Periods in the Zuni-Cibola Area, A.D. 1400–1680. In *Current Research on the Late Prehistory and Early History of New Mexico*, edited by Bradley J. Vierra, pp. 75–83. New Mexico Archaeological Council Special Publication No. 1. Albuquerque.

Arnold, Dean
1985   *Ceramic Theory and Cultural Process.* Cambridge University Press, Cambridge.

Bandelier, Adolph F.
1892   An Outline of the Documentary History of the Zuni Tribe. *Journal of American Ethnology and Archaeology* 3:1–115.

Bushnell, G. H. S.

1955   Some Pueblo IV Pottery Types from Kechipauan, New Mexico, U.S.A. In *Anais do XXXI Congresso Internacional de Americanistas, Sao Paulo—1954,* vol. 2, pp. 657–665. Editora Anhembi, Sao Paulo.

Costin, Cathy Lynne

1991   Craft Specialization: Issues in Defining, Documenting, and Explaining the Organization of Production. In *Archaeological Method and Theory,* vol. 3, edited by Michael B. Schiffer, pp. 1–56. University of Arizona Press, Tucson.

Costin, Cathy L., and Melissa B. Hagstrum

1995   Standardization, Labor Investment, Skill and the Organization of Ceramic Production in Late Prehispanic Highland Peru. *American Antiquity,* in press.

Doelle, William H.

1990   The Transitions to History in the Greater Southwest. In *Perspectives on Southwestern Prehistory,* edited by Paul E. Minnis and Charles E. Redman, pp. 225–227. Westview Press, Boulder, Colorado.

Ferguson, T. J.

1981   The Emergence of Modern Zuni Culture and Society: A Summary of Zuni Tribal History, A.D. 1450–1700. In *The Protohistoric Period in the North American Southwest, A.D. 1450–1700,* edited by David R. Wilcox and W. Bruce Masse, pp. 336–353. Anthropological Research Papers No. 24. Arizona State University, Tempe.

Ferguson, T. J., and E. Richard Hart

1985   *A Zuni Atlas.* University of Oklahoma Press, Norman.

Ferguson, T. J., and Barbara J. Mills

1982   *Archaeological Investigations at Zuni Pueblo, 1977–1980.* Zuni Archaeology Program Report No. 183. Pueblo of Zuni, Zuni, New Mexico.

Hagstrum, Melissa B.

1985   Measuring Prehistoric Ceramic Craft Specialization: A Test Case in the American Southwest. *Journal of Field Archaeology* 12:65–75.

Hodge, Frederick Webb

1918a   Excavations at Hawikuh, New Mexico. In *Explorations and Field Work of the Smithsonian Institution in 1917.* Smithsonian Miscellaneous Collections 68(12):61–72. Smithsonian Institution, Washington, D.C.

1918b   Excavations at the Zuni Pueblo of Hawikuh in 1917. *Art and Archaeology* 7(9):367–379.

1920a   The Age of the Zuni Pueblo of Kechipauan. *Indian Notes and Monographs* 3(2):41–60. Museum of the American Indian, Heye Foundation, New York.

1920b   Hawikuh Bonework. *Indian Notes and Monographs* 3(3):61–151. Museum of the American Indian, Heye Foundation, New York.

1921a   *Turquois Work at Hawikuh, New Mexico.* Leaflet No. 2. Museum of the American Indian, Heye Foundation, New York.

1921b   Work at Hawikuh. *El Palacio* 11(9):118.

1922   Recent Excavations at Hawikuh. *El Palacio* 12(1):1–16.

1924a   Excavations at Kechipauan, New Mexico. *Indian Notes* 1(1):35–36. Museum of the American Indian, Heye Foundation, New York.

1924b   Pottery of Hawikuh. *Indian Notes* 1(1):8–15. Museum of the American Indian, Heye Foundation, New York.

1924c   Snake-pens at Hawikuh, New Mexico. *Indian Notes* 1(3):111–119. Museum of the American Indian, Heye Foundation, New York.

1926   The Six Cities of Cibola, 1581–1680. *New Mexico Historical Review* 1(4): 478–488.

1937   *History of Hawikuh, New Mexico: One of the So-Called Cities of Cibola.* Southwest Museum, Los Angeles.

1939   A Square Kiva Near Hawikuh. In *So Live the Works of Man,* edited by Donald D. Brand and Fred E. Harvey, pp. 195–214. University of New Mexico and School of American Research, Albuquerque.

1952   Turkeys at Hawikuh. *Masterkey* 26(1):13–14. Southwest Museum, Los Angeles.

1966   Sequence of Pottery at Hawikuh. In The *Excavation of Hawikuh by Frederick Webb Hodge: Report of the Hendricks-Hodge Expedition, 1917–1923,* by Watson Smith, Richard B. Woodbury, and Nathalie F. S. Woodbury, pp. 141–150. Contributions from the Museum of the American Indian No. 20. Heye Foundation, New York.

Kintigh, Keith W.

1985   *Settlement, Subsistence and Society in Late Zuni Prehistory.* Anthropological Papers of the University of Arizona No. 44. University of Arizona Press, Tucson.

1990   Protohistoric Transitions in the Western Pueblo Area. In *Perspectives on Southwestern Prehistory,* edited by Paul E. Minnis and Charles E. Redman, pp. 258–275. Westview Press, Boulder, Colorado.

LeBlanc, Steven A.

1989   Cibola: Shifting Cultural Boundaries. In *Dynamics of Southwestern Prehistory,* edited by Linda S. Cordell and George J. Gumerman, pp. 337–369. Smithsonian Institution Press, Washington, D.C.

Longacre, William A., Kenneth L. Kvamme, and Masashi Kobayashi

1988   Southwestern Pottery Standardization: An Ethnoarchaeological View from the Philippines. *The Kiva* 53:101–112.

Lycett, Mark T.

1989   Spanish Contact and Pueblo Organization: Long-Term Implications of European Colonial Expansion in the Rio Grande Valley, New Mexico. In *Columbian Consequences, Volume 1: Archaeological and Historical Perspectives on the Spanish Borderlands West,* edited by David Hurst Thomas, pp. 115–125. Smithsonian Institution Press, Washington, D.C.

Mills, Barbara J.

1987   Ceramic Production and Distribution. In *Archaeological Investigations at Eight Small Sites in West-Central New Mexico,* by Patrick Hogan, pp. 145–154. Office of Contract Archeology, University of New Mexico, Albuquerque.

1989   *Ceramics and Settlement in the Cedar Mesa Area, Southeastern Utah: A Methodological Approach.* Unpublished Ph.D. dissertation, Department of Anthropology, University of New Mexico, Albuquerque.

Parnell, Roderick

1990   Mineralogy of Mesozoic and Cenozoic Source Materials. Ms. on file, Department of Geology, Northern Arizona University, Flagstaff.

Ramenofsky, Ann F.

1987   *Vectors of Death, the Archaeology of European Contact.* University of New Mexico Press, Albuquerque.

Rice, Prudence M.

1981   Evolution of Specialized Pottery Production: A Trial Model. *Current Anthropology* 22:219–240.

1987   *Pottery Analysis: A Sourcebook.* University of Chicago Press, Chicago.

1991   Specialization, Standardization, and Diversity: A Retrospective. In *The Ceramic Legacy of Anna O. Shepard,* edited by Ronald L. Bishop and Frederick W. Lange, pp. 257–279. University Press of Colorado, Niwot.

Riley, Carroll L.

1987   *The Frontier People: The Greater Southwest in the Protohistoric Period.* University of New Mexico Press, Albuquerque.

Shepard, Anna O.

1939   Technology of La Plata Pottery. In *Archaeological Studies in the La Plata District,* by Earl H. Morris, pp. 249–287. Publication No. 519. Carnegie Institution of Washington, Washington, D.C.

1953   Notes on Color and Paste Composition. In *Archaeological Studies in the Petrified Forest National Monument,* by Fred Wendorf, pp. 177–193. Bulletin No. 27. Museum of Northern Arizona, Flagstaff.

Sinopoli, Carla M.

1988   The Organization of Craft Production at Vijayanagara, South India. *American Anthropologist* 90:580–597.

Smith, Watson, Richard B. Woodbury, and Nathalie F. S. Woodbury
1966   *The Excavation of Hawikuh by Frederick Webb Hodge: Report of the Hendricks-Hodge Expedition, 1917–1923*. Contributions from the Museum of the American Indian No. 20. Heye Foundation, New York.

Snow, David
1982   The Rio Grande Glaze, Matte-Paint, and Plainware Tradition. In *Southwestern Ceramics: A Comparative Review*, edited by Albert H. Schroeder, pp. 235–278. The Arizona Archaeologist, Arizona Archaeological Society, Phoenix.

Sokal, Robert R., and F. James Rohlf
1981   *Biometry*. 2nd ed. W. H. Freeman and Co., San Francisco.

Spier, Leslie
1917   An Outline for a Chronology of Zuni Ruins. *Anthropological Papers of the American Museum of Natural History* 18(3):210–331.

Stein, Gil J., and M. James Blackman
1993   The Organizational Context of Specialized Craft Production in Early Mesopotamian States. *Research in Economic Anthropology* 14:29–59.

Toll, H. Wolcott, Thomas C. Windes, and Peter J. McKenna
1980   Late Ceramic Patterns in Chaco Canyon: The Pragmatics of Modeling Ceramic Exchange. *Society for American Archaeology Papers* 1:95–117.

Upham, Steadman
1982   *Polities and Power: An Economic and Political History of the Western Pueblo*. Academic Press, New York.

U.S. Bureau of Indian Affairs
1981   Zuni Oil and Gas Development: Comprehensive Environmental Assessment. Ms. on file, U.S. Bureau of Indian Affairs, Albuquerque Area Office, Albuquerque.

Walker, Frank Spencer
1992   *Chemical Differentiation of Clays by Atomic Spectroscopy*. Unpublished M.S. thesis, Department of Chemistry, Northern Arizona University, Flagstaff.

Watson, Patty Jo, Steven A. LeBlanc, and Charles Redman
1980   Aspects of Zuni Prehistory: Preliminary Report on Excavations and Survey in the El Morro Valley of New Mexico. *Journal of Field Archaeology* 7:201–218.

Windes, Thomas C.
1977   Typology and Technology of Anasazi Ceramics. In *Settlement and Subsistence Along the Lower Chaco River: The CGP Survey*, edited by Charles A. Reher, pp. 169–370. University of New Mexico Press, Albuquerque.

Woodbury, Richard B.

1956 The Antecedents of Zuni Culture. *Transactions of the New York Academy of Sciences*, Series No. 2, 18:557–563.

1979 Zuni Prehistory and History to 1850. In *Handbook of North American Indians, Vol. 9: Southwest*, edited by Alfonso Ortiz, pp. 467–473. Smithsonian Institution, Washington, D.C.

Woodbury, Richard B., and Nathalie F. S. Woodbury

1966 Appendix II: Decorated Pottery of the Zuni Area. In *The Excavation of Hawikuh by Frederick Webb Hodge: Report of the Hendricks-Hodge Expedition, 1917–1923*, by Watson Smith, Richard B. Woodbury, and Nathalie F. S. Woodbury, pp. 302–336. Contributions from the Museum of the American Indian No. 20. Heye Foundation, New York.

9

Problems in Analysis of Standardization and Specialization in Pottery

Barbara L. Stark

The idea that pottery made by specialists is more standard-ized than that of nonspecialists (Balfet 1965:166, 168, 176; Erich 1965:13; Linne 1965:27–28) is a long-standing one that has figured in economic ty-pologies and developmental schemes (Rathje 1975; Rice 1981; van der Leeuw 1977). Rice (1981:220) and Costin (1991) reviewed some of the archaeological indicators of specialization, ranging from the appearance of products, to concentrations of tools or by-products, to patterns of dis-tribution. If specialization and standardization are closely linked, then possibly one can infer aspects of the organizational context of production directly from archaeological collections without examining the actual locations of production (Costin 1991:32–43; Whittlesey 1974:102–103). Whittlesey (1974) and others (e.g., Hagstrum 1985; Longacre et al. 1988; Rice 1981; B. Stark and Hepworth 1982) built upon this possibility by comparing the diversity of archaeological pottery types or assemblages.

Researchers have made some progress in examining this topic ethno-graphically under better controlled conditions, but conclusions vary. Wright (1983) reported that Pakistani ethnographic data offer little sup-port for greater standardization in specialists' products, but M. Stark et al. (1991) found that increasing specialization in Philippine industries led to decreased variability in vessel sizes. Arnold and Nieves (1992) evaluated the effects of (1) manufacturing technique, (2) measurement procedures and tolerances, and (3) segments of the consumer market on variability in three vessel forms produced by one household of potters in Ticul, Yucatan, Mexico. They suggested that all three factors bear upon variation in vessel dimensions. Rigorous consideration of the circumstances affecting comparisons of standardization is crucial to evaluating the effects of specialization on products. Several factors are dissected below.

In this paper, I consider a set of ethnographic data. The link between specialization and standardization in non-wheel-made earthenware is inconsistent on the basis of two pairs of ethnographic industries. My analysis of two variables, orifice and maximum diameters, indicates that archaeological impressions of greater standardization in specialist-produced assemblages may be due as much to the ratio of producers to products as to the greater skill and practice of specialists.

The Concept of Standardization

Standardization of manufactured goods in the context of modern mechanized production implies controls of various sorts (e.g., dies, molds, and electronically controlled machining) to maintain an acceptable level of uniformity in parts and products. In the case of completely handmade goods, controls on uniformity depend heavily on the judgment and skill of the maker. Unless assembly of multipart items requires considerable uniformity, incentives to standardize may be modest, as can be shown by discussion of several alternative incentives to standardization. Stacking for kiln firing or for transport is easier in some cases with standard sizes (Rice 1987:202; Rottlander 1967:76; Whittlesey 1974), but stacking adjustments are possible for slight variations in size or shape. The functional roles that pots perform usually allow some variation in size or shape of vessels. Consumers may recognize and accept products even with some variation. The roles of the items in social communication may also be fulfilled despite a degree of variation. Commercial calculations in monetary economies encourage standardization (Rottlander 1967:77), but variations in vessel size or shape may involve only modest differences in raw material consumption. In fact, Birmingham (1975:382) noted that competitive Kathmandu specialists try to diversify their output to increase the chances of making a sale. Consequently, one can ask whether the commonly accepted link between specialization and standardization in pottery is well grounded.

Standardization—a high degree of uniformity in products—is relative to technological, functional, social, and individual factors. Examples of a particular kind of pot could be judged appropriate by both makers and users and yet vary in several respects, whether the pots were produced by nonspecialists or specialists. At the same time, the customary standards of a community where nonspecialist pottery is made may result in considerable similarity in products. Therefore, archaeologists are interested in differing degrees of standardization, not its presence or absence. The task is to make more precise the impressions frequently recorded about the contrast between specialist and nonspecialist products. For my purposes, *specialization* is defined as production for distribution to other households on more than a sporadic basis, such as might be involved in reciprocal gift-giving. Even though specialization, like standardization, forms a continuum, here it is convenient to restrict discussion to nonspecialists who produce primarily for their own household in contrast to specialists who produce in a household setting but primarily for exchange (see Costin [1991], Cowgill [1989], and Rice [1987:183–191; 1989] for additional discussion of the concept of specialization).[1]

Proximate Causes of Standardization

Anthropologists commonly mention two reasons for greater standardization in specialists' products. With regular, frequent pot making, motor skill and general experience presumably increase, producing fewer deviations from the kind of vessel the person is trying to create (Balfet 1965:165; Hagstrum 1985:68; Sears 1973:39). David and Hennig (1972:4–5, 23), for example, stressed that Fulani women are not very good potters partly because they learn the work haphazardly and do it infrequently.

A second reason involves the ratio of numbers of producers to consumers or to the total products in use. Many pottery attributes vary slightly according to the individual who produced them, as has been demonstrated in a variety of ethnographic cases (Costin 1991:4; DeBoer and Kaufman 1977; Friedrich 1970:340–341; Hardin 1977; Hill 1977; Kaufman 1977:11–14; Lauer 1974:158). Consequently, a representative sample of pottery used (and discarded) by a large community supplied, for example, by three specialists, will be less diverse than if every family makes its own pottery (Balfet 1965:176; Hagstrum 1985:69; Hill 1977:57).

Although market controls have been suggested as a factor affecting standardization, their effects are uncertain or at least variable. Arnold and Nieves (1992:110–111) found the least variation in a form destined for a tourist market and more variation in a form for a local market; still more variable were other vessels destined for middlemen, who resold them. Foster (1965:54) noted that potters may maintain a distinctive decoration or form for a particular market. (Perhaps this also aids consumer recognition of an accepted, good-quality product). Yet Birmingham (1975) and Foster (1965:52–53) argued that market competition may promote diversification of products. Increasing specialization may be associated with both diversification and standardization because growing specialization generally implies increased numbers of consumers or consumption levels; such growing demand may make it feasible to supply added, lower demand, functional types. (Economies of scale in production and distribution could also be expected to abet functional diversification.) Thus, diversity in kinds of products may grow simultaneously with increased standardization in each kind of product (Rice 1981:220). In addition to the "skill" and "ratio" factors, I address other matters as variables that researchers must control to make useful comparisons of product standardization.

To study standardization, one must consider several issues: choice of variables, the nature of assemblages to be compared, technology, and methods of analysis. I discuss below several factors that are important for ethnographic comparisons. Archaeological comparisons, however, pose additional severe problems, such as time-span differences and measurement differences (e.g., on sherds not vessels), which can drastically affect the apparent standardization of assemblages (Benco 1988:68).

Issues Affecting Analysis

Choice of Variables

Some variables relate to conspicuous aspects of pots that makers, whether specialists or nonspecialists, may strive to control in accordance with their own and consumer values. Stylistic variables may be readily imitated or constrained according to sociological and communication considerations (Plog 1980). (I use *stylistic* to describe characteristics that are largely unconstrained by practical function, in contrast to social or ideational function.)

Other, less obvious variables may not be so dependent on factors outside the production situation. For example, minor variations in the mix of temper and clay (within functional tolerances) may not be noticeable in a finished vessel. Minor metric variation within a functional size class, although not "invisible," may not be salient to the same extent as color or shape variation in, for example, painted designs. Less readily evident variables may be more useful when the effects of skill are to be measured than are obvious stylistic variables that communicate information (Costin 1991:35). Costin and Hagstrum's (1995) distinction between "intentional" and "mechanical" variables refers to this same issue, but judgments about ancient intentions are likely to rest upon inferences about the conspicuousness of attributes.

Comparisons require variables that are equally appropriate to different data sets. Many metric measurements fit this criterion, but painted design elements pose more problems (Plog 1980) because different industries may have noncomparable repertoires and uses of designs. See Hagstrum (1985) for exemplary controls to compare designs in analysis of standardization.

Attributes of vessel shape do not pose as many difficulties as design. Vessel form may incorporate aspects of both style and function. All vessels, however, have some parts that can be categorized formally, whereas all vessels do not bear designs. Unfortunately, detailed form analysis is generally not available for ethnographic collections. Although detailed form typologies are more common archaeologically, they are typically for sherds, making many inferences about form a complex step.

Variables and attributes should exhibit a comparable labor investment. Costin and Hagstrum (1995) discussed this issue in greater detail. Otherwise, a separate factor related to specialization is at stake. Reductions in labor investment may be characteristic of specialists' work under some circumstances, such as strong central administration and diminished competition. The resulting streamlined production may reduce variability in pottery. Hagstrum (1985), for example, assumed that streamlining is closely related to skill and marketing, whereas Feinman (1980) noted that it is related to the wider sociopolitical environment. In some cases, differentials in the sheer abundance or diversity of design attributes may reflect differentials in labor investments, a link that Hagstrum

(1985) demonstrated by conducting a study of design plus brush strokes and "gestures."

Assemblages and Producers

Information about the number of producers who created an assemblage is necessary to distinguish a skill from a ratio basis for standardization, which is the issue of particular concern here. Also relevant is the nature of the product assemblage—community-wide or workshop/household inventories. Only in ethnographic situations is it feasible to control precisely for the number of producers to resolve the relative roles of ratio and skill. Ideally, comparably sized, representative collections should also derive from comparable spans of production time or numbers of production episodes to minimize extraneous influences on variability, which might occur if initial preparation and use of materials or tools involves any break-in period. One would also wish to avoid sampling industries that are undergoing rapid technological or other change.

Current ethnographic data do not allow close control over production time or episodes, although the time spans represented are far smaller than those that are typical in archaeological data. The precision of archaeological chronologies poses a marked problem for interassemblage comparisons, but the problem is less severe within assemblages.

Partitioning Assemblages

Comparisons concerning degrees of standardization should be restricted within functional classes. For example, comparing cooking pots reduces extraneous considerations because other kinds of vessels may have different functional constraints. In Arnold and Nieves' (1992) study, a comparison of different markets also involved comparison of vessels with different functions, with the result that either factor could be responsible for the patterns in size standardization.

Metric comparisons should take size classes into account (Longacre et al. 1988). Size classes could also prove critical for other attributes; for example, some shape or decorative attributes vary across size classes because of shape-functional relationships or because of marked changes in the space available for decoration, respectively. Not uncommonly, vessels of a given function are "sized" (Matson 1965:280). Foster (1967:42), for example, commented that Tzintzuntzan potters have 12 to 14 recognized size classes for some kinds of pots (see also David and Hennig 1972:8, 10; Fontana et al. 1962:37). As in Shipibo-Conibo pottery, sometimes size classes establish functional differences (DeBoer and Lathrap 1979).

Inadvertent lumping of size classes will inflate variation in measurements that would not exist if a behaviorally or culturally significant boundary were known or approximated (Longacre et al. 1988). In an ethnographic setting, emic size classes may overlap, as will be shown below. For the archaeologist, confounded size classes could even appear as a unimodal distribution, despite the fact that two (or more) classes are represented, each with a different mean or mode. The only recourse is to examine the data for clear multimodality in measurements. However, the meaning of multimodality will still be confusing. Rice (1981:221) commented that it could reflect size classes or "the existence of multiple producers, each with his own slightly distinctive product." This latter, fine scale will not be perceivable with most archaeological collections, in which chronological controls do not permit identification of the work of an individual. However, variation among individual producers clearly shows in the ethnographic data considered below.

Metric comparisons across size extremes involve an allometric problem—an absolute variation, e.g., 1 cm in vessel diameter, is more evident on a small vessel than on a large one because it represents a higher percentage of the vessel diameter. This problem is a progressive or continuous one that can be controlled by comparing size classes that cover approximately the same range.

Technology

Finally, forming methods should be similar (Arnold and Nieves 1992). The most obvious distortion would be a comparison of mold-formed vs. hand-formed vessels. Archaeologists suspect that molds will be associated with specialists more than nonspecialists, but molds are by no means ubiquitous in specialist manufacture (B. Stark 1985). In many cases, including some considered below, partial molds constitute a concave mold for the base and lower part of a vessel that also supports the pot and aids in turning it during forming; partial molds can be expected to have little or no effect on some vessel dimensions. In an ethnographic situation, researchers may readily obtain information about manufacturing processes, but archaeologically this is often difficult.[2]

Raw materials differ and may affect the standardization of products. Some clays may be more difficult to work than others. Longacre et al. (1988:105) suggested differential shrinkage as a factor in standardization. Although a regular degree of shrinkage would not affect standardization, variable shrinkage would. Typically, however, researchers lack sufficiently detailed information to gauge the effects of shrinkage among extant data, especially whether this shrinkage is predictable.

Choice of Analytic Methods

One can use several quantitative measures to compare standardization in two assemblages (see Leonard and Jones [1989] for more extensive discussion of measures). Two aspects of variation are of interest: the number of attribute states of a variable and the frequencies of each attribute state. One might expect standardization to reduce the number of attribute states, e.g., fewer orifice diameters or lip forms, and to concentrate the cases in fewer of the attribute states that exist.

As initial descriptive measures for vessel size, the range, mean, and standard deviation are useful. Coefficients of homogeneity (or variation) also can portray patterns of relative diversity (Bronitsky 1978; Daddario 1980; Whallon 1968), but these measures do not provide for significance testing. Although often used, the coefficient of variation (standard deviation divided by the mean [Blalock 1972:88]) is not entirely satisfactory because it is sensitive to the mean of each population of measurements. Two industries might produce equally standardized vessels of a particular function but without identical means, and consequently the coefficients of variation would differ. Nevertheless, use of such a coefficient is desirable in lieu of inspection of standard deviations (e.g., Hagstrum 1985:69) because it compensates for the greater variation in measurements that might be expected with a higher mean (the allometric problem). Other approaches to ceramic diversity are discussed elsewhere (Braun 1980; Dickens 1980; Hagstrum 1985; Rottlander 1967).

Among parametric approaches, the F test compares variances between two populations of measurements, provided that the samples are normally distributed. However, the test is sensitive to violations of the normality assumption (unlike analysis of variance). Tests comparing variances for multiple samples are more appropriate in many cases because some of these are less sensitive to nonnormal distributions. One of them—the Q test (Burr 1974:345–347)—is used to compare three or more samples of different sizes. The test statistic is as follows:

$$q = \frac{\bar{v}\,(v_1 s_1^4 + \ldots + v_k s_k^4)}{(v_1 s_1^2 + \ldots + v_k s_k^2)^2}$$

where $v_i = n - 1$ and

$$\bar{v} = \sum_{i=1}^{k} \frac{v_i}{k}$$

and s_i = standard deviation
and n_i = sample size.

Burr (1974:449) provides the critical values.

A third major option involves diversity (or heterogeneity) indices, designed for nominal data. The two properties of variation are described in the ecological literature as *richness* and *evenness*. Richness means the number of nominal attributes in a distribution, and evenness means the degree of concentration within those categories. The Shannon-Weaver Index, H', combines these two characteristics and has been applied archaeologically (Braun 1985; Conkey 1980; Rice 1981; B. Stark and Hepworth 1982). Diversity indices have been described as difficult to interpret in the biological literature (Peet 1974) because of variations in terminology and attempts to link diversity to other properties of biological or ecological systems (Hurlbert 1971:585). Related problems affect archaeological applications (Leonard and Jones 1989); other indices measure richness or evenness alone. It is often preferable to separate the two properties to provide a clearer focus. The representativeness of samples and sample size are key problems for diversity indices (Jones et al. 1983; Kintigh 1984, 1989; McCartney and Glass 1990).

Thus, quantitative assessment of the degree of homogeneity of products is not simple. The comparisons of particular interest here are plagued by the difficulty of amassing sufficient nonspecialist observations for individual potters, and observations often reflect potting episodes that are well separated in time compared to those of specialists. Scant data for individual nonspecialist potters have a profound effect on statistical comparisons that can be made. The following discussion of ethnographic cases shows that the ratio effect may be significant in the traditional impression of greater homogeneity of specialist-produced assemblages. That impression has usually been ascribed to the specialists' greater skill, which, although important, may have been exaggerated. For each pair of industries discussed below, different formats of data are available, leading to separate consideration of each pair.

Two Pairs of Ethnographic Comparisons

Current ethnographic data are strikingly limited, but it is useful to examine them for clear-cut, obvious differences in variability between the products of specialists and nonspecialists. My analysis is confined to vessel orifice sizes and maximum diameters because of the constraints of available data. Throughout my discussion, I will couch the pros and cons of the comparisons in terms of the issues noted above; my aim is to match relevant samples and to anticipate the specific effects that any differences in the ethnographic contexts may have.

Although Rice (1989:112, 116) argued that comparisons of diversity among temporally or geographically removed industries should be avoided, the purpose in matching samples is to control for factors extraneous to those of interest (or to be specific about the consequences of particular factors). Temporal or geographic contiguity is no "magic bullet" that constrains irrelevance. For example, very different technologies and forms may be used within a single region, both contemporaneously and over time.

Paired Industries in the D'Entrecasteaux Islands, Papua

Lauer (1974) gathered data concerning nonspecialist production on Goodenough Island and specialist production on the Amphlett Islands; the two industries exhibit a general historical similarity in the pottery traditions. Amphlett pots are built up by adding and scraping clay slabs and coils, followed by paddling. Goodenough vessels are shaped by coiling, with no paddling. Lauer (1974:158) observed that the specialists produce pottery at a very low rate, around six vessels per month. Even though Amphlett pottery is important in exchange, the relatively infrequent production may not be sufficiently distinct in volume or frequency from nonspecialist production to yield differences in product standardization. Lauer's summary statistics (sample size, mean, and standard deviation) for orifice and maximum radii allow use of F or Q tests (table 9.1). Because no assessment of normality in the sample populations is possible, I applied Q tests.

Papuan specialists produce six categories of cooking pots, but nonspecialists produce only three kinds (in three hamlets). Specialist Type 6 has too few cases to be useful. I consider only nonspecialist vessel forms A and B because C is canoe shaped. B vessels are like A vessels, but with an interior partition. Amphlett specialist pottery came from Gumawana Island hamlets (the number of hamlets was not given). Types 1 and 4 were used as common household cooking pots; the other sizes were used for ceremonial or special occasions. Types 1 and 4 are, respectively, slightly smaller and larger than the nonspecialist cooking pots A and B in regard to mean orifice radius. Because maximum (shoulder) radius for type 1 is about the same as for nonspecialist cooking pots, comparisons of type 1 with types A and B are especially pertinent for evaluation of standardization.

Overall, coefficients of variation for specialist vessels are both larger and smaller than for nonspecialist vessels, but the more closely matched specialist types 1 and 4 have *higher* coefficients of variation than nonspecialist types A and B (table 9.1). The Q test yields a significant difference among types A, B, 1, and 4 for both variables (table 9.2), although not in the expected fashion. Because the three data sets for nonspecialist vessels do not differ significantly among themselves in variances based on a Q test, it is the contrast of specialist and nonspecialist products that yields a significant difference. The *nonspecialist* pottery, however, is more homogeneous, contrary to customary expectation.

It seems doubtful that Amphlett paddling would yield these results, but it might. It should be noted that Lauer (1974:190) found Amphlett pottery to have a more professional look overall, with some technological superiority, a greater labor investment, and more vessel forms; thus, variables other than vessel size may show effects of specialization. Although Papuan measurements do not lend support to the supposed link between standardization and specialization in regard to vessel size variation, lack of information about the number of producers for each data set precludes gauging the effects of imbalance in this factor. It is unlikely, but possible, that fewer nonspecialists were represented, thus reducing variability among their pots. Information about individual potters is available among the New World paired data that I consider next.

Table 9.1 Papuan Vessel Data

Category	N	Mean Orifice Radius (cm)	S.D.	Var.	C.V.
ORIFICE RADIUS					
Goodenough Island Nonspecialist Pottery					
Buduna Hamlet					
Form A	10	15.93	2.40	5.76	0.15
Form B	12	16.73	2.30	5.29	0.14
Manubuleya & Vedakala Hamlets					
Form A	15	15.53	1.90	3.61	0.12
Amphlett Islands Specialist Pottery					
Gumawana Island Hamlets					
Type 1	14	14.20	2.60	6.76	0.18
Type 2	18	23.13	2.20	4.84	0.10
Type 3	12	26.09	1.70	2.89	0.06
Type 4	36	18.04	3.80	14.44	0.21
Type 5	15	18.38	5.50	30.25	0.30

Paired Industries from Amazonia and the Guatemalan Highlands

Vessel measurements are available for cooking pots and water-carrying jars produced by Mayan specialists in highland Guatemala (Arnold 1978) and by Shipibo-Conibo nonspecialists (courtesy of Warren DeBoer, field data from 1971).

Guatemalan Specialists   Arnold (1978) studied Maya Indian pottery centers in the Valley of Guatemala. The women potters were full-time specialists who supplemented the family income produced by men, who farmed. Pottery was sold in markets in the region. Pottery-making diminished but did not cease in the rainy season (Arnold 1978:336, 346). The measurements were made on vessels at potters' workshops.

Table 9.1 *Continued*

Category	N	Mean Orifice Radius (cm)	S.D.	Var.	C.V.
MAXIMUM RADIUS					
Goodenough Island Nonspecialist Pottery					
Buduna Hamlet					
Form A	10	17.16	2.28	5.20	0.13
Form B	12	17.78	2.20	4.84	0.12
Manubuleya &					
Vedakala Hamlets					
Form A	15	17.03	2.10	4.41	0.12
Amphlett Islands Specialist Pottery					
Gumawana Island					
Hamlets					
Type 1	14	17.07	2.60	6.76	0.15
Type 2	18	26.25	2.10	4.41	0.08
Type 3	12	29.65	1.90	3.61	0.06
Type 4	36	21.59	3.80	14.44	0.18
Type 5	not applicable; see orifice radius				

Cooking pots were made in Sacoj Grande; water-carrying jars were made in Sacojito and Durazno. For each of these vessels Arnold (1978) recognized size classes, but he generally did not designate classes for the measured vessels. There is no assurance that all of the size classes are represented among the measurements, although they seem to be present. If this assumption were incorrect, the diversity of specialist pottery would increase and the statistical effect would not undermine any of the general points made here. I determined size classes by inspecting bivariate plots of orifice diameter, maximum diameter, and height to detect pairs of variables useful in segregating size groups.

Cooking pots in Sacoj Grande are made with partial molds that reach nearly to the maximum diameter of the vessel, with the upper part formed by hand in a modified coiling technique (Arnold 1978:336). Arnold (1978:

336) described cooking pots made in three capacities (5.2, 6.8, and 11.6 kg of corn), each with different uses, but size distinctions are hard to identify among the fired vessels produced by two potters in the same household (fig. 9.1). I segregated medium-capacity vessels for diversity analysis (table 9.3).[3]

Guatemalan water-carrying jars from Sacojito were made in two mouth sizes, but three capacity sizes (Arnold 1978:358–359). Potters measured the jars during forming to help control size (Arnold 1978:349), and partial molds were used for the bottom, with the remainder coiled by hand.[4] Tentative groups for both medium- and large-capacity jars can be defined in regard to maximum diameters (fig. 9.2). The two orifice sizes also can be tentatively identified, but they cross-cut the medium- and large-capacity vessels.[5] Sacojito jars have size ranges that are more similar to Amazonian water jars than are those from Durazno.

In Durazno, water-jar manufacturing methods were the same as those described for Sacojito, and the system of size classes may have been the

Table 9.2 Q-Test Statistical Decisions for a Hypothesis of No Significant
Difference Among Sets of Measurements for the
D'Entrecasteaux Islands[a] (alpha = 0.01)

Nonspecialist and Specialist Orifice Radii
Vessels A (Bud.), B (Bud.), A (Man. & Ved.), 4, and 1: Q = 0.416, df =16.4
reject

Nonspecialist and Specialist Maximum Radii
Vessels A (Bud.), B (Bud.), A (Man. & Ved.), 4, and 1: Q = 0.342, df = 16.4
reject

Nonspecialist Orifice Radii
Vessels A (Bud.), B (Bud.), and A (Man. & Ved.): Q = 0.380, df = 11.33
accept

Nonspecialist Maximum Radii
Vessels A (Bud.), B (Bud.), and A (Man. & Ved.): Q = 0.339, df = 11.33
accept

---

[a]Bud. = Buduna Hamlet; Man. & Ved. = Manubuleya & Vedakala Hamlets.

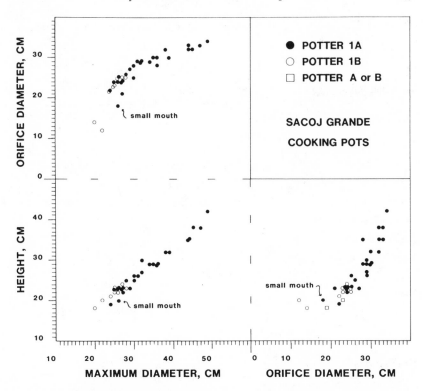

Figure 9.1 Guatemalan Sacoj Grande cooking pots. Arnold (1978) designated one vessel as small mouthed.

same (Arnold 1978:348–349, 358). The measurements derive from the work of five potters. Available data did not allow a distinction between medium- and large-capacity Durazno vessels; hence, measurements are pooled for these sizes (fig. 9.3).[6] Because it is difficult to decide if there are two orifice size classes cross-cutting all of the vessel capacity classes in Durazno, I employed two data sets: all Durazno orifice diameters pooled together, and orifice diameters only from the medium-to-large–capacity vessels.

Shipibo-Conibo Nonspecialists Women produce pottery primarily for their own families, but also in recent years, increasingly for tourists. The sample used here includes only pottery produced for domestic use (Warren DeBoer, personal communication 1982). The pottery was handmade by

Table 9.3 Descriptive Statistics for Guatemalan and Amazonian Vessels by Potters

Group & Vessel Type	N	Range (cm)	Mean (cm)	S.D.	C.V.
SHIPIBO-CONIBO					
Fam. 17, large brewing, ori. diam.	4	46.5–68	55.37	9.48	0.17
Fam. 17, large brewing, max. diam.	4	60–77	69.25	7.41	0.11
Fam. 17, water jars, ori. diam.	5	11–14	12.1	1.51	0.12
Fam. 19, water jars, ori. diam.	5	11–15	13.3	1.48	0.11
Fam. 20, water jars, ori. diam.	6	13.5–22.5	18.5	3.79	0.20
GUATEMALA					
Sacoj Grande					
SG1A, medium cooking, ori. diam.	20	21–31.5	26.62	2.94	0.11
SG1A, medium cooking, max. diam.	20	23.5–39	30.45	4.59	0.15
SG1B, medium cooking, ori. diam.	6	21.5–25	23.58	1.46	0.06
SG1B, medium cooking, max. diam.	6	24–28	25.83	1.47	0.06
Sacojito					
SJ3, medium-large–capac. water jars, large ori.	21	13–18	14.76	1.46	0.10
SJ3, medium-large–capac. water jars, small ori.	8	7–10	8.62	1.12	0.13
SJ3, large-capac. water jars, max. diam.	18	31–38	33.69	2.20	0.07

Table 9.3 *Continued*

Group & Vessel Type	N	Range (cm)	Mean (cm)	S.D.	C.V.
SJ3, medium-capac. water jars, max. diam.	14	27.5–36	32.03	2.03	0.06
SJ7, medium-large–capac. water jars, large ori.	13	13–15.5	13.88	0.68	0.05
SJ7, medium-large–capac. water jars, small ori.	8	7–10.5	8.75	1.10	0.13
SJ7, medium-capac. water jars, max. diam.	20	28–31	29.67	0.69	0.02
SJ8, medium-large–capac. water jars, small ori.	4	9–11	9.87	0.85	0.09
SJ8, medium-large–capac. water jars, large ori.	19	11.5–15	13.55	0.70	0.05
SJ8, large-capac. water jars, max. diam.	13	32–35	33.30	0.90	0.03
SJ8, medium-capac. water jars, max. diam.	10	25.5–28	27.05	0.92	0.03
Durazno					
D2, small-capac. water jars, small ori.	6	7–9	8.33	0.75	0.09
D2, small-capac. water jars, max. diam.	6	14–14.5	14.33	0.25	0.02
D6, medium-large–capac. water jars, large ori.	13	9.5–11	10.19	0.48	0.05
D6, medium-large–capac. water jars, max. diam.	13	21.5–24	23.00	0.79	0.03
D7, medium-large–capac. water jars, large ori.	5	11.5–12	11.80	0.27	0.02
D7, medium-large–capac. water jars, max. diam.	6	28.5–32.5	29.58	1.53	0.05

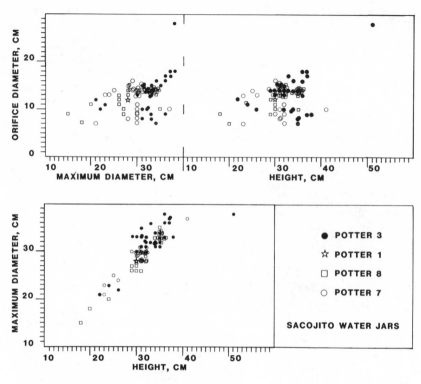

Figure 9.2 Guatemalan Sacojito water jars.

coiling. The Shipibo-Conibo live in small to medium-sized villages interrelated by kin ties. Measurements were derived from pottery produced in five villages, located within about 225 km (direct distance) of each other.

Quenti vessels are used for cooking and come in three sizes with different primary functions: *quenti ani* (large) for brewing, *quenti anitama* (medium) for cooking foods, and *quenti vacu* (small) for medicinal preparations (fig. 9.4). The food-cooking pots are the most appropriate category to compare to Guatemalan medium cooking pots in regard to both size and function. Shipibo-Conibo jars are made in four sizes with different functions. The medium size (*chomo anitama*) is primarily for carrying water (fig. 9.5).

It is important to underscore that different bases have been used to establish size classes in the two ethnographic settings: (1) inspection of values for the specialist industries, and (2) emic designations in the nonspecialist industry (in part, because inspection of values could not identify the size classes). My guess is that this could have the effect of increasing variability in the nonspecialist data, a bias that would enhance the contrast with specialist products.

Comparisons of New World Industries   Individual variation among potters is striking in both production contexts. In several instances, size classes were indistinct when the work of many producers was pooled (figs. 9.4, 9.5, and 9.6), yet plots for individual producers (or families, in the case of the Shipibo-Conibo) show relatively clear distinctions. Families 22, 17, and 6 are Shipibo-Conibo examples (figs. 9.4 and 9.5), and potters 3, 7, and 8 are Sacojito examples (fig. 9.6). Individual producers often had distinct "operational" size classes that differed slightly from those of other producers, despite the fact that all shared the same community-wide conceptual scheme. David and Hennig (1972:8, 10) observed a similar phenomenon. Nicholson and Patterson's (1985:236) plots of vessel

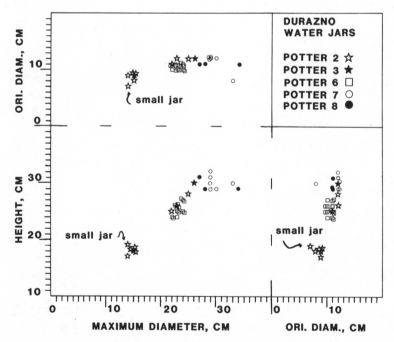

Figure 9.3 Guatemalan Durazno water jars. Arnold (1978) designated one vessel as a small jar.

measurements taken from two potters in a specialized Egyptian industry also revealed individual variation in sizes. Arnold (1978:345) also demonstrated such variation in a plot of modes for molded tortilla griddle diameters for three potters in Mixco, Guatemala.

In Shipibo-Conibo households 2, 3, and 14, the people assigned comparably sized vessels to *different* function/size classes (see also Fontana et al. 1962:80; Nicholson and Patterson 1985:234). I assume that some

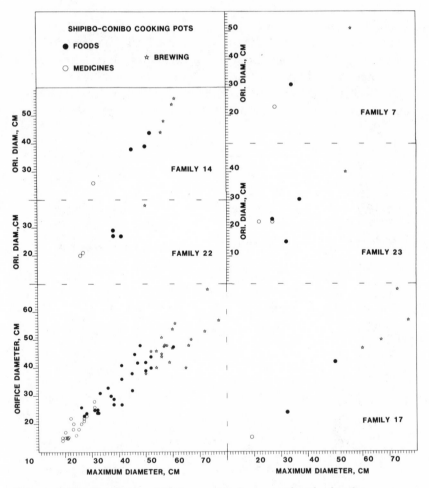

Figure 9.4 Shipibo-Conibo cooking vessels. Separate plots for families are combined in lower left plot.

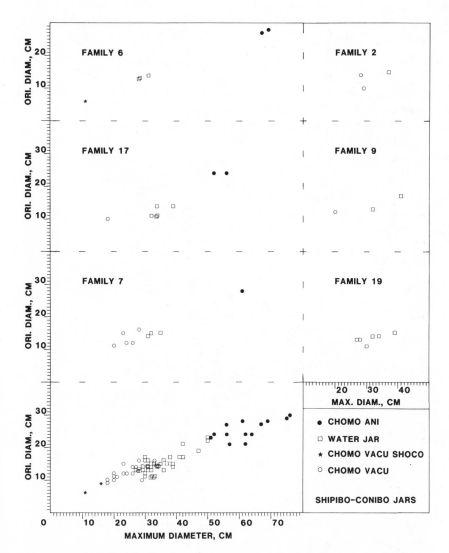

Figure 9.5 Shipibo-Conibo jars. Separate plots for families are combined in lower left plot.

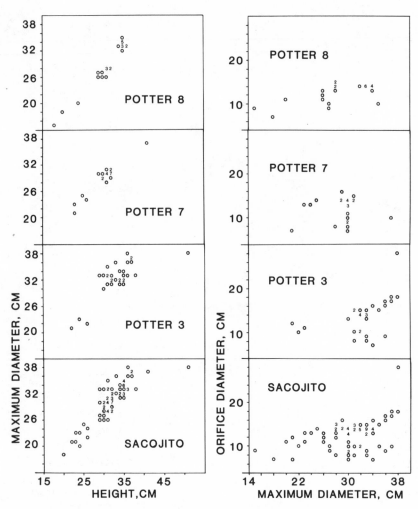

Figure 9.6 Sacojito water jars. Separate plots for producers are combined in lowest plots. Numbers in plots represent multiple vessels.

functional requirements are not so stringent that a given size of vessel cannot fulfill different functions, dependent on the needs, circumstances, and perhaps concepts of particular households. Size classes have some degree of practical flexibility, a fact that is compatible with variation in operational size classes. The reason for this variation is uncertain. In some cases, nonspecialists may have tailored sizes to suit the family situation.

Family needs could vary with the domestic cycle, among other factors. In market situations, specialists may produce variants that aim at different consumers; a consumer, in turn, may adjust to changing needs by searching out convenient variants within a size class. Variation in operational size classes means that the ratio effect may be quite powerful in conditioning typical archaeological assemblages, at least in regard to vessel sizes. Other kinds of variables, e.g., complex painted designs, would likely be more responsive to skill.

Researchers can examine the skill vs. ratio effect by evaluating variation in products by individual potters. Do specialists, as individuals, exhibit less variation in their products? The chief obstacle has been noted already—a nonspecialist will have few pots of a particular function. In comparisons of coefficients of variation by potter, I use only those cases with measurements on at least four vessels of a particular function or size class (table 9.3; fig. 9.7).

As a group, the five nonspecialist Shipibo-Conibo coefficients are consistently high (all have very low sample sizes), but several specialist Guatemalan values, based on better sample sizes in some instances, are about as high. Some specialists equal or exceed the nonspecialists in coefficients of variation (e.g., some water jars made by Sacojito potter 3 or cooking pots made by Sacoj Grande potter 1A). The specialists show individual differences in how closely they hold to a given size. It is not surprising that specialists' water jars exhibit more low coefficients of variation than do vessels of Shipibo-Conibo potters because the specialists measure pots during manufacture. In contrast, specialist cooking pots are more variable than water jars, perhaps because measurement is not part of the manufacturing process.

Despite the potential differences in clays or other confounding factors, it is useful to establish whether Amazonian nonspecialist and Guatemalan specialist products differ significantly in size variability. Coefficients of variation suggest that Amazonian nonspecialist vessels vary more in size, but the sample is small. In a more rigorous assessment, Q tests can be applied to comparisons of three or more potters (table 9.3), but comparisons cannot closely match specialists with nonspecialists except for the orifices of water jars, which are judged to differ significantly (alpha = 0.01, for comparison of Sacojito large-sized orifice diameters for medium-to-large–capacity vessels and orifice diameters for Shipibo-Conibo jars; Q = 0.570; degrees of freedom = 10.5). Is the significance solely due to the contrast between specialist and nonspecialist vessels?

The three Shipibo-Conibo variances are not significantly different from one another (an expectable result, given the sample sizes; $Q = 0.576$; degrees of freedom $= 4.3$), but the three Sacojito specialist measures *are* significantly different among themselves ($Q = 0.501$; degrees of freedom $= 16.67$). Thus, the differences detected when the two industries are analyzed together reflect not only the contrast of specialists and nonspecialists, but also significant variability among the specialists themselves. Significant variability among specialist measures is also evident for maximum diameters among Durazno medium-to-large–capacity water jars and Sacojito medium- and large-capacity jars ($Q = 0.25$; degrees of freedom $= 12.4$). Thus, individual specialist variability is as marked a factor as any skill advantages enjoyed by the specialists.

The data show that individual variation among specialists is significant and can be as great as that exhibited by nonspecialists. The data also address three other factors that bear on comparisons of standardization among industries: allometric effects, manufacturing technology, and different functional forms. The allometric effects, however, are not severe among these data (fig. 9.8). In regressions of the mean against the stan-

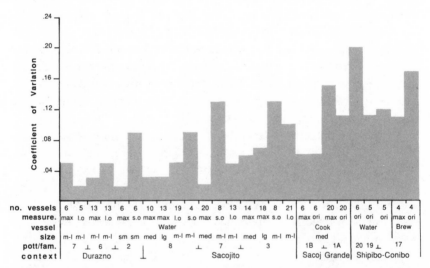

no. vessels	measure	vessel size	pott/fam	context
6	max	m-l	7	Durazno
5	l.o	m-l		
13	max	m-l	6	
13	l.o	m-l		
6	max	sm	2	
6	s.o	sm		
10	max	med		
13	max	lg		
19	l.o	m-l	8	Sacojito
4	s.o	m-l		
20	max	med		
8	s.o	m-l	7	
13	l.o	m-l		
14	max	med		
18	max	lg	3	
8	s.o	m-l		
21	l.o	m-l		
6	max ori	med	1B	Sacoj Grande (Cook)
6	max ori		1A	
20	max ori			
20	max ori			
6	ori		20	Water (Shipibo-Conibo)
5	ori		19	
5	ori			
4	max ori		17	Brew
4				

Figure 9.7 Bar graph of coefficients of variation for each type of vessel for each potter. For measurements, "max" is maximum diameter, "l.o" is large orifice, "s.o" is small orifice, and "ori" is orifice diameter. For sizes, "m-l" is medium to large, "sm" is small, "med" is medium, and "lg" is large.

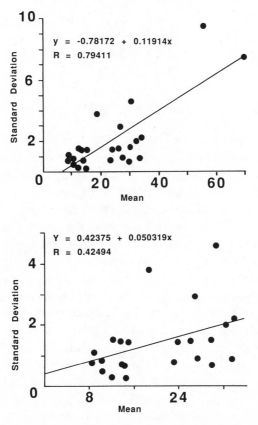

Figure 9.8 Regressions of means against standard deviations for potters in Table 3. Upper graph shows all cases. In lower graph, two high values are omitted (Shipibo-Conibo brewing vessels).

dard deviation, inclusion of the extremely large Shipibo-Conibo brewing pots (fig. 9.8, top graph) is the primary reason for the tendency for bigger vessels to have a correspondingly larger standard deviation. Removal of the brewing pots shows a much weaker relationship (fig. 9.8, bottom graph). Manufacturing technology proved to have only modest effects on standardization with respect to the partial molds used for the lower part of vessels in Guatemala; maximum diameters of the Guatemalan pots were not consistently less variable than orifice diameters (see Benco 1988:68). In these instances, the necessity for closely matching samples in regard to technology was not very marked.[7] The data, however, also show possible noteworthy differences in the degree of variation between different functional forms. The coefficients of variation among specialists' water jars are generally lower than those among cooking pots.

The Ratio Effect: An Alternative to "Skill"

The ethnographic comparisons discussed here are too few to derail the traditional expectation of a link between specialization and standardization owing to specialists' greater skill, but the comparisons are disquieting. In the Papuan case, comparisons did not establish that specialists produced more standardized vessel sizes. However, the modest specialist output, the lack of knowledge concerning the number of producers (preventing control for the ratio effect), and slight differences in forming methods make interpretation of these data inconclusive.

Beyond a healthier skepticism about the consistency of a contrast between specialist and nonspecialist products, one can make a specific case for substantial effects due to the ratio of producers to products on the basis of Amazonian and Guatemalan data. Operational size classes that varied by the individual producer and the functional flexibility of pots of a particular size suggest that assemblages of vessels used in a community, whether they are of specialist or nonspecialist origin, will blend diverse sizes that reflect the number of producers. Coefficients of variation among individual specialist's products differed significantly, which also strengthened the ratio effect. Perhaps the Amazonian nonspecialists tend to make more variably sized vessels than do Guatemalan specialists (coefficients of variation suggest this, but sample limitations prevent a more definitive statement). If so, skill limitations are no more compelling a reason than the following: production was certainly episodic and was likely tailored to immediate needs in a manner that was not comparable to specialist production as it was represented among the measurements taken at potters' workshops.

The ratio effect rather than the skill effect may well be a strong contributor to many archaeologists' impressions of greater standardization in specialist pottery. Because a few specialized pottery-producing communities, workshops, or producers could supply vessels to a surrounding population, it is not surprising that archaeologists and ethnographers may have registered noteworthy similarity in such pottery. Skill and practice may not constitute as profound an influence on assemblages as researchers have thought. The traditional expectation concerning skill could reflect an ethnocentric bias that ascribes greater competence to specialists in complex societies.

In the meantime, archaeological attempts to monitor specialization that rely exclusively on standardization cannot be strongly warranted. Rather, measurement of standardization should be combined with powerful ancillary data (Costin 1991). Examples of such data include evidence from some actual production locations concerning the mode of production (e.g., Pool and Santley 1992; Santley et al. 1987; Santley et al. 1989) and information concerning the spatial distributions of pottery (e.g., B. Stark and Heller 1987; B. Stark et al. 1985; Toll 1981). One particularly useful line of analysis for some archaeological situations examines local vs. nonlocal (presumably specialist-produced) pottery *within* a particular site or assemblage, thus controlling for time (B. Stark et al. 1985; Whittlesey 1974). However, evidence is accumulating that shows that archaeological industries may be mixed in degree of specialization, in some cases for the same products (Curet 1993; Santley et al. 1989; B. Stark 1992). Consumer archaeological assemblages may blend the effects of diverse production contexts. In such cases, interpretation of differences in degree of standardization among different categories of vessels may be difficult, and the distribution system(s) will likely not function the same for different modes of production.

Among the many potential archaeological variables, vessel forms should prove particularly useful because of the indications that specialization is associated with an increased diversity of forms and increased standardization within each. Both overall vessel form and attributes of form can be examined. Nicholson and Patterson (1985:234) found that rim form was specific to the potter, even though the potters themselves believed that this variable alone was insufficient for recognition of an individual's work. I have found it difficult to obtain adequate archaeological samples of reliable vessel-size measurements from sherds, which makes shape categories a useful alternative. Sheehy (1986) demonstrated that with very large data sets, problems in acquiring enough size measurements may be overcome by controlling for the proportion of arc represented. In general, archaeological studies of standardization must proceed cautiously (e.g., Costin 1991; Costin and Hagstrum 1995), given the currently problematic relation of standardization and specialization. In particular, comparisons of standardization require consideration of the possible biases introduced by factors such as the selection of suitable variables for analysis, the nature and partitioning of assemblages, technology and raw materials, and analytic methods.

Acknowledgments

My investigation of pottery standardization began under NSF grant BNS-79-12896. Warren DeBoer generously provided unpublished data and many valuable suggestions, and the study would not have been possible without his cooperation. I drafted this paper in 1986 and revised it to add the Papuan data, to use the Q statistic, and to note related papers that have subsequently been published. I presented an earlier version at the 1991 Southwestern Anthropological Association meeting in Tucson, Arizona, at a symposium that Miriam Stark organized; I appreciate her invitation to participate. I am grateful to Lynette Heller for able contributions as a research assistant at various points during the analysis. James Collins provided helpful references. Dean Arnold, Keith Kintigh, Prudence Rice, Dennis Young, and anonymous reviewers made constructive suggestions. Despite the many improvements in the paper that resulted from their comments, for which I thank them, none is responsible for deficiencies and errors, for which I claim my usual credit.

Notes

1. Rice (1991:270) remarked that my consideration of the skill vs. ratio effect "misses the point . . . that specialist/intensive production by definition means a (relatively) small number of producers." I believe that my definition of specialization is clearly stated. The concept of specialization is not the issue. Rather, I address what effects the mode of production has upon products and for what reason(s). Are specialists more skilled? Clearly variations in skill exist, but they may not be consistently associated with the mode of production. Consideration of the ratio effect focuses on individual (or workshop) variability in products and the effect that the number of producers has upon assemblages. Suppose, for the sake of argument, that there are no differences in skill between specialists and nonspecialists. Will the resultant assemblages exhibit similar variability?—not if individuals (for a variety of reasons) produce the same kind of products but with slightly (or markedly) different attributes.

2. One example of the resultant problems concerns temper. Suppose that the size and amount of temper particles are selected as paste variables for

analysis. Natural sorting of particles that occurred in the clay may be responsible for observed patterns, or the potters' selection of temper and manner of adding it to the clay may play a role, particularly the use of baskets, cloth, or screening to winnow particles. Nature, the skill of the potter, and technological devices may not be separable if one depends solely on archaeological observations in a collection of vessels or sherds.

3. Figure 9.1 shows bivariate plots of the three measurements on cooking pots. Plots of maximum diameter against height or orifice diameter indicate a cluster of five larger vessels, but small-capacity vessels are not very distinct, reflecting the closer ideal capacities of 5.6 and 6.8 kg (vs. 11.6 kg). Three vessels seem likely to fall into the smaller size class on the basis of maximum diameter plotted against orifice diameter (those with orifices of 20 cm or less). Consequently, the medium-capacity vessels analyzed will range from 21 to 32 cm in orifice diameter, but with only one case included at 32 cm because all other orifices of 32 cm or greater pertain to the putative large-capacity class (table 9.3).

For maximum diameter, medium cooking pots will range from 24 to 39 cm. Use of this range sets aside the two smallest maximum-diameter values signaled by a gap in the distribution of maximum diameter against orifice diameter (between 23 and 24 cm) in lieu of any clearer division in maximum diameter values. Note that a couple of the smaller values in the medium group are dubious, which may add to the diversity of the specialist values.

4. For potter 3, records were not clear about whether the measured vessels were fired or unfired. Because I group the measurements by 1-cm increments and it is unlikely that dramatic shrinking would occur with firing, I included measurements from potter 3. Among other categories of vessels, however, I excluded unfired vessels whenever sample size permitted.

5. Three capacity classes are not very distinct in the plot of maximum diameter against height except for the small size (fig. 9.2). Potter 3 made one aberrant vessel, which is particularly tall and wide mouthed; it will be ignored in subsequent analysis. Minimally a small-capacity class can be distinguished on the height-against-maximum-diameter plot (division of maximum diameter at 25 cm; of height, at 27 or 28 cm), but the number of cases is too low for standardization analysis. There may be two larger capacity clusters (dividing at about 33 cm in height), but they are quite close, with some intermediate values; in this situation, with the work of so few potters represented, distinction of medium from large capacities is much less certain. I include the maximum diameter values for vessels with 33 cm height in both the medium- and large-capacity groups because it is uncertain to which they are most pertinent.

The two orifice sizes said to be recognized may be reflected in a division between 11 and 12 cm (excluding small-capacity vessels, which seem to have a distinct pair of orifice sizes). The previous distinction between medium- and large-capacity vessels can be tested for any effect on orifice diameter by using chi-square. The chi-square test compares medium- and large-capacity vessels in regard to the frequencies of orifice diameters; two vessels with a height of 33 cm are not assigned to either capacity class for this analysis. For chi-square, it was necessary to group data into the following categories to form adequate cell counts: 7–10 cm, 11–14 cm, and 15–18 cm for orifice diameters. With two degrees of freedom, chi-square was 0.93, which suggests no significant difference at the 0.05 level for a one-tailed test. Consequently, I pool medium- and large-capacity classes in regard to large orifice diameters.

Some Sacojito jars are decorated, but some are plain. To determine if these two categories differ in regard to orifice diameter, it is best to compare decorated vs. plain vessels by potter 3. (Comparisons across potters may confound the individual variation of potters with any effects of decoration because all other decorated vessels are the work of potter 7.) Potter 3 produced 10 decorated and 14 plain jars. For the Fisher-Yates exact test (Siegel 1956:96–104), data for plain and decorated jars were grouped in two categories: 7–12 cm and 13–18 cm for orifice diameters. The contingency table can be constructed to use tables provided by Finney (1948). There is no significant difference at the 0.05 level. Consequently, for analysis of standardization in orifice diameter, I pool decorated and plain jars and the two possible capacity classes, medium and large.

6. A plot of maximum diameter against height for Durazno shows a cluster of small values (less than 20 cm in maximum diameter), which includes the one vessel that Arnold (1978:398) labeled as a small jar (fig. 9.3). There appear to be two closely spaced larger clusters, but they tend to be distinct in regard to potters. Therefore, it is unclear whether they represent size classes or individual potter's operational size categories. A conservative stance is to treat them as a single size class, possibly medium-to-large, because it will tend to increase the diversity of the specialist data and will not create a bias in the expected direction; the corresponding range for maximum diameter is 22–34 cm. Plots of orifice diameter against either height or maximum diameter show only slight differences in orifice diameter for the small- and medium-to-large–capacity groups. Small-capacity vessels all have orifices of less than 10 cm, but only one medium-to-large–capacity vessel does (fig. 9.3). The medium-to-large group typically has orifices of 10–12 cm. For Durazno, unlike Sacojito, the two orifice size classes that are recognized seem to be linked strongly to the capacity classes.

7. Specialist potters in Mixco, another Guatemalan community, predominantly manufactured completely molded tortilla griddles (Arnold 1978:337–345). In cases in which size classes could be readily distinguished, e.g., potter 2, coefficients of variation were consistently quite low (0.01, 0.02, and 0.02), as would be expected with use of complete molds.

References Cited

Arnold, Dean E.

1978   The Ethnography of Pottery Making in the Valley of Guatemala. In *The Ceramics of Kaminaljuyu, Guatemala,* edited by Ronald K. Wetherington, pp. 327–400. Pennsylvania State University Press, University Park.

Arnold, Dean E., and Alvaro L. Nieves

1992   Factors Affecting Ceramic Standardization. In *Ceramic Production and Distribution: An Integrated Approach,* edited by George J. Bey III and Christopher A. Pool, pp. 93–113. Westview Press, Boulder, Colorado.

Balfet, Hèléne

1965   Ethnographical Observations in North Africa and Archaeological Interpretation: The Pottery of the Maghreb. In *Ceramics and Man,* edited by Frederick R. Matson, pp. 161–177. Aldine Publishing Co., Chicago.

Benco, Nancy L.

1988   Morphological Standardization: An Approach to the Study of Craft Specialization. In *A Pot for All Reasons: Ceramic Ecology Revisited,* edited by Charles C. Kolb and Louanna Lackey, pp. 57–72. Laboratory of Anthropology, Temple University, Philadelphia.

Birmingham, Judy

1975   Traditional Potters of the Kathmandu Valley: An Ethnoarchaeological Study. *Man* 10:370–386.

Blalock, Herbert M., Jr.

1972   *Social Statistics.* 2nd ed. McGraw-Hill Book Co., New York.

Braun, David P.

1980   Appendix I, Experimental Interpretation of Ceramic Vessel Use on the Basis of Rim and Neck Formal Attributes. In *The Navajo Project: Archaeological Investigations, Page to Phoenix 500 KV Southern Transmission Line,* by Donald C. Fiero, Robert W. Munson, Martha T. McClain, Suzanne M. Wilson, and Anne H. Zier, pp. 171–228. Research Report 11. Museum of Northern Arizona, Flagstaff.

1985   Ceramic Decorative Diversity and Illinois Woodland Regional Integration. In *Decoding Prehistoric Ceramics,* edited by Ben A. Nelson, pp. 128–154. Southern Illinois University Press, Carbondale.

Bronitsky, Gordon

1978   Postclassic Maya Plainware Ceramics: Measures of Cultural Homogeneity. In *Papers on the Economy and Architecture of the Ancient Maya,* edited by Ronald Sidrys, pp. 142–154. Monograph VIII. Institute of Archaeology, University of California, Los Angeles.

Burr, I. W.

1974   *Applied Statistical Methods.* Academic Press, New York.

Conkey, Margaret W.

1980   The Identification of Prehistoric Hunter-Gatherer Aggregation Sites: The Case of Altamira. *Current Anthropology* 21:609–630.

Costin, Cathy L.

1991   Craft Specialization: Issues in Defining, Documenting, and Explaining the Organization of Production. In *Archaeological Method and Theory,* vol. 3, edited by Michael B. Schiffer, pp. 1–56. University of Arizona Press, Tucson.

Costin, Cathy L., and Melissa B. Hagstrum

1995   Standardization, Labor Investment, Skill and the Organization of Ceramic Production in Late Prehispanic Highland Peru. *American Antiquity,* in press.

Cowgill, George L.

1989   The Concept of Diversity in Archaeological Theory. In *Quantifying Diversity in Archaeology,* edited by Robert D. Leonard and George T. Jones, pp. 131–141. Cambridge University Press, Cambridge.

Curet, Antonio

1993   Regional Studies and Ceramic Production Areas: An Example from La Mixtequilla, Veracruz, Mexico. *Journal of Field Archaeology* 20(4):427–440.

Daddario, Joanne T.

1980   *Ceramic Productive Specialization and Sociopolitical Complexity in the Prehistoric Plateau Southwest: A Test of the Relationship.* Unpublished Master's thesis, Department of Anthropology, Arizona State University, Tempe.

David, Nicholas, and Hilke Hennig

1972   The Ethnography of Pottery: A Fulani Case Seen in Archaeological Perspective. *McCaleb Module* 21:1–29. Addison-Wesley Modular Publications, Reading, Massachusetts.

DeBoer, Warren R., and S. A. Kaufman

1977   Developments in Ethnoarchaeology: Examples from the Upper Amazon. Paper presented at the 42nd Annual Meeting of the Society for American Archaeology, New Orleans.

DeBoer, Warren R., and Donald W. Lathrap

1979   The Making and Breaking of Shipibo-Conibo Ceramics. In *Ethnoarchaeology: Implications of Ethnography for Archaeology,* edited by Carol Kramer, pp. 102–138. Columbia University Press, New York.

Dickens, Roy S., Jr.

1980   Ceramic Diversity as an Indicator of Cultural Dynamics in the Wood-
        land Period. *Tennessee Anthropologist* 5(1):34–46.

Erich, R. W.

1965   Ceramics and Man: A Cultural Perspective. In *Ceramics and Man*, edited
        by Frederick R. Matson, pp. 1–19. Aldine Publishing Co., Chicago.

Feinman, Gary

1980   *The Relationship Between Administrative Organization and Ceramic Produc-
        tion in the Valley of Oaxaca.* Unpublished Ph.D. dissertation, Depart-
        ment of Anthropology, City University of New York, New York.

Finney, David J.

1948   The Fisher-Yates Test of Significance in 2 x 2 Contingency Tables. *Bio-
        metrika* 35:145–156.

Fontana, Bernard L., William J. Robinson, Charles W. Cormack, and
Ernest E. Leavitt, Jr.

1962   *Papago Indian Pottery.* University of Washington Press, Seattle.

Foster, George M.

1965   The Sociology of Pottery: Questions and Hypotheses Arising from
        Contemporary Mexican Work. In *Ceramics and Man*, edited by Freder-
        ick R. Matson, pp. 43–61. Aldine Publishing Co., Chicago.

1967   *Tzintzuntzan: Mexican Peasants in a Changing World.* Little, Brown, Boston.

Friedrich, Margaret H.

1970   Design Structure and Social Interaction: Archaeological Implications of
        an Ethnographic Analysis. *American Antiquity* 35(3):332–343.

Hagstrum, Melissa B.

1985   Measuring Prehistoric Ceramic Craft Specialization: A Test Case in the
        American Southwest. *Journal of Field Archaeology* 12(1):65–75.

Hardin, Margaret A.

1977   Individual Style in San Jose Pottery Painting: The Role of Deliberate
        Choice. In *The Individual in Prehistory: Studies of Variability in Style in
        Prehistoric Technologies*, edited by James N. Hill and Joel Gunn, pp.
        109–136. Academic Press, New York.

Hill, James N.

1977   Individual Variability in Ceramics and the Study of Prehistoric Social
        Organization. In *The Individual in Prehistory: Studies of Variability in Style
        in Prehistoric Technologies*, edited by James Hill and Joel Gunn, pp.
        55–108. Academic Press, New York.

Hurlbert, Stuart H.

1971   The Nonconcept of Species Diversity: A Critique and Alternative Para-
        meters. *Ecology* 52(4):577–586.

Jones, George T., Donald K. Grayson, and Charlotte Beck
1983   Artifact Class Richness and Sample Size in Archaeological Surface As-
        semblages. In *Lulu Linear Punctated: Essays in Honor of George Irving
        Quimby*, edited by Robert C. Dunnell and Donald K. Grayson, pp.
        55–73. Anthropological Papers No. 72. Museum of Anthropology, Uni-
        versity of Michigan, Ann Arbor.

Kaufman, S. A.
1977   *Individual Variations and the Reconstruction of Prehistoric Patterns of Arti-
        fact Production: A Test from the Late Neolithic Site of Divostin, Jugoslavia.*
        Unpublished Ph.D. dissertation, Department of Anthropology, City
        University of New York, New York.

Kintigh, Keith W.
1984   Measuring Archaeological Diversity by Comparison with Simulated
        Assemblages. *American Antiquity* 49(1):44–54.
1989   Sample Size, Significance, and Measures of Diversity. In *Quantifying
        Diversity in Archaeology*, edited by Robert D. Leonard and George T.
        Jones, pp. 25–36. Cambridge University Press, Cambridge.

Lauer, Peter K.
1974   *Pottery Traditions in the D'Entrecasteaux Islands of Papua.* Occasional Pa-
        pers in Anthropology No. 3, University of Queensland, Australia.

Leonard, Robert D., and George T. Jones (editors)
1989   *Quantifying Diversity in Archaeology.* University of Cambridge Press,
        Cambridge.

Linne, Sigvald
1965   The Ethnologist and the American Indian Potter. In *Ceramics and Man*,
        edited by Frederick R. Matson, pp. 20–42. Aldine Publishing Co.,
        Chicago.

Longacre, William A., Kenneth L. Kvamme, and Masashi Kobayashi
1988   Southwestern Pottery Standardization: An Ethnoarchaeological View
        from the Philippines. *The Kiva* 53(2):101–111.

McCartney, Peter H., and Margaret F. Glass
1990   Simulation Models and the Interpretation of Archaeological Diversity.
        American Antiquity 55(3):521–536.

Matson, Frederick R.
1965   Ceramic Queries. In *Ceramics and Man*, edited by Frederick R. Matson,
        pp. 277–287. Aldine Publishing Co., Chicago.

Nicholson, Paul, and Helen Patterson
1985   Pottery Making in Upper Egypt: An Ethnoarchaeological Study. *World
        Archaeology* 17(2):222–239.

Peet, Robert K.

1974   The Measurement of Species Diversity. *Annual Review of Ecology and Systematics* 5:285–307.

Plog, Stephen

1980   *Stylistic Variation in Prehistoric Ceramics: Design Analysis in the American Southwest.* Cambridge University Press, Cambridge.

Pool, Christopher A., and Robert S. Santley

1992   Middle Classic Pottery Economics in the Tuxtla Mountains, Southern Veracruz, Mexico. In *Ceramic Production and Distribution: An Integrated Approach,* edited by George L. Bey III and Christopher A. Pool, pp. 205–234. Westview Press, Boulder, Colorado.

Rathje, William L.

1975   The Last Tango in Mayapan: A Tentative Trajectory of Production-Distribution Systems. In *Ancient Civilization and Trade,* edited by J. A. Sabloff and C. C. Lamberg-Karlovsky, pp. 409–448. University of New Mexico Press, Albuquerque.

Rice, Prudence M.

1981   Evolution of Specialized Pottery Production: A Trial Model. *Current Anthropology* 22:219–240.

1987   *Pottery Analysis: A Sourcebook.* University of Chicago Press, Chicago.

1989   Ceramic Diversity, Production, and Use. In *Quantifying Diversity in Archaeology,* edited by Robert D. Leonard and George T. Jones, pp. 109–117. Cambridge University Press, Cambridge.

1991   Specialization, Standardization, and Diversity: A Retrospective. In *The Ceramic Legacy of Anna O. Shepard,* edited by Ronald L. Bishop and Frederick W. Lange, pp. 257–279. University Press of Colorado, Niwot.

Rottlander, Rolf C. A.

1967   Is Provincial-Roman Pottery Standardized? *Archaeometry* 9:76–91.

Santley, Robert S., Phillip J. Arnold III, and Christopher A. Pool

1989   The Ceramic Production System at Matacapan, Veracruz. *Journal of Field Archaeology* 16:107–132.

Santley, Robert S., Ponciano Ortiz C., and Christopher A. Pool

1987   Recent Archaeological Research at Matacapan, Veracruz: A Summary of the Results of the 1982–1986 Field Seasons. *Mexicon* 9(2):41–48.

Sears, William H.

1973   The Sacred and the Secular in Prehistoric Ceramics. In *Variation in Anthropology: Essays in Honor of John C. McGregor,* edited by Donald W. Lathrap and J. Douglas, pp. 31–42. Illinois Archaeological Survey, Urbana.

Sheehy, James L.
1986   Product Standardization and Ceramic Production in Tlajinga 33, Teoti-
        huacan. Paper presented at the 51st Annual Meeting of the Society for
        American Archaeology, New Orleans.

Siegel, Sidney
1956   *Nonparametric Statistics for the Behavioral Sciences.* McGraw-Hill Book
        Co., New York.

Stark, Barbara L.
1985   Archaeological Identification of Pottery Production Locations: Ethno-
        archaeological and Archaeological Data in Mesoamerica. In *Decoding
        Prehistoric Ceramics*, edited by Ben A. Nelson, pp. 158–194. Southern
        Illinois University Press, Carbondale.
1992   Ceramic Production in La Mixtequilla, Veracruz, Mexico. In *Ceramic
        Production and Distribution: An Integrated Approach*, edited by George J.
        Bey III and Christopher A. Pool, pp. 175–204. Westview Press, Boulder,
        Colorado.

Stark, Barbara L., and L. Heller
1987   Vessel Forms at La Ciudad. In *La Ciudad: Specialized Studies in the Econ-
        omy, Environment and Culture of La Ciudad, Part I and II*, edited by Joanne
        E. Kisselburg, Glen E. Rice, and Brenda L. Shears, pp. 41–73. Anthropo-
        logical Field Studies No. 20. Arizona State University, Tempe.

Stark, Barbara L., Linda Heller, Frederick W. Nelson, Ronald Bishop,
Deborah M. Pearsall, and David S. Whitley
1985   El Balsamo Residential Investigations: A Pilot Project and Research Is-
        sues. *American Anthropologist* 87:100–111.

Stark, Barbara L., and J. T. Hepworth
1982   A Diversity Index Approach to Analysis of Standardization in Pre-
        historic Pottery. In *Computer Applications in Archaeology 1982: Confer-
        ence Proceedings*, pp. 87–104. University of Birmingham, Birmingham,
        England.

Stark, Miriam T., William Longacre, and Kenneth Kvamme
1991   Ethnoarchaeological Perspectives on Ceramic Specialization: Four
        Philippine Examples. Paper presented at the 62nd Annual Meeting of
        the Southwestern Anthropological Association, Tucson.

Toll, H. Wolcott
1981   Ceramic Comparisons Concerning Redistribution in Chaco Canyon,
        New Mexico. In *Production and Distribution: A Ceramic Viewpoint*, edited
        by Hillary Howard and Elaine L. Morris, pp. 83–121. BAR International
        Series 120. British Archaeological Reports, Oxford.

van der Leeuw, Sander E.

1977   Towards a Study of the Economics of Pottery Making. In *Ex Horreo,* edited by B. L. van Beek, R. W. Brandt, and W. Groenman-van Waateringe, pp. 68–76. Albert Egges van Giffen Instituut voor Prae-en Protohistorie, Universiteit van Amsterdam, Amsterdam.

Whallon, Robert, Jr.

1968   Investigations of Late Prehistoric Social Organization in New York State. In *New Perspectives in Archeology,* edited by Sally R. Binford and Lewis R. Binford, pp. 223–244. Aldine Publishing Co., Chicago.

Whittlesey, Stephanie M.

1974   Identification of Imported Ceramics Through Functional Analysis of Attributes. *The Kiva* 40(1–2):101–112.

Wright, Rita

1983   Standardization as Evidence for Craft Specialization: A Case Study. Paper presented at the 82nd Annual Meeting of the American Anthropological Association, Chicago.

10

Paradigms and Pottery

The Analysis of Production and Exchange in the American Southwest

Stephen Plog

Perhaps more than any other recent publication, this set of papers epitomizes both change and stability in the nature of archaeological research in the prehistoric American Southwest. From the very beginning of these studies, the abundant ceramics that litter the surface of so many Southwestern archaeological sites have been a major focus, whether for purposes of typology, chronology building, and spatial-temporal frameworks or for studies of social organization, exchange, and interaction. Of particular relevance to the theme of this volume, some of the earliest investigations of New World ceramic production were conducted in the Southwest beginning in the 1930s by the peerless Anna O. Shepard. From the perspective of that long history, a volume on Southwestern ceramics is hardly a new phenomenon. This volume is simply another important member of a long and honored lineage.

The above characterization, however, glosses over significant differences—some fairly obvious and others more subtle—between the papers in this volume and those in previous books on the pottery of the Southwest. Although I acknowledge Shepard's numerous and significant contributions, I believe that Barbara Mills and Patricia Crown, by assembling an entire volume of papers on ceramic production in the Southwest, have shown that the nature of archaeological research has significantly changed. Shepard is "peerless" in two senses of the word; the quality of her research was outstanding, and unfortunately few scholars chose to continue her pioneering analyses of ceramic technology. Compared to the sporadic nature of such studies even during the decades of the 1970s and 1980s, the studies in this volume, along with others published elsewhere (e.g., Bishop et al. 1988; Douglass 1987; Neitzel and Bishop 1990) foretell a major change in research direction over the next decade.

Such transitions inevitably raise questions regarding the reasons for the change. I believe that the paucity of earlier studies was partly due to the considerable technical skills required to conduct them—skills taught in few graduate programs in archaeology. This lack of training, however, must also be explained, particularly in light of the significant insights that Shepard's (e.g., 1939, 1965) studies provided—e.g., the importation of thousands of vessels into Chaco Canyon—and the fact that those insights were largely ignored for several decades. In retrospect, it seems obvious that the explanatory framework within which most Southwestern archaeologists operated was the primary reason for the lack of production studies. That framework was based (for time periods after ca. A.D. 700) on the assumption of egalitarian, autonomous farming villages in which all of the basic tools required for day-to-day life were produced within the village. Those tools included ceramic vessels. Archaeologists believed that vessel production by each and every household was the typical pattern during almost every prehistoric period and in virtually every geographic area. Why study ceramic production when household production was presumably ubiquitous? Thus, books on Southwestern ceramics published just over a decade ago (Schroeder 1982) rarely even mention the possibility of variation in the organization of production. As Kuhn (1962:53) has argued, until a discipline "has learned to see nature in a different way—the new fact [Shepard's evidence for exchange, in this instance] is not quite a scientific fact at all."

Over the last 15 years, two forces have increased our focus on ceramic production and exchange, and it is important to recognize both in order to place the articles in this volume in their proper context. One fundamental factor is that methods of mineralogical and chemical characterization have become more accessible, allowing more precise determination of the locations of production. The Conservation Analytical Laboratory at the Smithsonian Institution and the National Bureau of Standards (through the help and cooperation of Lambertus van Zelst, Ronald Bishop, and James Blackman), in particular, have provided several Southwestern archaeologists with the facilities and training for important studies of the nature of ceramic production and exchange.

Nevertheless, I believe that the accessibility of these analytic tools is not the primary reason for the recent emphasis on production and exchange studies. The new emphasis evolved more from the development of new frameworks to explain cultural change in the Southwest, frameworks that are based on different theoretical perspectives and different assumptions than those that guided much of the archaeological research in the past. Some of these new models postulated the development of significant social differentiation in some sections of the prehistoric Southwest and typically argued that greater differentiation is tied in various ways to exchange relationships (Lightfoot 1984; Lightfoot and Feinman 1982; Sebastien 1991; Upham 1982).

At the same time, other researchers (e.g., Braun and Plog 1982; S. Plog 1980; Wills 1988) postulated exchange relationships for areas and time periods that probably had no significant sociopolitical complexity. From this perspective, exchange is viewed as an expected characteristic of almost all societies, from mobile hunter-gatherers living in small bands to people living in urban centers characterized by economic specialization (e.g., Ford 1972; Spier 1928). Even simple reciprocal exchange among households, however, can result in the movement of significant numbers of items over sizeable areas and, thus, can have a considerable impact on the artifactual assemblages of individual villages (Allen 1984; Crown, this volume).

Although these two general models differ in specifics, they both emphasize relationships between groups in explanations of cultural stability and change; thus, they stress the need to place Southwestern villages in broader regional contexts. Both types of models postulate that exchange relationships are not limited to regions where natural resources are differentially distributed or where shortages of agricultural land force segments of the population to consider nonagricultural occupations. Rather, those relationships develop because of a variety of demographic, social, economic, religious, and political factors, and the items traded include not only exotics, such as turquoise and macaws, but also nonexotics, such as ceramics and chipped-stone raw materials.

Certainly most scholars familiar with the current literature on the prehistoric Southwest are aware of the differences between earlier explanatory frameworks and those advanced more recently. They have structured much of our discourse regarding Southwestern prehistory. Many of the articles in this volume either explicitly or implicitly attempt to evaluate these frameworks. Nevertheless, I believe it is important to emphasize the differences here for two reasons, the foremost of which is their relevance to the papers in this volume. Whether someone is inclined to accept one of the more recently advanced alternative perspectives or the prior model of autonomous villages, more precise determinations of the exact nature of production and of intensities of exchange become mandatory. The issues addressed in this volume thus lie at the very center of the current debate. When the articles in this volume are compared, it is clear that differences in the reconstructions of the magnitude and intensity of ceramic exchange and production are not simply narrow disputes about those components of prehistoric behavior, but are also parts of much broader debates over the ways the prehistoric Southwestern societies were organized and evolved.

The second reason for emphasizing the differences between explanatory frameworks is to highlight that the debate is not between theoreticians and empiricists. It is not uncommon (sometimes in print, but more often in conversation) to see arguments for household production and consumption characterized as "empirically grounded," in contrast to arguments for exchange that are pejoratively labeled "conjectural" or "speculative." The alternative models described above are not paradigms in the broadest sense that Kuhn (1962) used that word (nor do I want to unearth the rhetoric of the 1960s or imply that Southwestern archaeology is undergoing a revolution). These models, however, do have impacts very comparable to those that Kuhn described for scientific paradigms. They "exert a deep hold on the scientific mind," leading to "incommensurable ways of seeing the world and practicing science in it" (Kuhn 1962:4, 5). Thus, different scholars see the same "facts" in very different ways because fact and theory are not separable. One scholar's "reasonable assumption" is another's "problematic assertion" (e.g., Sullivan 1992) because assumptions are tied to theoretical perspectives.

Sullivan's (1988) review of evidence for ceramic production in the northern Southwest serves as an excellent example of the latter points. He stated (1988:23) that, with the exception of two cases, "Southwestern sites rarely have disclosed convincing feature and artifact evidence of on-site pottery-making and pottery-firing areas." Yet, after summarizing 15 "representative, but not exhaustive" cases where some evidence of production had been recovered (9 of the 15 were considered "strong" cases), he concluded (p. 31) "that pottery was made at all types of large and small settlements" and argued that it may therefore be necessary to revise "centralized ceramic-production models." This conclusion is consistent with Sullivan's defense of the traditional model of prehistoric South-western societies, which postulates that ceramic production was characteristic of most households.

As one who has been an advocate of some of the alternative models, I, however, place the 15 sites that Sullivan discusses in the context of the many hundreds of sites that have been excavated in the Southwest where convincing evidence of production is lacking. Many of the strong cases are sites (e.g., Pueblo Bonito, Show Low Ruin, Kiet Siel, and Snaketown) that are much larger than average or atypical in other ways and, thus, are not good models for the areas and time periods when hundreds of small villages dotted the landscape. In addition, more than 50 percent of the utility pottery found at Pueblo Bonito was imported during some periods. The presence of production facilities at a site is thus compatible with the import or export of significant numbers of vessels. Noting the simple presence of production facilities does not begin to address the many questions that have been raised about degrees of specialized production or the differential exchange of different ceramic types and wares. Sullivan's sweeping conclusions are thus, from my point of view, so inconsistent with the data he presented that they are perplexing. We simply see the *same facts* in, to use Kuhn's words, very different and incommensurable ways.

Given the impoverished studies on the history of technology and production, we simply do not at present have a clear conception of the range of variation in production and exchange. However, now that questions about exchange and production are so central to current discourse, studies such as those presented in this volume will become a common and significant path toward resolving the current debates. I am therefore optimistic about the directions being taken in current research. At the same time, it is critical that we ask what must be done to move toward resolution, to the point where the individual studies of particular sites, areas, or time periods are not isolated pieces of information, but can be placed within a broader characterization of variation in production and exchange behavior.

The Production and Organizational Continua

As research progresses, I believe it is important that we keep in mind several issues that are underscored in this volume. Among the most central is that we should measure exchange and production on a continuum. As noted in several chapters, production should not be dichotomized as either specialized or unspecialized, but should be measured as much as possible on a continuous scale ranging from production by each household in each village to specialized production by a single household or work group in only one village in a region. Similarly, we should not limit our discussions of exchange to noting presence or absence, but should describe variation along a number of dimensions (F. Plog 1977) and examine the relationships among exchanges of different ceramic wares or different materials (Wilson and Blinman, this volume). Oversimplified descriptions of exchange and production will only result in oversimplified understandings of cultural change.

This desire for greater specificity must, however, be tempered by the quality of our data and the precision of our methods of measurement. Even in the best studies conducted to date, there is typically little evidence that allows us to address directly the question of variation among households *within a village*. As Hegmon et al. (this volume) note, several potters in a single village may exploit the same raw material sources, making their products chemically and mineralogically indistinguishable. Thus, in most studies of Southwestern ceramic exchange, we are (at present) essentially asking questions about whether production of a given ceramic type did or did not occur within a village as a whole, rather than addressing variation in production at the household level.

Our goal of continuous measurement should not be restricted to measurements of production and exchange, however. We vastly oversimplify organizational variation in human societies when we conclude that status differential is either present or absent, that groups are either egalitarian or complex. To understand the evolution of Southwestern societies and to assess the extent to which production and exchange are linked to social differentiation and political development, we must measure *variation* along all of these dimensions—both our models and our methods must allow for continuous measurement.

Sample Size and Variation

Characterizations of production along a continuum are inseparable from the consideration of sample size (in terms of both the number of settlements sampled and the number of sherds analyzed) and variation within a sample. Here again we must avoid over-generalizations that may obscure complex patterns. Evidence of production in more than one village in a given region does not mean that all villagers were producers. Evidence of local (or nonlocal) production of a given ceramic type does not mean that all vessels of that type were produced locally (or imported). Evidence that all examples of one ceramic type were produced locally does not eliminate the possibility that other types were produced elsewhere. These caveats regarding the problems of inferring from small samples to larger populations are particularly important because the multivariate statistical techniques that are often necessary for the analysis of complex data sets (e.g., trace-element frequencies from instrumental neutron activation analysis) focus attention on samples that fit patterns, not samples that deviate from those patterns. Important exceptions to central tendencies may thus be minimized, if not overlooked.

The study of Hopi yellow-firing pottery from northern Arizona by Bishop et al. (1988) can be used as an illustration. They characterized 169 vessels using instrumental neutron activation analysis and then employed multivariate analysis of the trace-element frequencies to identify primary-paste-composition reference groups that were site specific. Given the pioneering nature of their study, they cautiously suggested (1988:325) that only 103 vessels that could be assigned to one of three primary paste groups and were recovered from the presumed locus of production could "be assumed to have been locally produced." Based on these vessels, Bishop et al. (1988:333) concluded that "the evidence of ceramic production on the Hopi mesas between A.D. 1300 and 1600 would appear to support a model of production wherein Hopi villagers at each site had equal access to resources and manufactured ceramics that were used on-site."

Although I recognize the significant general pattern that Bishop et al. (1988) identified, I also note that they could not determine a production locus for numerous samples with the available information. At least 12 vessels belonged to one of the primary paste groups, yet were found at sites other than the inferred locus of production (p. 330, Table 6); 32 vessels were assigned to secondary paste-composition reference groups (p. 323, Table 2); and 34 vessels were not assigned to either a primary or a secondary group. Thus, a minimum of 39 percent of the vessels analyzed did not fit the criteria that Bishop et al. employed to identify local production. The possibility remains that two of every five vessels were not locally produced. Their argument that the data support a model of local production and consumption therefore seems premature (although the analysis continues [De Atley et al. 1991], and the authors are pursuing further source identification), given that we are ultimately interested in the production of all samples, not just those that fit the dominant pattern.

Units of Study

In a region where ceramics have been studied so intensively for so long, it is tempting to start our analyses by assuming that we already know how to sort the pottery into categories. Of particular relevance here is the common use of individual ceramic types to define separate populations for chemical or mineralogical characterization. Although this method may be appropriate in some instances, in other cases such categories may hinder our analyses. As Shepard (1965:85) argued, "the very method of classifying sherds—by reference to norms (pottery types)—obscures the record of change."

There are three specific issues that are of concern. First, distinctions among Southwestern ceramic types (as opposed to distinctions among wares) are typically made on the basis of stylistic characteristics rather than on aspects of material composition. Material distinctions are undoubtedly relevant to efforts to identify patterns of chemical or mineralogical composition, but stylistic distinctions may not be. Second, the use of types assumes that the boundaries between categories are discrete. Numerous studies (e.g., Abbott and Walsh-Anduze, this volume; Neitzel 1984; S. Plog 1991) have shown that the mutually exclusive clusters of attributes that are the foundation of type descriptions have little empirical reality in many cases. Rather than discrete classes, the categories (i.e., types) overlap. Recent theoretical perspectives (S. Plog 1991) also raise the possibility that the existence of discrete types should not be expected in all times and places, but will depend on the nature of social dynamics. Third, as Abbott and Walsh-Anduze (this volume) demonstrate, these typological systems are based on certain assumptions about the causes of ceramic variation. By accepting those systems, we impose those assumptions on our data and unconsciously remove some dimensions of variation that we are striving to study.

The study by Abbott and Walsh-Anduze is an exciting example of the new understandings that can be achieved when analytic units are carefully defined in a manner consistent with the questions being asked. Their conclusion—that the pattern of temporal change may not have been the result of uniform changes in production across a region as assumed by traditional typologies, but rather was a product of changes in local production and exchange relationships—is strikingly similar to findings in the Chevelon drainage of east-central Arizona (S. Plog 1980). The latter discovery was also made when we eschewed traditional type definitions and instead employed petrographic and simpler microscopic identifications to define analytic groups. Traditional ceramic typologies, therefore, should be used as analytic units only with extreme caution, if at all.

Context

One of the key points emphasized by most of the articles in this volume is that we must pay increasing attention to the contexts in which ceramics are produced and used. Vessels are not simply containers that vary in utilitarian function, but may also play important and active roles in various social and religious affairs. As a result, vessel characteristics may have as much to do with those affairs as they do with the desire to make strong, durable containers suitable for processing or storing foods. Our attempts to explain similarities and differences or degrees of variation in ceramics must go beyond traditional factors, such as economic change or migration, and beyond the more recent emphasis on exchange, to consider a broader range of variables and relationships.

Zedeño (this volume), for example, suggests that the sudden appearance of Roosevelt Red Ware (more typically referred to as Salado Red Ware [Crown 1994]) in the Grasshopper region at the end of the thirteenth century was a result of in-migration of people from the north as the Colorado Plateau was abandoned because of a serious drought. Before the change, decorated vessels (both bowls and jars) were primarily black-on-white; afterward most bowls were Salado Red Ware and most jars continued to be black-on-white. Zedeño argues that the immigrants "brought a few [Salado Red Ware] bowls with them and began to manufacture . . . bowls with local clays"; this, in turn, "stimulated the adoption of a foreign ware by mountain potters." Alternatively, Montgomery and Reid (1990:95) proposed that the Salado Red Ware may have been "a low-fire solution to ceramic manufacture encouraged by increased residential stability" because "sedentism reduces the movement of pots and thus relaxes the need for the mechanical strength of high-fired ceramics."

In both studies, primarily economic factors (migration resulting from drought and greater residential stability) are the hypothesized causes of the production of Salado Red Ware.

Both explanations, however, fail to account for one of the most interesting aspects of the change—the strong association between bowls and early Salado Red Ware, on the one hand, and between jars and Cibola White Ware, on the other. If increasing residential stability relaxed the need for mechanical strength, why weren't all decorated vessels Salado Red Ware? Also, if immigrants brought a new pottery tradition that was then imitated by the indigenous inhabitants, why was that tradition limited to the manufacture of bowls? Although it could be argued that immigrants could have carried bowls more easily, this does not explain why there is little or no change in the relationship between form and vessel color after the hypothesized migration. The strong association between ware (color) and form suggests that new explanations must be sought in the contextual and symbolic dimensions of the vessels. Crown's (1994) recent proposal that the symbolic aspects of the painted designs on the Salado Red Ware may have signaled participation in an emerging cult is one particularly intriguing hypothesis along the line that I am suggesting.

Context is also important in the interpretation of the standardization measures that receive considerable attention in this volume. Some contexts of use, particularly those related to social relationships or ritual affairs, may demand considerable standardization in vessel characteristics that is unrelated to either the number of producers or the ratio of producers to consumers and has little to do with production efficiency (see Hegmon et al., this volume). For that reason, standardization measures are not straightforward indexes of productive specialization.

Conclusions

"It is becoming increasingly apparent that the actual point of manufacture of several types may be much less widespread than was originally thought, it being possible that only a few families, or perhaps, villages, made most types and traded them to surrounding areas" (McGregor 1965:101).

John McGregor's statement is one of the few made before 1980 that hypothesize that specialized ceramic production in the Southwest may have been common. Many similar proposals have been advanced in recent years based on new conceptions of the structure and organization of prehistoric societies and tantalizing bits of new evidence. The paucity of detailed studies of ceramic technology and production in the years following the initial studies by Anna Shepard has always hindered tests of these hypotheses, but the papers in this volume illustrate an important shift in ceramic research toward the investigation of such issues. Although there is at present little consensus on the nature of production or the implications of production and exchange data for questions of social organization and differentiation, that is not surprising given the complexities involved in understanding the modes of production of even a single ware in a single area. These papers demonstrate that significant progress is being made and that the debate over issues of production, exchange, and cultural change has really just begun.

References Cited

Allen, Jim

1984   Pots and Poor Princes: A Multidimensional Approach to the Role of Pottery Trading in Coastal Papua. In *The Many Dimensions of Pottery: Ceramics in Archaeology and Anthropology*, edited by Sander E. van der Leeuw and Alison C. Pritchard, pp. 407–463. Albert Egges van Giffen Instituut voor Prae-en Protohistorie, Universiteit van Amsterdam, Amsterdam.

Bishop, Ronald L., Valetta Canouts, Suzanne P. De Atley, Alvin Qoyawayma, and C. W. Aikens

1988   The Formation of Ceramic Analytical Groups: Hopi Pottery Production and Exchange, A.D. 1300–1600. *Journal of Field Archaeology* 15:317–337.

Braun, David P., and Stephen Plog

1982   Evolution of "Tribal" Social Networks: Theory and Prehistoric North American Evidence. *American Antiquity* 47:504–525.

Crown, Patricia L.

1994   *Ceramics and Ideology: Salado Polychrome Pottery*. University of New Mexico Press, Albuquerque.

De Atley, Suzanne P., Valetta Canouts, and Ronald Bishop

1991   Modeling Changes in Technological Style and Organizational Structure of the Hopi Yellow Ware Tradition, A.D. 1300 to 1600. Paper presented at the 56th Annual Meeting of the Society for American Archaeology, New Orleans.

Douglass, Amy A.

1987 *Prehistoric Exchange and Sociopolitical Development: The Little Colorado White Ware Production-Distribution System.* Ph.D. dissertation, Arizona State University, Tempe. University Microfilms, Ann Arbor.

Ford, Richard I.

1972 Barter, Gift, or Violence. In *Social Exchange and Interaction,* edited by Edwin Wilmsen, pp. 21–45. Anthropological Papers No. 75. Museum of Anthropology, University of Michigan, Ann Arbor.

Kuhn, Thomas S.

1962 *The Structure of Scientific Revolutions.* University of Chicago Press, Chicago.

Lightfoot, Kent G.

1984 *Prehistoric Political Dynamics: A Case Study from the American Southwest.* Northern Illinois University Press, De Kalb.

Lightfoot, Kent G., and Gary Feinman

1982 Social Differentiation and Leadership Development in Early Pithouse Villages in the Mogollon Region of the American Southwest. *American Antiquity* 47:64–86.

McGregor, John C.

1965 *Southwestern Archaeology.* University of Illinois Press, Urbana.

Montgomery, Barbara K., and J. Jefferson Reid

1990 An Instance of Rapid Ceramic Change. *American Antiquity* 55:88–97.

Neitzel, Jill E.

1984 *The Regional Organization of the Hohokam in the American Southwest: A Stylistic Analysis of Red-on-Buff Pottery.* Ph.D. dissertation, Arizona State University, Tempe. University Microfilms, Ann Arbor.

Neitzel, Jill E., and Ronald L. Bishop

1990 Neutron Activation of Dogoszhi Ceramics: Production and Exchange in the Chacoan Regional System. *The Kiva* 56:67–85.

Plog, Fred

1977 Modeling Economic Exchange. In *Exchange Systems in Prehistory,* edited by Timothy K. Earle and Jonathon E. Ericson, pp. 127–140. Academic Press, New York.

Plog, Stephen

1980 *Stylistic Variation in Prehistoric Ceramics.* Cambridge University Press, Cambridge.

1991 Sociopolitical Implications of Stylistic Variation in the American Southwest. In *The Uses of Style in Archaeology,* edited by Margaret W. Conkey and Christine A. Hastorf, pp. 61–72. Cambridge University Press, Cambridge.

Schroeder, Albert H. (editor)

1982   *Southwestern Ceramics: A Comparative Perspective.* The Arizona Archaeologist No. 15. Arizona Archaeological Society, Phoenix.

Sebastien, Lynne

1991   Sociopolitical Complexity and the Chaco System. In *Chaco & Hohokam: Prehistoric Regional Systems in the American Southwest,* edited by Patricia L. Crown and W. James Judge, pp. 109–134. School of American Research Press, Santa Fe.

Shepard, Anna O.

1939   Technology of La Plata Pottery. In *Archaeological Studies in the La Plata District,* by Earl H. Morris, pp. 249–287. Publication No. 519. Carnegie Institution of Washington, Washington, D.C.

1965   Rio Grande Glaze-Paint Pottery: A Test of Petrographic Analysis. In *Ceramics and Man,* edited by Frederick R. Matson, pp. 62–87. Viking Fund Publications in Anthropology 41. Aldine Publishing Co., Chicago.

Spier, Leslie

1928   *Havasupai Ethnography.* American Museum of Natural History Anthropological Papers Vol. 29, Part 3, pp. 81–392. New York.

Sullivan, Alan P., III

1988   Prehistoric Southwestern Ceramic Manufacture: The Limitations of Current Evidence. *American Antiquity* 53:23–35.

1992   Book Review: The Architecture of Social Integration in Prehistoric Pueblos. *The Kiva* 57:271–276.

Upham, Steadman

1982   *Polities and Power: An Economic and Political History of the Western Pueblo.* Academic Press, New York.

Wills, W. H.

1988   *Early Prehistoric Agriculture in the American Southwest.* School of American Research Press, Santa Fe.

11

Creativity and Craft

Household Pottery Traditions in the Southwest

Melissa B. Hagstrum

The hallmark painted styles of Southwestern pottery traditions, whether prehistoric, protohistoric, or contemporary, capture the imagination of people who behold them. Ceramic decorative styles, vessel shapes, and materials of manufacture are subjects of delight and inquiry, presenting an astonishing array of distinctive regional and temporal expressions. Despite the creativity that these pottery traditions portray, the organization of ceramic craft production in the American Southwest appears remarkably uniform through time, across varied landscapes, and amidst many ethnic groups—an observation to challenge and enrich the conceptions of craft specialization.

At the heart of each production scheme described in this volume is the household, whose autonomy and flexibility are well suited to the scope of demographic, sociopolitical, and ecological conditions detailed in these studies. Spanning the seventh through seventeenth centuries A.D. and set in the mountains, deserts, and highland valleys of the greater Southwest, this volume's papers provide insight into factors structuring household ceramic manufacture among the prehistoric Anasazi, Hohokam, and Mogollon and the protohistoric Zuni. The scarcity of reliable resources, which constrained the family, produced similarities in the social organization of production recognizable throughout the Southwest.

Cultural coping strategies included many kinds of social interactions that are commonly preserved in the material record by distinctive craft technologies.

Prehistoric Southwestern painted pottery is one such technology that can provide insight into ancient social, political, and economic dynamics. Throughout the region, pottery was crafted early on by family artisans and later by specialists, but all worked in domestic contexts (e.g., see the papers in this volume). Anna Shepard (Kidder and Shepard 1936; Shepard 1942, 1965) pioneered petrography as a way to characterize Rio Grande ceramic composition and challenged the common wisdom that Southwestern pottery production was "one of the regular household tasks of every Pueblo woman, that each town was in this regard self-sufficient" (Kidder and Shepard 1936:xxiii). Ever since Shepard's contribution, subsequent compositional analyses have amplified her initial finding, as the papers here attest (see also Bishop et al. 1988). Although continuity in the household organization of Southwestern craft production persisted across space and time, strategies for exchanging and distributing pots varied widely geographically and temporally, underscoring the adaptability of the household farm and craft studio.

Southwestern pottery, despite being crafted in household contexts, is distinguished by creativity and beauty. Traditionally, "cottage craft industries" worldwide have been made by hands that tilled the soil and worked clay or fiber, wood or leather, metal or stone—household activities undertaken to sustain self and family. Most of the world's artisans throughout history have taken turns at food production and craft production seasonally, year in and year out. The simple fact that artisans worked at home and engaged in the generalized subsistence activities characteristic of domestic production in no way diminishes the high artistic standard achieved by legions of these household craft producers.

Design studies of Southwestern painted pottery, dating to Ruth Bunzel (1929) and Anna Shepard (1948), highlight skill and sophistication, practice and patience in craftsmanship (for more recent studies see, e.g., Hegmon 1986; Plog 1980; Washburn 1977). One may ponder the labor and expertise devoted to these painted pottery traditions. Indeed, the pottery's aesthetic qualities, beyond instilling a measure of pleasure in everyday existence, hold clues to cultural mechanisms.

The theoretical understanding of craft specialization originates in studies of complex society (e.g., Brumfiel and Earle 1987; Childe 1951; Clark and Parry 1990; Costin 1991; Earle 1981; Feinman 1986; Peacock 1982; Rice 1981, 1991; Santley 1984; Sinopoli 1988; van der Leeuw 1977) and traces a typological continuum from family and household to factory and industry. Craft specialists in hierarchical society are defined according to their economic support base, i.e., whether they are self-supporting, independent craftsmen or artisans attached to patron institutions or elites (Earle 1981). Independent specialists customarily produce utility goods for a broad market of elites and commoners alike—cookware, storage pots, and pots for carrying things. Attached specialists generally produce two kinds of goods: (1) utility items for institutional consumption; e.g., Inka aryballoid jars for storing and serving maize beer at state installations; and (2) luxury items for social and political elites; e.g., textiles, such as Inka kumpi cloth, which serve as visible symbols of status and authority for elites who possessed them (Brumfiel and Earle 1987; Clark 1986; Earle 1987; Hodder 1982; Marcus 1974).

Because sociopolitical integration and economic specialization were comparatively limited in the prehistoric Southwest (Johnson 1989; the papers in this volume), the production context of all crafts may be characterized as independent (Hegmon et al., this volume). This fact beckons archaeologists to develop that portion of the craft-specialization continuum focusing on the household unit of production (Hegmon et al., this volume; Wilson and Blinman, this volume). The twin goals of researchers should be to elaborate the independent artisan's process encompassing food-getting and craft-making activities, typically undertaken within the family circle, and to establish the roles of the potter's craft in subsistence and social strategies.

This set of papers has aroused my interest in Southwestern painted pottery for its aesthetic appeal and its home-based production scheme. Neither of these aspects of the American Southwestern ceramic tradition has received the attention it merits: the creativity of Southwestern potters, artistically and strategically, was an important component of household production strategies in this region. These papers provide a catalyst for developing a more comprehensive framework to understand the role of the household in craft manufacture and its specialization in segmentary societies. My commentary will weave together notions concerning the artistry of the Southwestern potter and the centrality of the household for dealing with craft and agricultural production. As these concepts reinforce the pillars of the Southwestern pottery tradition, I will look at the roles of uncertain food production, social mobility and commodity exchange, creativity and making objects special, and socio-political organization.

Household Production: Why the Family Farm and Craft Studio Work

The difficulty for human survival posed by arid Southwestern land-scapes in prehistory is well documented (e.g., Dean 1988; Minnis 1985). The archaeological record of Southwest settlement and subsistence systems generally reveals a pattern of small, short-lived communities engaged in precarious cultivation supplemented by wild resources (Johnson 1989; Zedeño, this volume). The unpredictability of rainfall patterns and temperature extremes, together with the overall scarcities of water and arable land, make for wide swings in the annual harvests of Southwestern agriculturalists. Successful adaptation to these conditions rested on small-scale social groups—the family and household—whose autonomy and flexibility ensured that decisions and responses to environmental uncertainty and crisis, whether natural or cultural, were unencumbered and implemented with ease (Hagstrum 1989, 1995). Indeed, the autonomous household would appear to be the basic building block in segmentary societies.

The papers in this volume pinpoint the self-sufficient farming household as the key production unit for ceramic manufacture. Prehistoric Southwestern pottery traditions delimited elemental technological enterprises: labor recruitment was founded on kinship ties, craft technologies were simple and widely available, resource access was generally unrestricted, and moreover, the distribution of craft goods appears not to have been limited to any particular segment of society (Crown, this volume; Habicht-Mauche, this volume; Johnson 1989). Production of this kind generally frees artisans to establish work patterns to accommodate all household activities, whether economic, social, or ceremonial. Scheduling such activities in complementary ways minimizes competition among tasks and work hands.

Focusing on the internal processes of the farming-artisan household sharpens the understanding of self-sufficiency as a goal and practice for family management, scheduling, and provisioning. Food production and craft manufacture form the fabric of the independent artisan's everyday life (Hagstrum 1989, 1995). Both tasks, complements in the domestic sub-sistence economy, sustain the family. Household self-sufficiency in terms of labor requirements for farming and craft activity is a most effective economic strategy. In accomplishing the regular and recurring daily, monthly, and yearly tasks, the family work team can be juggled easily.

Because they do not achieve complete self-sufficiency, households rely on various mechanisms linking them to the outside world. Thus, inter-acting with people through ceremonial activities and other ways of ex-changing items and information would have provided sustenance and knowledge for people making their way in a difficult arid environment. Mobility, moreover, appears to have been a key strategy for coping with local stress and for taking advantage of distant opportunity (Johnson 1989; Zedeño, this volume).

Assessing the Organization of Ceramic Production

To delineate the organization of ceramic production in the case studies presented here, all authors have employed ceramic compositional analy-sis, pinning down patterns of resource use and areal extent of pottery distribution. Because most archaeological evidence concerning the orga-nization of ceramic production is indirect (Wilson and Blinman, this vol-ume), the strength of these papers is their pairing of material characteri-zations with other indicators of productive organization. Hegmon et al., Crown, and Mills (all in this volume) assess standardization in attributes related to vessel shape, Hegmon et al. assess standardization in attri-butes related to manufacturing technique and design execution, and Crown assesses labor invested in the execution of painted decoration.

Stark's (this volume) treatment of issues encountered in using mea-sures of standardization to infer specialized pottery manufacture are well considered for archaeological ceramics. Her ethnographic work pro-vides a forum for evaluating this problematic relationship in archaeolog-ical settings, for which researchers must isolate material evidence for the individual processes of production, consumption, and distribution; con-trol for time; and shun ethnocentric bias. Mills (this volume) highlights the key cautions in using standardization as an indicator of specializa-tion: (1) standardization is a relative concept requiring case comparisons to establish contexts for production schemes (Rice 1991); (2) standardi-zation is best reflected in ceramic assemblages by controlling for size and shape classes (Longacre et al. 1988); and (3) the critical underlying variable in assessing standardization is the ratio of producers to consumers (Stark, this volume).

To understand the nature of household craft production in the prehistoric and protohistoric Southwest, Hegmon et al. (this volume) specify three basic modes of production defining the independent artisan strategy: (1) unspecialized household production, where every family makes its own pottery; (2) dispersed household specialization, where a few households make crafts for other families in the same community; and (3) community specialization, where a few households make crafts for families in other communities throughout a region (Costin 1991). All of these strategies couple food production with craft production at the household level, and all are influenced by the many factors structuring technological systems: the geographic distribution of suitable raw materials, the subsistence emphases of populations, the technological complexities associated with different wares, and the utilitarian and social roles of vessels (Wilson and Blinman, this volume). These modes of production, moreover, encompass a broad range of distributional strategies (addressed by papers in this volume) that emphasize the flexibility of the household.

This trio of household production schemes suggests trends in sociopolitical and economic organization—increasing population size and organizational complexity together with increased reliance on agriculture. These developments, as Wilson and Blinman (this volume) emphasize, were cyclical rather than unidirectional. This cyclic pattern (in the short run)—the trajectory of which was aimed toward population densities aggregated in large communities (in the long run)—underscores the importance of household adaptability. The paper by Mills (this volume), analyzing production strategies immediately preceding and postdating European contact with the protohistoric Zuni, possibly illustrates an exception to the trajectory just described, but certainly demonstrates household adaptability in the face of crisis.

A caveat is in order: the typology of production outlined here provides a heuristic structure focusing on the role of the household in Southwestern ceramic-production strategies. Although these organizational strategies form a continuum with messy overlaps and boundaries for analysis, modal differences are indeed distinct. These modes of production, moreover, may have overlapped spatially and temporally in the past as well.

Dispersed household specialization and community specialization likely display considerable overlap in the record, making assessment difficult in some archaeological cases. A fruitful strategy would be to consider several parameters that affect specialization: context, concentration, scale, and intensity of craft production (Costin 1991; Hegmon et al., this volume). Likewise, Rice's (1991) formulation, specifying resource, site, and producer specialization, provides another analytic approach (Crown and Hegmon et al., this volume). Finally, analysis of the range of pottery in an individual archaeological assemblage, rather than analysis of a single type, gives insight into the various structures of production and economic interaction of a social group (Costin and Hagstrum 1995). Craft production schemes are multidimensional and thus require careful consideration of all pertinent contextual information.

Unspecialized Household Production

The domestic mode of production, where each family makes crafts for its own use, defines a generalized economy underscored by self-sufficiency (Sahlins 1972). Although no endogamous human social group can claim complete self-reliance, the domestic mode of production broadly characterizes a constellation of autonomous producers. No person or task is specialized, so socioeconomic interdependence beyond the domestic group is minimal.

Unspecialized household production thus affords maximum autonomy and flexibility because the domestic group meets its own basic needs for survival. This self-sufficiency, in turn, affords maximum mobility—the family can decide to move on a whim because of the group's small size and its lack of administrative bureaucracy.

Mobility, whether of families or larger social configurations, may be recognized as an adaptive strategy under contrasting circumstances, in times of plenty and in times of want. Early in Southwestern prehistory, the hunter-gatherer strategy prevailed in the face of low population densities and relative resource abundance (Cordell 1984). In later prehistory, social mobility provided a mechanism for surviving ecological disaster (e.g., the Great Drought at the end of the thirteenth century, as described by Zedeño, this volume) and cultural crisis (e.g., the population decimation wrought by European contact, as described by Mills, this volume).

Although most of the papers in this volume do not discuss unspecialized household production per se, it is clear that the form and functioning of the relatively autonomous farming household was central in Southwestern ceramic production schemes.

Dispersed Household Specialization

In its simplest form, dispersed household specialization may be described as a mere step past the domestic mode of production (unspecialized household production). Family producers make a few craft goods beyond their household needs, thereby establishing exchange relationships with other families. Producing families are dispersed throughout the consuming population within the same community. Because the household defines the unit of production, this organizational scheme affords the same opportunity for mobility that was outlined for unspecialized household production, for two key reasons: (1) the family remains the unit of production and is basically autonomous and flexible; and (2) ceramic resources, suitable for pottery making, are generally ubiquitous throughout the Southwest (Cordell and Plog 1979).

Dispersed household specialization is a strategy common to most of the studies in this volume and was probably common throughout much of the prehistoric and protohistoric Southwest. Although it encourages some economic interdependence, it preserves household flexibility.

Community Specialization

Community household specialization differs from dispersed household specialization primarily in the spatial distribution of both producers and their goods (Hegmon et al., this volume). The specialized community likely localizes family pottery-making work groups near resources, providing opportunities for pooling labor, tools, and transportation. Whereas the wares of community specialists are distributed to other communities (involving greater distances and suggesting both regional and formalized exchange systems), those of dispersed specialists are distributed to members of the potters' own community (involving shorter distances and suggesting local exchange systems).

Because community craft specialists produce goods for individuals outside of their own local districts (see especially Abbott and Walsh-Anduze, and Habicht-Mauche, this volume), a larger population is dependent on specialist producers to meet its basic needs. In turn, specialists are dependent on the population's larger demand for goods to sustain their own livelihoods. Dependence encourages specialization and results in the increased economic integration of a society (Hagstrum 1985).

The Currency of Things: Why Craft Specialization
Exists in the Southwest

Material culture provides a way for people to ally themselves with one another. The simple acts of making an object and giving it away or trading it for something else create webs of social and economic ties that buffer people in many ways, corporeal and spiritual, against difficult conditions for survival. In the Peruvian Andes today, for instance, pots are manufactured to use in food preparation, serving, and storage as well as to barter, in established contexts, for food the family needs, either because it could not be grown in its own fields (ecological niche; e.g., maize cannot be grown reliably above a 3,400-m elevation), or because the household happened upon a shortfall (ecological risk; e.g., lack of rain or untimely frost). Pots are exchanged throughout the region defined by the highland valley at festival markets held during the harvest season. Such a system distributes resources, food, and craft throughout a regional network (Hagstrum 1989).

Resource variability, risk, and social networks are topics of interest and importance to archaeologists for understanding adaptations to arid conditions in the Southwest (e.g., Rautman 1993). Regional social networks are thought to play a key role in the members' ability to assess and deal with environmental variability in nonhierarchical societies (e.g., Braun and Plog 1982). This line of reasoning suggests that social networks distribute risks and benefits arising from environmental variability by providing a way for people to monitor conditions in more remote areas: networks define social groupings for population movement, and facilitate decision making (Rautman 1993). The archaeological record preserves evidence of recurrent use of those cultural options, with material correlates, for coping with resource variability and risk.

Pottery has been used to evaluate social interaction and movement in several ways, including design similarity (e.g., Plog 1980) and technological (e.g., Zedeño, this volume) and material signatures (e.g., all papers, this volume). Such analyses of ceramic vessels can indicate either exchange of vessels themselves or social contact that results in adoption of similar design patterns, manufacturing techniques, or resource use. Whether designs or techniques were copied in local pottery production (Zedeño, this volume) or whether actual vessels were imported are both alternatives that suggest a level of contact that would facilitate group mobility and food exchange between regions (Rautman 1993).

Nutritional requirements may have opened the channels for trade in regions marked by environmental contrasts (e.g., the Plains and the Pueblos [Spielmann 1982]), but craft goods certainly coursed through those channels to meet basic survival needs and to keep the channels open for the passage of food and people in stressful circumstances (Rautman 1993). People did indeed march along these routes to pursue more favorable conditions when their own situations became unproductive (Johnson 1989; Zedeño, this volume). Likewise, regions marked by environmental redundance (e.g., the Rio Grande pueblos [Ford 1972]) suffer unpredictable environmental fluctuations that may affect pockets within the region. In such settings, the craft economy may be structured by artificial specialties to promote exchanges and to foster security between trading partners when food for one is in short supply.

Social Mobility

One of the salient features of the American Southwest was its agricultural marginality. Environmental variability in spatial and temporal terms underlies shifting patterns of settlement and land use throughout the region—a strategy befitting societies defined as segmentary and structured on the autonomous household. The relationship of social mobility and the organization of ceramic manufacture may be best described by unspecialized or dispersed household production schemes, although one can certainly envision events in Southwestern prehistory that would have prompted the movement of community specialists, still structured by the more-or-less autonomous household.

I have already mentioned the currency of pots (other crafts obviously would also be pertinent) in founding and maintaining social networks, a crucial means of buffering people against the short-term ecological vagaries of this part of the world. I also suggested that, in times of particular hardship (the Great Drought is an extreme discussed by Zedeño, this volume), people would likely trace the same pathways their material goods had traveled because this was the mechanism for keeping abreast of distant prospects. The insights from Zedeño's work highlighting the roles of population movement and technological transfer suggest profitable ways to decipher subtleties and complexities in the Southwestern ceramic record that bear on the social and economic interactions engendered by environmental misfortune. Understanding the movement of pots through a region requires compositional analysis and provides clues to the "currency of things." Understanding social mobility requires both compositional and technological analysis, as Zedeño specifies, and offers possibilities of unscrambling periods of ethnic coresidence. Habicht-Mauche's (this volume) analysis of the Santa Fe Black-on-white pottery from the Rio Grande Coalition period illustrates clearly a broad social network based on the currency of pottery, ensuring mutual access to local shared resources and information about more distant resources.

It strikes me that the widespread distribution of Salado polychromes in the fourteenth century may be a phenomenon partially attributable to movements of both pots and people. Crown's work (this volume), demonstrating that the polychromes were used for predominantly domestic purposes, supports my views concerning the centrality of the household in ceramic production and consumption and has implications for the relationship of craft economy and sociopolitical organization (discussed below).

Commodity Exchange

Commodity exchange suggests a formalized and perhaps routinized aspect of this notion I call *the currency of things,* as the research on Classic period Rio Grande glaze wares (Habicht-Mauche, this volume) and Hohokam red wares (Abbott and Walsh-Anduze, this volume) demonstrates. The critical variable is the scale of economic integration encompassing socially distant groups. *Commodification*—a process whereby goods once produced primarily for local consumption become manufactured in larger quantities for distribution outside the local district—describes the same mechanism referred to above, sustaining social supports to lean on in times of local strife (Habicht-Mauche, this volume).

In the Rio Grande region, shifts in settlement structure resulting from population growth and aggregation in large communities are reflected in the ceramic record. The production and consumption pattern of decorated pottery shifted from that described by a dispersed household model (with informal links throughout the region) to one best portrayed as community specialization (within a highly integrated regional economic system; Habicht-Mauche, this volume). The synchronic occurrence of glaze ware specialization and population aggregation is intriguing. Manufacturing glaze ware involved a specialized technology and lead, a resource limited in geographical distribution (a clear example in which site specialization, resource specialization, and product specialization [Rice 1991] intersect).

Abbott and Walsh-Anduze (this volume) recognize a similar pattern in the late Classic period red wares of the Phoenix Basin. They interpret that the social contexts of recovery of these ceramics (more prevalent in burials than trash and in ceremonial precincts near platform mounds) indicate formalized distribution by socially distant parties. This exchange structure suggests both economic and social integration, which forged interdependent links through a ceremonial network and reciprocal social obligations. I think what was most important about the currency of things in the Southwest was the social-buffering mechanism that material objects reinforced, whether on a relatively ad hoc or on a formal basis.

Creativity in the Ceramic Arts:
Why Southwestern Pottery is Beautiful

An appreciation of the technical mastery and visual appeal of Southwestern painted pottery unites scholars, travelers, Native Americans, and pot hunters alike. Academic, avocational, and illicit interest in prehistoric artifacts tells the same story over and over around the world. The draw of an exquisite handmade object clearly transcends tens of thousands of years, belying a common human passion for creativity and craft.

Anthropologists address the arts and crafts of human groups as cultural phenomena, identifying forms and functions in economic, political, spiritual, social, and practical terms. To conclude my commentary, I will speak of the aesthetic appeal of Southwestern pottery traditions as a behavioral response in an uncertain environment for food production and as an expression of sociopolitical organization in nonhierarchical societies.

Creativity and Craft

What is striking about the creation of art and craft, whether past or present, is the universal human proclivity to make the products special and the human tendency to respond to such specialness. The activities involved in making something special, as in decorating or embellishing a pot, entail both taking pains to execute the tasks and taking those tasks seriously. Taking pains to make something special is a way of being more certain of achieving one's intention, of convincing others and oneself that the activity is worth doing (Dissanayake 1988, 1992). When such activity is attached to life-serving activities, such as exchanging food for sustenance and maintaining social alliances for security, the decorative elaboration of pottery may actually have an essential element, to enhance survivorship. Why are pots decorated? Nature does not leave advantageous behavior to chance; she makes it pleasurable, such as eating and sex.

Politics and Pottery

The relationship between developing craft specialization and the evolution of early states has recently been understood, among other things, to be rooted in the strategies emergent elites use to maintain or increase their political authority (Blanton and Feinman 1984; Brumfiel and Earle 1987; Friedman and Rowlands 1977; Pollock 1983). In this scenario, elites employ craftsmen and their products to further their political agendas. These prestige craft goods, customarily exotic personal ornaments, are shaped from materials, whose access is restricted (either by cost or code), according to labor-intensive techniques (acquired and executed by highly skilled artisans).

   This thumbnail sketch of the relationship of politics and crafts in complex society provides counterpoints to foster the understanding of this relationship in nonhierarchical societies. By definition, political authority, agenda, and prestige do not play roles in acephalous societies. Although access to resources may be restricted in nonranked as in ranked social formations by geographical circumscription and territorial boundaries, the denial of access to resources on political grounds, especially to drive up value, is absent. The material assemblages of egalitarian societies, moreover, are generally characterized by goods fashioned from locally available, rather than exotic, resources.

   In the absence of these roles and constraints, household artisans may embellish a craft, such as pottery (whose main ingredient, clay, is widely available across the Southwest), particularly if that craft were central in the subsistence economy. Were I writing about craft specialization in the Inka-period Andes, I would focus on the political economy and discuss why Inka cloth is beautiful. Cloth, unlike pottery, can be elaborated with costly materials and invested with increasing amounts of labor ad nauseam: gold threads, exotic bird feathers, and rare dyes can be added; the density of weave and intricacy of pattern can be made ever finer and more complex.

Pottery does not have the nearly infinite possibilities for costly elaboration that cloth has, but it does have infinite possibilities for plastic and painted embellishment. The captivating array of Southwestern pottery, shaped by remarkable hands that also tilled the soil, illustrates that such embellishment is restricted only by human creativity and ingenuity— limited limitations, indeed.

Conclusions

I have simplified and streamlined many intricacies of the work presented in this volume for the sake of argument and emphasis. I do not think I have overstated my case for the ubiquity of the household organization of pottery production throughout the Southwest nor my case for specialized manufacture to describe much of the Southwestern ceramic record. I am aware that mere mention of the word *specialization* in the Southwest (and in many other areas, for that matter) raises the hackles of some archaeologists. This is unfortunate. I imagine the term may evoke images of workshops, assembly lines, and heavy equipment—potters' wheels and kilns—which are clearly inappropriate for any conceptualization of ceramic manufacture in this region.

Instead, if archaeologists think of specialization as embodying the simple notions of people relying on one another and sharing with one another, then they will have a concept worth exploring in the realm of Southwestern ceramic craft production. The core meaning of specialized production is the creation of interdependencies; everything else is economic, political, and ideological embellishment that is appropriate for and vital in only specific situations.

The humble farming household is remarkably elastic in terms of what it can do and when it does it. Householders are remarkably clever in the achievements (in productivity and creativity) they attain with little in the way of wherewithal. The household production unit is a flexible component of human social organization, an enduring solution to the problems of production, whether of food or craft (Netting 1989). This point is reiterated and illustrated beautifully by the papers in this volume.

Acknowledgments

I would like to voice my gratitude to the editors and authors for providing a stimulating body of work to think and write about, particularly because this area of the world and its ceramics are so dear to me. I would also like to thank Tim Earle and Richard Lawson, my mentors and muses, for standing by me with encouraging words all along the way.

References Cited

Bishop, Ronald L., Valetta Canouts, Suzanne De Atley, Alvin Qoyawayma, and C. W. Aikens
1988   The Formation of Ceramic Analytical Groups: Hopi Pottery Production and Exchange, A.D. 1300–1600. *Journal of Field Archaeology* 15:317–337.

Blanton, Richard E., and Gary M. Feinman
1984   The Mesoamerican World System: A Comparative Approach. *American Anthropologist* 86:673–682.

Braun, David P., and Stephen Plog
1982   The Evolution of "Tribal" Social Networks: Theory and Prehistoric North American Evidence. *American Antiquity* 47:504–525.

Brumfiel, Elizabeth M., and Timothy K. Earle
1987   Specialization, Exchange, and Complex Societies: An Introduction. In *Specialization, Exchange, and Complex Societies*, edited by Elizabeth M. Brumfiel and Timothy K. Earle, pp. 1–9. Cambridge University Press, Cambridge.

Bunzel, Ruth L.
1929   *The Pueblo Potter: A Study of Creative Imagination in Primitive Art.* Columbia University Press, New York.

Childe, V. Gordon
1951   *Social Evolution.* Meridian Books, World Publishing, Cleveland.

Clark, G.
1986   *Symbols of Excellence: Precious Metals as Expressions of Status.* Cambridge University Press, Cambridge.

Clark, John, and William J. Parry
1990   Craft Specialization and Cultural Complexity. *Research in Economic Anthropology* 12:289–346.

Cordell, Linda S.
1984   *Prehistory of the Southwest.* New World Archaeological Record Series. Academic Press, Orlando.

Cordell, Linda, and Fred Plog

1979   Escaping the Confines of Normative Thought: A Reevaluation of Puebloan Prehistory. *American Antiquity* 44:405–429.

Costin, Cathy L.

1991   Craft Specialization: Issues in Defining, Documenting, and Explaining the Organization of Production. In *Archaeological Method and Theory*, vol. 3, edited by Michael. B. Schiffer, pp. 1–56. University of Arizona Press, Tucson.

Costin, Cathy L., and Melissa B. Hagstrum

1995   Standardization, Labor Investment, Skill and the Organization of Ceramic Production in Late Pre-Hispanic Highland Peru. *American Antiquity*, in press.

Dean, Jeffrey S.

1988   A Model of Anasazi Behavioral Adaptation. In *The Anasazi in a Changing Environment*, edited by George J. Gumerman, pp. 25–44. Cambridge University Press, Cambridge.

Dissanayake, E.

1988   *What is Art For?* University of Washington Press, Seattle.

1992   *Homo Aestheticus: Where Art Comes From and Why*. Free Press, New York.

Earle, Timothy K.

1981   Comment on P. Rice, Evolution of Specialized Pottery Production: A Trial Model. *Current Anthropology* 22(3):230–231.

1987   Specialization and the Production of Wealth: Hawaiian Chiefdoms and the Inka Empire. In *Specialization, Exchange, and Complex Societies*, edited by Elizabeth M. Brumfiel and Timothy K. Earle, pp. 64–75. Cambridge University Press, Cambridge.

Feinman, Gary M.

1986   The Emergence of Specialized Ceramic Production in Formative Oaxaca. In *Economic Aspects of Prehispanic Highland Mexico*, edited by B. L. Isaac, pp. 347–373. Research in Economic Anthropology, supp. 2. JAI Press, Greenwich, Connecticut.

Ford, Richard I.

1972   Barter, Gift, or Violence: An Analysis of Tewa Intertribal Exchange. In *Social Exchange and Interaction*, edited by Edwin. N. Wilmsen, pp. 21–45. Anthropological Papers No. 46. Museum of Anthropology, University of Michigan, Ann Arbor.

Friedman Jonathon, and Michael J. Rowlands

1977   Notes Towards an Epigenetic Model of the Evolution of "Civilization." In *The Evolution of Social Systems*, edited by Jonathon M. Friedman and Michael J. Rowlands, pp. 201–276. Duckworth Publishing Co., London.

Hagstrum, Melissa B.

1985   Measuring Prehistoric Ceramic Craft Specialization: A Test Case in the American Southwest. *Journal of Field Archaeology* 12(1):65–75.

1989   *Technological Continuity and Change: Ceramic Ethnoarchaeology in the Peruvian Andes.* Ph.D. dissertation, University of California, Los Angeles. University Microfilms, Ann Arbor.

1995   Household Autonomy in Peasant Craft Specialization. In *Empire and Domestic Economy: Transformations in Household Economics of Xauxa Society Under the Inka,* edited by Terrance N. D'Altroy and Christine A. Hastorf. Smithsonian Institution Press, Washington, D.C.

Hegmon, Michelle

1986   Information Exchange and Integration on Black Mesa, Arizona, A.D. 931–1150. In *Spatial Organization and Exchange: Archaeological Survey on Northern Black Mesa,* edited by Stephen Plog, pp. 256–282. Southern Illinois University Press, Carbondale.

Hodder, Ian

1982   Theoretical Archaeology: A Reactionary View. In *Symbolic and Structural Archaeology,* edited by Ian Hodder, pp. 1–16. Cambridge University Press, Cambridge.

Johnson, Gregory A.

1989   Dynamics of Southwestern Prehistory: Far Outside—Looking In. In *Dynamics of Southwest Prehistory,* edited by Linda S. Cordell and George J. Gumerman, pp. 371–389. Smithsonian Institution Press, Washington, D.C.

Kidder, Alfred V., and Anna O. Shepard

1936   *The Pottery of Pecos,* vols. 1 and 2. Papers of the South West Expedition No. 7. Phillips Academy, Andover, and Yale University Press, New Haven.

Longacre, William A., Kenneth L. Kvamme, and Masashi Kobayashi

1988   Southwestern Pottery Standardization: An Ethnoarchaeological View from the Philippines. *The Kiva* 53:101–112.

Marcus, Joyce

1974   The Iconography of Power Among the Classic Maya. *World Archaeology* 6:83–94.

Minnis, Paul E.

1985   *Social Adaptation to Food Stress: A Prehistoric Southwestern Example.* University of Chicago Press, Chicago.

Netting, Robert McC.

1989   Smallholders, Householders, Freeholders: Why the Family Farm Works Well Worldwide. In *The Household Economy: Reconsidering the*

Domestic Mode of Production, edited by Richard R. Wilk, pp. 221–244. Westview Press, Boulder, Colorado.

Peacock, D. P. S.

1982   *Pottery in the Roman World: An Ethnoarchaeological Approach.* Longman, London.

Plog, Stephen

1980   *Stylistic Variation in Prehistoric Ceramics: Design Analysis in the American Southwest.* Cambridge University Press, Cambridge.

Pollock, Susan

1983   *The Symbolism of Prestige.* Ph.D. dissertation, University of Michigan, Ann Arbor. University Microfilms, Ann Arbor.

Rautman, Allison E.

1993   Resource Variability, Risk, and the Structure of Social Networks: An Example from the Prehistoric Southwest. *American Antiquity* 58(3):403–424.

Rice, Prudence M.

1981   Evolution of Specialized Pottery Production: A Trial Model. *Current Anthropology* 22(3):219–240.

1991   Specialization, Standardization, and Diversity: A Retrospective. In *The Ceramic Legacy of Anna O. Shepard,* edited by Ronald L. Bishop and Frederick W. Lange, pp. 257–279. University Press of Colorado, Niwot.

Sahlins, Marshall

1972   *Stone Age Economics.* Aldine Publishing Co., Chicago.

Santley, Robert S.

1984   Obsidian Exchange, Economic Stratification, and the Evolution of Complex Society in the Basin of Mexico. In *Trade and Exchange in Early Mesoamerica,* edited by Kenneth G. Hirth, pp. 43–86. University of New Mexico Press, Albuquerque.

Shepard, Anna O.

1942   *Rio Grande Glaze Paint Ware: A Study Illustrating the Place of Ceramic Technological Analysis in Archaeological Research.* Contributions to American Anthropology and History No. 39. Publication No. 528. Carnegie Institution of Washington, Washington, D.C.

1948   *The Symmetry of Abstract Design with Special Reference to Ceramic Decoration.* Contributions to American Anthropology and History No. 47. Publication No. 574. Carnegie Institution of Washington, Washington, D.C.

1965   Rio Grande Glaze-Paint Pottery: A Test of Petrographic Analysis. In *Ceramics and Man,* edited by Frederick R. Matson, pp. 62–87. Viking Fund Publications in Anthropology No. 41. Wenner-Gren Foundation for Anthropological Research, New York.

Sinopoli, Carla

1988   The Organization of Craft Production and Vijayanagara, South India. *American Anthropologist* 90(3):580–597.

Spielmann, Katherine A.

1982   *Inter-societal Food Acquisition Among Egalitarian Societies: An Ecological Study of Plains/Pueblo Interaction in the American Southwest.* Ph.D. dissertation, University of Michigan, Ann Arbor. University Microfilms, Ann Arbor.

van der Leeuw, Sander E.

1977   Towards a Study of the Economics of Pottery Making. In *Ex Horreo,* edited by B. L. van Beek, R. W. Brandt, and W. Groenman-van Watteringe, pp. 68–76. Albert Egges van Giffen Instituut voor Prae-en Protohistorie, Universiteit van Amsterdam, Amsterdam.

Washburn, Dorothy K.

1977   *A Symmetry Analysis of Upper Gila Area Ceramic Design.* Papers of the Peabody Museum of American Archaeology and Ethnology Vol. 68. Harvard University, Cambridge.

INDEX

ABOUT THE EDITORS

BARBARA J. MILLS is an associate professor in the Department of Anthropology, University of Arizona, and a research associate of the Zuni Archaeology Program, Pueblo of Zuni. She has worked throughout the Anasazi and Mogollon regions, especially in the Zuni, Mimbres, Chaco, and Mogollon Rim areas. Since 1993, she has directed the University of Arizona's Archaeological Field School. She recently completed direction of the analyses of ceramics excavated from more than 100 sites, which resulted in the publication *Across the Colorado Plateau: Archaeological Investigations along the Transwestern Pipeline Expansion Project; Ceramic Interpretations* (with Christine E. Goetze and María Nieves Zedeño; Office of Contract Archaeology and the Maxwell Museum of Anthropology, University of New Mexico, 1993). Other recent publications include "Community Dynamics and Archaeological Dynamics: Some Considerations of Middle-Range Theory" in *The Ancient Southwestern Community* (University of New Mexico Press, 1994) and "Abandonment at Zuni Farming Villages" (with Nan Rothschild, T. J. Ferguson, and Susan Dublin) in *Abandonment of Settlements and Regions* (Cambridge University Press, 1993).

PATRICIA L. CROWN is a professor in the Department of Anthropology, University of New Mexico. Having conducted research in the Anasazi, Mogollon, and Hohokam areas, she is particularly interested in macroregional processes of change in the Southwest, including the origins of pottery production and the fourteenth-century shift to polychrome manufacture. Recent publications include a comprehensive study of fourteenth-century pottery, *Ceramics and Ideology: Salado Polychrome Pottery* (University of New Mexico Press, 1994) and an edited volume comparing two major regional systems in the Southwest, *Chaco and Hohokam* (edited with W. James Judge, School of American Research Press, 1991).